The Hidden Foundation

The Hidden Foundation

Cinema and the Question of Class

David E. James and Rick Berg, editors

University of Minnesota Press
Minneapolis
London

The Louis and Hermione Brown Humanities Support Fund at Occidental College assisted in the preparation of this book.

Published by the University of Minnesota Press
111 Third Avenue South, Suite 290, Minneapolis, MN 55401-2520
Printed in the United States of America on acid-free paper

Library of Congress Cataloging-in-Publication Data

The hidden foundation : cinema and the question of class / David E.
James and Rick Berg, editors.
    p.   cm.
Includes index.
ISBN 0-8166-2704-5 (hc)
ISBN 0-8166-2705-3 (pb)
    1. Motion pictures—Political aspects.   2. Motion pictures—Social
aspects.   3. Social classes.   I. James, David E., 1945– .
II. Berg, Rick.
PN1995.9.P6H5   1996
791.43′652062—dc20   95-22733

It is always the direct relation of the owners of the conditions of production to the direct producers which reveals the innermost secret, the hidden foundation of the entire social construction.

—*Karl Marx, Capital, III:47*

Contents

Chapter 1
Introduction: Is There Class in This Text?

David E. James

Academic Identity Politics

The present collection of essays was occasioned by specific institutional events. At the 1989 meeting of the Society for Cinema
Studies, the professional organization of film and television scholars in the United States, one of its several internal interest groups,
the Task Force on Race and Class, voted to dissolve and reconsti-
tute itself as the Task Force on Race. The decision to sever institutional consideration of class from that of race and to jettison the
former occurred at a moment when demands for increasing the
presence of people of color in higher education and for increasing
attention to ethnically oriented film practices were regaining some
of the momentum lost in the previous decade and a half. And although nothing like justice has been done to those concerns, let
alone to the wider social conditions to which they speak, still substantial attention to what has become known as "multiculturalism" did come of the initiative. But the zero-sum rules of academic
identity politics ensured that ground gained by one marginalized
discourse would be lost by another.

After a decade that had been as devastating practically for the
global working class as it had been theoretically for Marxism, the
fact that in this case the loser was class should have come as no
surprise—except to anyone who had followed the rhetoric of the

1

curricular debates of the late Reagan era. Commonplace in both justifications of and attacks on attempts to diversify core humanities programs had been the claim that received canons and methodologies were being supplemented in ways that reflected the interests of previously excluded peoples, specifically those defined by "class, race, and gender." But although feminism had transformed the humanities in the twenty years since the burgeoning of the women's liberation movement, and inroads were certainly being made by peoples of color, consideration of class was almost entirely absent from the humanities generally and film studies in particular. In an age of unprecedented extensions of the limits of discourse, one topic alone remained unspeakable.[1]

Although this repression reflects conditions in many aspects of American society, it has been most immediately determined by the functions of the academy itself, where the very developments that allowed sexual and ethnic identity groups to find their agendas simultaneously ensured the silencing of class theory. The social movements of the 1960s and then the mutually incommensurate micropolitics that split the left thrived in the university largely to the extent that they negotiated the personalization of the political into academic practices. Thus, in the case of feminism, the struggle for women's rights generally, the struggle to increase the presence of women in higher education, and the struggle to empower women as cultural producers all played their part in the struggle to develop feminist hermeneutics and historiography in the university, and were all understood as interdependent components of a broadly unified cultural initiative. Both the trace and the medium of the interdependence of these projects was a new, postmodernist discourse, a mixed autobiographical and critical mode based (to use Lyotard's terms; see Lyotard 1984) on narrative rather than science, whose immense rhetorical and analytic force was supplied by the heritage of shared subjectivity discovered in consciousness-raising.

Subsequent identity groups aspired to their own similarly united fronts, in which advances in academic theory, disseminated through para-academic institutions, would both nourish and be nourished by advances in the relevant constituencies in society at large. But whereas in the academy and on its slopes these interdependencies made possible great gains in the theoretical consideration of ethnic and sexual identity, the practice of constructing academic programs around the political interests of academics themselves in fact inhibited the emergence of parallel discourses around class. First, the crucial component that might have created an equivalent identity group was not present; the working class is not generally admitted into higher education, certainly not to elite research universities where theoretical work is done, in sufficient numbers to create the critical mass of working-class-identified subjects that could develop such a theoretical offensive in class terms.[2] Second, where affirmative action programs did fortuitously occasion the enrollment of working-class women or working-class people of color to these institutions, they were admitted (and interpellated) not *as* working class, but under the designation of their sexual or ethnic identities, identities that were subsequently invoked and affirmed by a panoply of methodologies, courses, journals, and other apparatuses, while their class background was ignored and any residual class consciousness and class loyalties they might have had were systematically inhibited.

And so third, although all other identities have been eminently assimilable to the bourgeois academy, allowing female, black, and queer people to live privileged lives as female, black, and queer academics, such a richly rewarded career as the voice and image of a social identity is not even theoretically possible for a working-class person. Apart from a few exceptional moments—notably the exploitation of peripatetic adjuncts in some cases and the brief period of graduate school exploitation in others—a tenured life of college teaching and research is not alienated labor. Whatever its anxieties, it provides more of the rewards and satisfactions of bourgeois life than of the exigencies and perils of the proletarian's.[3] In this respect, the best a person from the working class can hope for is precisely that, to be *from* the working class, and in this displacement to be deprived of the possibility of speaking either as or for the working class, or even as or for her- or himself.[4] The back of a working-class identity must be broken across the abyss of a class migration to a station where feelings of pride and success will always be gnawed by estrangement and betrayal.[5]

Such institutional repression of working-class consciousness is not accidental. As Samuel Bowles and Herbert Gintis (1976) have shown, reforms in the U.S. educational system have historically entailed the extension of privileges; but the schooling of the previously excluded has always been determined by the requirements of their roles in the structural transformations of capital: in the early nineteenth century, when public day schools replaced the family to complement the developing factory system; in the Progressive Era, when the expansion of high schools saw the common curriculum sacrificed to the ideology of vocationalism, with special tracking for working-class children that broke the control of trade unions in skill training; and since World War II, where acceptance of demands for expanded access to higher education by minorities and women has simultaneously satisfied corporate and state needs for technical, clerical, and other service skills—the creation of a reserve army of underemployed white-collar labor.[6] There is no reason not to suppose that contemporary curricular reforms and admissions programs are part of a similar historical process. However humanly necessary and objectively good they currently seem to be, and however they empower those few, selected members of minority groups that they incorporate, they are similarly instrumental in displacing class consciousness and otherwise legitimating and reproducing the class structure of a diversified postmodern economy. And indeed, despite pockets of resistance, multiculturalism has itself long been a major corporate priority.

The point here is not to propose an academic identity politics based on class. The university already—sometimes loudly, sometimes silently—sustains a bourgeois identity politics, and a working-class identity politics within it will be structurally infeasible as long as the university maintains its present functions, that is to say, as long as the present social order and its systemic dependence on exploitation lasts. And in any case, whatever impossible identity working-class intellectuals sustain is fundamentally different from all others; rather than seeking to create a society in which its own interests are paramount, it looks forward to its own supersession, either in the terms of Marx's own proposal that "a *real* possibility of emancipation" demands the formation of "a class which is the dissolution of all classes," or in the now century-old commitment by socialism to oppose "not only the exploitation and oppression of wage workers, but also every form of exploitation and oppression, be it directed against a class, a party, a sex, or a race."[7] Where they are not simply unimaginable, such conceptions are now so ubiquitously denigrated that it would be absurd to expect academic film studies to be or even want to be the arena where their credibility could be restored. Accordingly, this collection of essays has been obliged to begin from the recognition of two absences: the absence of a generally accepted theory of class and of its articulation with other forms of structural social division, and hence the absence of any single systematic or comprehensive theory of the way class could inform the study of cinema. While recognizing the dangers of empiricism, the contributors to this volume have therefore proceeded inductively, attempting to think some actual instances of cinema, using the concept of class in whatever form it might have been available. Keeping this provisionality in mind, a synopsis of some of the overall issues involved in the concept of class may still have its uses.[8]

Classical Marxism

Marx himself never systematically developed a theory of class, and in fact he died leaving the manuscript of volume 3 of *Capital* unfinished a few lines after he had asked the crucial question, "What constitutes a social class?" (441). Nevertheless, in his work and in the traditions of Marxism, class is one of the key theoretical formulations. Fundamentally, it designates a position in the economic structure of society. As each historical era finds its own way of organizing material production, around the raw materials, tools, factories, and so on from which goods are produced (*the means of production*), it generates specific social divisions. These social divisions are classes; the relation between them is "the hidden foundation" of the social formation, and their conflictual interaction has driven history through a series of stages, or *modes of production*. If the latest of these, capitalism, were ever to exist in a pure form, it would allow two social positions in relation to the means of production: that of the few capitalists, who own them, and that of the many workers, who own nothing but their ability to work, which they are obliged to sell in order to live and from which the capitalists extract and appropriate more value than the labor power itself costs to reproduce. Capitalist society consists in essence, then, of two classes, bourgeois and proletarian. Marx expected nineteenth-century capitalism to continue to develop the conflict between these until the proletariat would communally seize control of the means of production for themselves, eventually to create a society without a division between exploiter and exploited, "the *abolition of all classes* and . . . *a classless society"* (220). Beyond this premise of the historically specific, adversarial relation between capitalists and workers, almost everything in Marx about class is debatable. A number of issues, however, are both primary and recurrent: the apparent existence of classes or class fractions other than those of capitalist and worker; the relation between the objective and subjective components of a class position; and the modes of activity in spheres outside the economic that follow from a given position in production.

The period in which Marx wrote was not one of pure capitalism, but rather one in which capitalism was in the process of replacing the previous mode of production, feudalism, with its class division between landowners and peasants, while glimpses of a future socialism were already perceptible. Class positions remaining from a previous era, as well as those harbingers of the next, thus complicated the social polarization. In the early 1880s, when he was writing the last page of *Capital,* Marx observed that whereas "middle and intermediate strata even here obliterate lines of demarcation," nevertheless "three great social classes" existed: "wage-labourers, capitalists and landlords" (441–42). But because the last two of these, vestigial of feudalism, were progressively assimilating to capital, the situation as a whole fundamentally ratified the polarization thesis announced more than thirty years before in *The Communist Manifesto:* "Society as a whole is more and more splitting up into two great hostile camps, into two great classes directly facing each other: Bourgeoisie and Proletariat" (474).

Marx's prediction of the inevitability of class polarization was challenged as early as the 1890s, when, largely as a result of gains made by the labor movement, class conflict appeared to be diminishing in Western Europe and economic crises and the immiseration of the proletariat seemed, if anything, to be becoming less likely. *Revisionism,* initially theorized by Eduard Bernstein, proposed that class fractions between capitalist and proletariat would not disappear, but would continue to expand. The expansion of these middle classes indicated a reconciliation of the class conflicts of early capital and the progressive amelioration of workers' conditions through electoral politics of the kind that produced the traditions of social democracy. In the longer perspective, the proliferation of such fractions and other social reforms, together with the failure of the working class to emerge as the agent of revolutionary change in the Western democracies, has continued to challenge Marx's teleology, while simultaneously authorizing social movements premised on reconciliation between classes, or on structural division along lines other than class.

Marxism itself has provided several responses to these challenges. While in the West recent deindustrialization and the expansion of service and high-technology sectors have allowed a small number of blue-collar workers to rise economically, a much greater number of previously skilled and unionized workers have slid down into unskilled service jobs and even unemployment, creating a new social polarization with a new and highly fragmented working class that traditional forms of working-class organization find difficult to access. And in any case, Marx's expectation of increasing class polarization was predicated on capitalism's assimilation of the entire global economy, and although he may not have theorized this fully, others did, most notably Lenin, in his diagnosis in *Imperialism, the Highest Stage of Capitalism* of the shift from the industrial to the financial form of capital as the vehicle of its expansion. Today, as the relocation of heavy manufacturing industries from the West to East Asia reconfigures the global division of labor and as the capitalist world market has come to control even the vestigial instances of precapitalist production, the New World Economy, and other similar umbrellas for the unregulated internationalization of capital may temporarily obscure class polarization in the First World, but only as the exploitation of First World proletariat is refracted in core-periphery relations and the spatial extension of capitalism generally. Thus, employing a simple, objective definition of class (the bourgeois are those who receive surplus value and are in a position to reinvest it; all others are proletarian), Immanuel Wallerstein has argued that worldwide the process of increasing dependence on wage labor has continued, so that polarization remains "a historically correct hypothesis, not a false one . . . provided we use as the unit of calculation . . . the capitalist world-economy" (Balibar and Wallerstein 1991, 128).

The other, entirely different response to the apparent plurality of classes is to make a distinction between an objective position in relation to production (like Wallerstein's above, for example) and one that includes other factors, such as the notion that in the actual historical organization of classes, economic relations interact with political and ideological processes, especially the consciousness of specific historical subjects.[9] Marx himself proposed the basis for this latter in a distinction between class *an sich* and class *für sich*, first adumbrated in 1847 in *The Poverty of Philosophy:* industrialization, he argued, has in fact "transformed the mass of the people of the country into workers. The combination of capital has created for this mass a common situation, common interests. This mass is thus already a class as against capital, but not yet for itself" (218). But neither the specific point at which a social aggregate constituted around production actually forms a class nor the role played by ideological self-consciousness in the process was fully explained. Thus, in a parallel discussion of small peasants in mid-century France in *The Eighteenth Brumaire of Louis Bonaparte,* Marx implied the need for quite extensive activity outside the realm of the purely economic for a class formation properly to congeal. The peasants were, he argued, "a vast mass . . . which live in similar conditions"; but they were nevertheless so isolated from each other in the process of their work that they remained politically inchoate, "much as potatoes in a sack form a sackful of potatoes" (608):

> In so far as millions of families live under economic
> conditions of existence that divide their mode of life, their
> interests and their culture from those of other classes, and
> put them in hostile contrast to the latter, they form a class.
> In so far as there is merely a local interconnection among
> these small peasants, and the identity of their interests
> begets no unity, no national union and no political
> organisation, they do not form a class. They are
> consequently incapable of enforcing their class interest in
> their own name. (608)

In his commentaries on the revolutions in nineteenth-century France, particularly *The Eighteenth Brumaire* (1852) and *The Civil War in France* (written in 1871), Marx explored the process by which class as an economic category is re-created in the more complex forms of class as a political category and function. The process includes the overlapping of modes of production to produce multiple class fractions (the aristocracy of finance, the industrial bourgeoisie, the middle class, the petty bourgeois, the army, the lumpenproletariat, the intellectual lights, the clergy, the rural population, as well as the proletariat proper of France in 1848, for example), the shifting alliances among these as they form "ruling blocs," the consolidation of such blocs in the formation of the state, and the subsequent degree of the state's autonomy and/or its implementation of specific class interests, either overtly or through some form of masquerade.

The question of class consciousness that runs through all these considerations is framed by the issues of ideology and ideological determination generally. Again, key formulations are not a little ambiguous. In *The German Ideology* (written 1845–46), Marx proposed a schema according to which the class that controls material production is also able to control mental production, with the result that the "ideas of the ruling class are in every epoch the ruling ideas. . . . The ruling ideas are nothing more than the ideal expression of the dominant material relationships" (172). Elsewhere, most clearly in the summary statement of the general principles of historical materialism in *A Contribution to the Critique of Political Economy* (1859), he strongly implied that different classes possess different ideologies: if "it is not the consciousness of men that determines their being, but, on the contrary, their social being that determines their consciousness" (4), then, because different classes have different social beings, their different consciousnesses must follow.

Because intentional social reorganization would seem to require some degree of conscious opposition to the received status quo, the Marxist tradition has produced a number of positions about the consciousness of the agents of such historical change, especially about working-class self-consciousness. One tradition emphasizes its importance: Rosa Luxembourg, for example, believed that the working class could generate its own class consciousness through its own mass political action, and in *History and Class-Consciousness* Georg Lukács (1971) argued that although the working class is the only class capable of true self-knowledge, practically speaking the conditions of working-class people's lives inhibit the emergence of self-knowledge, necessitating its construction from outside by the party, a position fully developed by Lenin. On the other hand, the need for or possibility of such a self-consciousness posited in this "Hegelian" tradition has been denied by "structural" Marxists, notably Louis Althusser and Nicos Poulantzas. Referencing the antihumanism of late Marx, instanced in his claim in *Capital* that he was dealing with individuals "only in so far as they are the personifications of economic categories, embodiments [or bearers, *Träger*] of economic categories, embodiments of particular class-relations and class-interests" (297), Althusser theorized classes as objective social structures, whose nature and development are independent of any immanent subjectivity, even in the working class itself.

Multiplied by the details of subsequent political history as well as by transformations in the nature of capital, these indeterminacies in Marx have generated the body of Marxist class theory. This is beyond even the meagerest summary here, but three issues do merit mention: the main non-Marxist theories of class, debates about class in contemporary sociology, and "post-Marxist" attacks on the primacy of the working class in left politics.

Other Theories of Class

Besides Marx, the main contributor to classical sociological theories of class was Max Weber (1864–1920), who conceived of class somewhat more loosely as a specification of "life chances," defined not by a position in productive relations but by one in market relations, determined by ownership of property and possession of skills and education. He subsumed the resulting plurality of market situations into four "social classes": the working class; the petty bourgeoisie; technicians, specialists, and lower-level management; and those who were privileged through property and education. In addition to rejecting Marx's notion of necessary structural conflict among these groups, he rejected any distinction between conscious and unconscious positioning, and hence the possibility of economistic historical development. (*The Protestant Ethic and the Spirit of Capitalism*, his analysis of the origins of modern society, thus emphasizes the role of ideology, specifically Calvinism, as producing rather than reflecting economic transformation.) The importance of economic class for Weber is further qualified in its relation to an alternative formulation, that of the "status group," according to which individuals derive social identity from common cultural patterns, including consumption and other lifestyle priorities.

Postwar U.S. sociology effected various forms of Marx-Weber synthesis in functionalist theories of the relation between (objective) class formation and (subjective) class action. The most prominent neo-Weberian, John Goldthorpe, for example, devised a class scheme, closely resembling those used by market researchers and census bureaus, that combined market and work situations to differentiate seven levels aggregated into three categories: service, working, and intermediate classes. On the basis of this analysis, he then explored the degree to which these positions have produced actual demographic identities capable of social action and also tracked social mobility across class positions (Crompton 1993, 57–60, 63–69).[10]

Erik Olin Wright, on the other hand, retained the Marxist principle of class positions generated in production; his work has attempted to demonstrate that the plurality of new middle classes may actually be reduced back to primary economic relations, so as to sustain the polarization thesis. To the bourgeoisie, proletariat, and petty bourgeoisie—the three basic positions developed in orthodox Marxism in respect to ownership or nonownership of the means of production—he added three *contradictory* class locations: managers and supervisors, small employers, and semiautonomous wage earners. Occupants of these locations are contradictorily determined; managers, for instance, do not own the means of production, yet they do control both means of production and labor power, whereas semiautonomous wage earners do not own or control the material means of production, nor do they sell their labor power (Wright 1985, 19–57). In subsequent work, as he shifted his emphasis from forms of domination to processes of exploitation, Wright (1989) was forced to double the number of classes in the occupational scheme, as well as to develop increasingly sophisticated theoretical and statistical procedures to map synchronic positions and mobility among them. Although he has not been able to produce a model that can satisfactorily account for multiple intermediary classes, he has not abandoned either the general project or its Marxist foundations.

Given the economic emphasis of these Weberian and neo-Marxist traditions, it is not surprising that their reverberation in cultural studies has been slight; but other Marxist-Weberian sociologies oriented toward consumption, particularly symbolic consumption, have been heard, most notably the work of Pierre Bourdieu.[11] His *Distinction: A Social Critique of the Judgement of Taste* (1984), a self-designated "ethnography of France," synthesizes a Marxist understanding of class as an objective structural position in relation to production with an extensive system of stratification based on subjective values—a broadly Weberian attention to symbolic practices, including lifestyles and consumption preferences. Occupation categories supply the major social strata (working, middle, and upper classes) and the internal divisions within them, but positions in these—and the operations of power generally—are seen as sustained through other social and cultural factors, which Bourdieu defines as educational and cultural "capital." An individual's or social group's possession of social and cultural capital produces a characteristic system of dispositions, which Bourdieu calls the *habitus*—"the internalized form of class condition and of the conditioning it entails" (101). Together, the economic, social, and cultural conditions constitute class: "Social class is not defined solely by a position in the relation of production, but by the class habitus which is 'normally' (i.e., with a high statistical probability) associated with that position" (372).

Generally, Bourdieu argues, the hierarchies of occupation and taste are homologous; higher social class reproduces itself with better education, which produces more cultural capital, leading to superior social standing and power, including a greater capacity to process works of "legitimate" culture. But there are significant variations within the three major class divisions that reflect not only the different overall volume of a given capital, but also its different "composition," that is, the relative proportions of the economic, social, and cultural forms. These variations engender the different tastes and consumption habits of the various groups within each stratum. Within the dominant class, for example, the economic capital of industrial employers dominates their cultural capital, whereas the opposite is the case for intellectuals (115); for recreation, then, the former prefer golf, "with its aristocratic etiquette, its English vocabulary and its great exclusive spaces, together with extrinsic profits, such as the accumulation of social capital," whereas the latter get high ascetically, in mountaineering, for example, which "offers for minimum economic costs the maximum distinction, distance, and spiritual elevation" (219).

Distinction is based on surveys taken in France, some as long ago as 1963. In anglophone countries thirty years later, neither the occupational class patterns that are its basis nor the codes of cultural differentiation are nearly as clear; a working-class taste for *La Traviata* against a haute bourgeois taste for *The Well-Tempered Clavier* will not register in a leveled cultural milieu where both works are denigrated as "high" culture. The understanding of cultural preferences is, moreover, strongly deterministic, and although it allows for extremely fine gradings of class location and is extraordinarily responsive to cultural factors that internally stratify occupational categories, it makes no place for individual or subcultural resistance to them or movement through them. Nevertheless, the demonstration of how class situation not only permeates and controls all forms of subjectivity, but in fact constitutes it—in Bourdieu's words, how a class "condition" in fact "impos[es] conditionings" (101)—remains a powerful challenge to the end-of-class ideologies that now dominate the academic study of culture. Of these, Ernesto Laclau and Chantal Mouffe's use of poststructural theory to authorize the replacement of class by other forms of identity in radical politics has become widely fashionable.

In their *Hegemony and Socialist Strategy* (1985), Laclau and Mouffe develop a "post-Marxism" in which the proletariat's inability to hegemonize over the "New Social Movements" has caused the disintegration of the historical role proposed for it in Marxism:

> What is now in crisis is a whole conception of socialism which rests upon the ontological centrality of the working class, upon the role of Revolution, with a capital "r," as the founding moment in the transition from one type of society to another, and upon the illusory prospect of a perfectly unitary and homogeneous collective will that will render pointless the moment of politics. The plural and

multifarious character of contemporary social struggles has finally dissolved the last foundation for that political imaginary. (2)

Their revisionism is distinguished by its highly sophisticated repertoire of discourse theory drawn especially from Saussure, Wittgenstein, Foucault, and Derrida—a theoretical apparatus that they use to read the classic Marxist texts from Bernstein to Althusser deconstructively. Their reading, they claim, discloses the persistence of a fundamental economic determinism that has caused all Marxists to give an ontological priority to the working class, even in social analyses that propose forms of class alliance; although a plurality of social actors are recognized, the search for a "true working-class subject" forces their reduction back into class politics. Against such an essentialism and against a totally undifferentiated pluralism, they argue the need for new forms of "*social logics* which . . . acquire their meaning in precise conjunctural and relational contexts where they will always be limited by other—frequently contradictory—logics; but none of them has absolute validity, in the sense of defining a space or structural moment which could not in its turn be subverted" (142–43).

Laclau and Mouffe have encountered some resistance from the left.[12] Their historical rereading of the Marxist tradition has been criticized as reductionist, a straw-man caricature that conceals the actual complexity of the relations between the economic and political developed in it, and the argument that economic production does generate social relations and hence classes prior to their discursive articulation has been reasserted. The political programs their conclusions project have likewise been dismissed as merely a new pluralism or as so abstract and vague as to be virtually useless. But because some version of the crisis in Marxist theory they describe is all but axiomatic in the entire New Left tradition (articulated in its essentials thirty years earlier by C. Wright Mills) as well as in many postwar Marxisms (Eurocommunism, for example), by and large the academy has received their work with relief and gratitude. Their argument that class need no longer be considered *the* hegemonic formation of political alterity in a model of "radical democracy" that still necessarily included a socialist dimension, "the abolition of capitalist relations of production" (192) has slipped into justification for the abandonment of class as even one among other categories of resistance—a specifically anti-working-class politics that their subsequent writings have endorsed. Here we cannot explore that process in the realm of political thought, but a virtually identical itinerary may be traced in the displacement of class from two of the bodies of cultural theory engendered by the New Left, 1970s film theory and 1980s cultural studies.

The Displacement of Class from Film Theory and Cultural Studies

Especially after the Comintern adopted Popular Front policies, in the late 1930s many forms of populist film culture in which class politics were paramount flourished across Western Europe and the United States; but in the renewal of radical politics after the 1950s the importance of class was radically diminished, especially in the United States.[13] The reasons for this are complex, though beyond whatever plausibility remains to arguments for "American exceptionalism," clearly the revelations about Stalin, followed by the Cold War and McCarthyism, had virtually destroyed any popular currency Marxism might still have had. With the notable exceptions of the Black Panthers and certain sectors of the Vietnam War resistance, the main social movements of the 1960s, such as those for civil rights and women's liberation—the immediate sources of contemporary ethnic and sexual identity politics—developed more in opposition to Marxism than in articulation with it. But in France, following the success of the union of students and workers in the May events and the challenge to Gaullism, the vocabulary of cultural criticism was not only self-consciously Marxist, but its Marxism was to some degree class oriented. So initially were both radical film and radical film theory in the period immediately after 1968. The subsequent evaporation of class from this Marxism and then the general failure of French Marxism reverberated through the anglophone adoption of French film theory, particularly around the heritage of Althusser.

Of Althusser's various interventions—the proposal of the autonomy of economic, political, and ideological practices; the theory of the epistemological break between the conceptual frameworks of the early and the late Marx; the replacement of a Hegelian, humanist conception of the subject by one determined by the lived social structures—the most fateful for film studies was his theory of ideology. Given his strictures on Marx's early Hegelian writings, it is ironic that Althusser should have taken up the general model of ideology proposed in *The German Ideology,* that is, as pandemic and consistent in the social formation as a whole rather than class specific. As early as 1967, he recognized the limitations that resulted; he was "not equipped for an adequate treatment of certain questions," and so he "did not examine . . . the 'fusion' of Marxist theory and the *workers' movement . . .* did not examine the *concrete forms of existence* of this 'fusion' (organization of the class struggle—trade unions, parties—the means and methods of direction of the class struggle by these organizations" (1977, 15). But he never redressed the deficiency, and with the sole exception of the autonomy allowed to certain intellectual activity designated as science (or "theoretical practice"), all the other social, material, and ideological apparatuses that call the subject into being were understood as promoting each other uniformly, and were lived so completely and across all social classes as to amount to a general conditioning that structured even the unconscious. Developed through Lacanian psychoanalysis, this theory of ideology was appropriated by film studies with a similar essentialism; the ideological effects of cinema were seen as socially uniform because they were intrinsic to its apparatus, to the historical conditions of its invention, and to all cases of its use apart from deliberate avant-gardist ruptures of its fundamental and enabling mechanism, primary identification.

Because the British importation of French theory took place in the mid-1970s at exactly the time when its psychoanalytic component was being most forcefully developed, the early 1970s concern with the rediscovery of early Soviet cinema (also imitated from French journals) was hardly in place before a psychoanalytic theory of the subject was dropped like a cuckoo's egg into the nest of historical materialism. Thus, to take one example, in the 1974 special issue of *Screen* devoted to a reconsideration of Brecht as exemplary for a contemporary revolutionary cinema, his use of techniques of formal rupture and negation as a means to critical distanciation were re-presented through a Freudian rather than a Marxian theory of fetishism (Heath 1974). The combination of semiology and psychoanalysis that constituted *Screen's* Marxism, especially as it moved to disentangle a purely Lacanian concern with subject formation from its previous Althusserian concern with ideology, was challenged in both Britain and the United States—in the first case, from a position that sought to sustain concern with working-class cultural values (e.g., Buscombe et al. 1975, 129–30), and in the second, where *Jump Cut* was beginning to nurture a populist radical film criticism that did include elements of class consciousness, from a working-class feminist position (e.g., Lesage 1974). But with the fading of the suspicion of Freud common in U.S. feminism in the early 1970s, Lacanian psychoanalysis came to dominate U.S. film theory almost entirely. As it did so, the only social difference that film theory could thenceforth register was the specificity psychoanalysis itself could theorize, that is, sexual difference. After this point, given that even the historically specific family structure was not admissible as a mediating agency in the structuration of the unconscious and of language around the phallus or its lack, the main currents of cinema studies had no theoretical means of addressing issues of class. That they have neither had any desire to do so has been confirmed in the generally parallel itinerary followed by the other New Left tradition of cultural criticism, cultural studies.

The founders of British cultural studies—Richard Hoggart, Raymond Williams, and E. P. Thompson—were committed to working-class politics; Hoggart and Williams were themselves of working-class origin. Their early critical and historiographical writing was informed by their political commitments as well as by their address to specific constituencies, especially as they found them through their participation in adult education programs for working-class people. In this, their project paralleled later feminist practices, even though (in the case of Williams and Hoggart) its autobiographical component was displaced into novels, rather than combined with criticism to form the mixed objective/ subjective mode that made early feminist writing so powerful. Initially, their project entailed not the repression of class content from Marxism so much as the gradual discovery that European Marxism could in some cases supply a vocabulary for the analysis of working-class culture. With the conspicuous exception of Thompson's (1978) attack on Althusserianism and "theory" in general and his own correlative subjectivist (and empiricist) theory of class as something that "happens when some men, as a result of common experiences (inherited or shared), feel and articulate the identity of their interests as between themselves, and as against other men" (1963, 9), British cultural studies profited from the translation into English of the texts of Western Marxism: Lukács, the Frankfurt school and, especially, Gramsci. By the early 1970s, "a decisive second . . . break into a complex Marxism" (Hall 1980a, 25) allowed researchers at the Birmingham Centre for Contemporary Cultural Studies decisively to jettison Anglo-American structural-functionalist sociology, and so to produce the mid-1970s projects of reading working-class life for its "lived meanings," and the initial studies of deviant subcultures, schooling, and workplace relations, as well as sophisticated metatheoretical considerations (e.g., Clarke, Critcher, and Johnson 1979). These were thoroughly informed by Althusser, but structural Marxism's inability to pose the concept of class from within a general theory of ideology, and its lack of a theoretical means of conceptualizing ideological resistance, made it less and less useful, especially as text-based, semiological studies were increasingly linked to sociological studies of actual audiences. The consequent "turn to Gramsci"—a turn away from the concept of monolithic, virtually irresistible ideological determination toward that of a dialectical relation among the interests of several classes under the hegemony of one of them—was incompatible with the *Screen* problematic.

Birmingham's implicit challenge to Althusserianism and "*Screen* theory" was taken up by Rosalind Coward (1977). Admitting (more than charitably) that "in *Screen* itself, there has been little work which deals explicitly with the problems of class analysis," she nevertheless argued that its Lacanian theories of subject formation invalidated the Birmingham Centre's papers in which "the ideological and political are finally reduced to being an expression of a class interest or position" (75–76). Denying reductionism, Birmingham retorted that *Screen*'s view of the autonomy of discursive practices and the refusal of any "determinacy in, articulation with or pertinent specific effects for other levels of the social formation" (Chambers et al. 1977, 116) discredited any theory of ideology it might otherwise propose, certainly any Marxist one. Presumably spurred by this interchange, the Media Group at Birmingham spent the next year (1977–78) studying *Screen* theory and reevaluating its own premises, but without finding anything to make them amend their position. Stuart Hall's (1980b) summary response again attacked *Screen*'s exclusive concern with the psychoanalytic construction of the subject as an essentialism that excluded any other determination the social formation in its historically specific forms might exert, and made any concept of ideological struggle impossible. In advancing Birmingham's alternative, David Morely ([1980] 1992) did invoke Michel Pêcheux's concept of an inter-discourse, by which the differential effects of specific discursive practices are seen as inflecting the uniformity of primary subject positioning; but practically his work was still based on Hall's "decoding" model, published some seven years earlier. Indeed, his empirical studies of the reception of British television news programs (made with Charlotte Brunsden) presupposed precisely the self-identical, humanist subject of which *Screen* had worked so hard to dispose.

The progress of this and of Morely's independent work was not, however, immune to the prevailing currents. The early study of the *Nationwide* audience was overtly concerned with class, and had demonstrated very clear, if nondirect, correlations between class position and patterns of decoding.[14] But Morely's discontent with the imprecision of the model of the class structure used, which might well have prompted him to develop a more sophisticated model, instead caused him to abandon class for an exclusive concern with gender. His subsequent studies of the contexts of television reception still focused on working-class families, but because they were *all* working-class, class was a constant; it thus became invisible in all the analyses, which in any case made no attempt to explore the class specificity of the gender relations discovered, or to compare them with gender relations in more privileged families. Though Morely eventually recognized that "gender analysis was prioritized more exclusively than had originally been intended, and the effectivity of this particular factor was isolated from that of others—such as class and age" (160), he has not returned to class.

Otherwise, in attempting to combine a historically and socially specific semiotics with a nonreductionist sociology, and in walking a thin line between recognition of the ways people actively and creatively make over industrial culture to their own uses and ac-

knowledgment of the constraints that surround such interventions, Morely's work has been representative of the best of 1980s
media studies. In general, however, what has become the main current of cultural studies in the United States has abandoned not
only Birmingham's concern with the working class, but also the
Marxist and feminist critical components of the early projects.
What Morely himself designated as "the 'don't worry, be happy'
school of (principally American) cultural studies" (11) is largely
accommodationist, preoccupied with affirmative models of the
consumption of industrial culture as itself a form of empowerment, the site of resistance. Where the heat of *Screen* theory had
boiled off Althusser's Marxism, so, amid the political defeats and
defeatism of the Reagan/Thatcher era, the lowlier ambitions of
cultural studies drained the Marxism out of Gramsci.[15]

In this situation—and in a period of ferociously renewed attacks
on the working class—the present editors organized a number of
panels at Society for Cinema Studies conferences after the dissolution of the Task Force on Race and Class. We hoped to find ways
in which the question of class might again have a place on the
agenda of film and cultural studies, especially in its articulation
with questions of race and gender. Most of the essays assembled
here were initially presented at these panels; the remainder were
solicited. Given the enormity of the project itself, the overall un-
fashionableness of the topic, and the difficulty of finding scholars
who were both capable of writing about class and willing to do so
in a field apparently so inimical, we realize that the task is only just
begun. Whatever the intrinsic value of these essays, the one quality
they have in common is that they all open or reopen a vantage
point from which we can see all the other work that remains to be
done.

Notes

1. There are, of course, exceptions: some work in labor history; less in literary criticism, with Barbara Foley's recent (1993) study of proletarian fiction especially noteworthy; and some essays in cinema studies, for example, Auster and
Quart (1978), Biskind and Ehrenreich (1980), Hansen (1983), Jameson (1990),
Kleinhans (1974), Mayne (1982), Nichols (1972), Ross (1991), Ryan and Kellner
(1988), Sklar (1975), Stead (1989), Traube (1992), and several essays in the col-

lection edited by Sklar and Musser (1990). Hansen and Philipson (1990) have assembled essential articles on socialist feminism.

2. See Bowles and Gintis (1976, especially 209–13) for a survey of statistics on the stratification of higher education by family income. Bourdieu (1988, 44) notes that only 6.7 percent of French professors come from working-class families.

3. Erik Olin Wright (1979) surveyed various models of the class position of intellectuals—that they are workers, that they belong to several different classes, that they are part of the petty bourgeoisie, and that they are part of a profession-managerial class—and concluded that they occupy contradictory locations.

4. Bourdieu (1984) points out that the intellectual who attempts to put him- or herself in the place of the worker can actually experience neither the conditionings that position imposes nor, especially, the necessity that informs those conditionings; but he also points out that migration out of the working class makes "true" representations of working-class experience similarly unavailable for people who "originate from these classes" (372–74, 587 n. 1–2). His whole section on the determination of working-class culture by the experience of domination is very important.

5. *Strangers in Paradise: Academics from the Working Class* (Ryan and Sackrey 1984) is a collection of autobiographical essays typically illustrating the fact that "to grow up working class, then to take on the full trappings of the life of the college professor, *internalizes the conflicts in the hierarchy of the class system within the individual, upwardly mobile person*" (5). This principle, that of the "hidden injuries of class," is adopted from the book of that title (Sennett and Cobb 1973), an account of the experience of working-class people in Boston.

6. Bowles and Gintis's (1976) "reproduction theory" of capitalist education, with its general principle that any "adequate explanation" of "the evidently critical relationship between education and the capitalist economy . . . must begin with the fact that schools produce workers" (10), recognizes that the "authoritarian classroom does produce productive workers, but it also produces misfits and rebels" (12), but it does not develop the alternative function. Bowles and Gintis's work is usefully supplemented by an important text from a quite different tradition, Paul Willis's *Learning to Labor: How Working Class Kids Get Working Class Jobs* ([1977] 1981), an ethnography of the forms of cultural resistance mobilized by working-class youth, which nevertheless assures their reproduction as working-class. In its contrast with Bowles and Gintis's functionalism—which can find hope only in "a socialist movement [and] the creation of working-class consciousness" to replace "the divisive and fragmented consciousness of U.S. working people" (285)—Willis's recognition of the "deep disjunctions and desperate tensions within social and cultural reproduction" that allows for "challenging and subversive and . . . threatening" subcultural contestation (175) was a major contribution to the Gramscian phase of British cultural studies.

7. The first quote here is from *Contribution to the Critique of Hegel's Philosophy of Right*, in Tucker (1978, 64; all subsequent references to Marx's writ-

ings in this chapter are to this edition). The second quote is the statement of the Erfurth Program, as cited by Przeworski (1977, 381).

8. Johnson (1979) provides a useful overview of Marxist theories of class, especially as they affect issues of culture. Other useful introductions may be found in Bottomore (1983, 74–78) and Crompton (1993, 23–29).

9. Przeworski (1977) provides an especially useful survey of the history of this position in Marxist thought.

10. Crompton (1993) has constructed an excellent—and user-friendly—overview of the history and present state of debates about class in sociology. In addition to the theoretical class schemes deriving from the traditions of Marx and Weber, she considers other categories of class indexes, such as "commonsense" hierarchies based on occupation and subjective scales of social status.

11. Brubaker (1985) usefully surveys Bourdieu's work, though he underestimates the importance of social position in relation to production in Bourdieu's model of class identity.

12. Wood (1986) is especially useful in placing Laclau and Mouffe's disarticulation of the political from the economic in the "retreat from class" of 1970s anglophone post-Althusserianism generally, especially in the work of Barry Hindess and Paul Hirst.

13. A notable exception here is the school of radical historians fostered by William Appleman Williams at the University of Wisconsin, who in 1959 founded the seminal journal *Studies on the Left*. For an overview of this left historiography, see Wiener (1991). The continued relevance of this school's corporate liberalism thesis—that corporate capital's appropriation of popular protest movements within the ideology of liberalism prevents their challenging capitalism itself on specifically socialist grounds—is intrinsic to the present project.

14. The conclusion was "that patterns of decoding should not be seen as being simply determined by class position, but by the way in which social position articulates with the individual's position in different discursive formations" (Morely [1980] 1992, 116). So whereas there were great differences in the decodings made by people of different classes, there were also differences within classes. Within working-class reception of *Nationwide,* for example, Morely found a "profound difference in decodings between those groups which are nonunion, or are simply 'members' of unions, and those groups with an active involvement in the discourses of trade unionism—although the two categories of groups have the same working-class background. . . . union officials tend to produce forms of negotiated decoding; the shop stewards produce a fully oppositional form of decoding . . . and simply inactive union members . . . tend to reproduce dominant decodings" (116). Morely's conclusions here, which strikingly resemble Bourdieu's general model described above, were read, however, especially in the United States, as if they demonstrated that there were *no* correlations between decoding and class. See Morely ([1980] 1992, 12–13) for his complaints about these misreadings, and his attempts to clarify.

15. For an overview of the erasure of the critical component in 1980s Gramscianism, see Harris (1992). Morely ([1980] 1992, 1–41) also reviews some of the same issues.

Works Cited

Althusser, Louis. 1977. *For Marx*. London: New Left Books.

Auster, Albert, and Leonard Quart. 1978. "The Working Class Goes to Hollywood." *Cineaste*, 9, no. 1, 4–7.

Balibar, Etienne, and Immanuel Wallerstein. 1991. *Race, Nation, Class: Ambiguous Identities*. London: Verso.

Biskind, Peter, and Barbara Ehrenreich. 1980. "Machismo and Hollywood's Working Class." *Socialist Review*, 50/51, 109–30.

Bottomore, Tom, ed. 1983. *A Dictionary of Marxist Thought*. Cambridge: Harvard University Press.

Bourdieu, Pierre. 1984. *Distinction: A Social Critique of the Judgement of Taste*. Cambridge: Harvard Unversity Press.

———. 1988. *Homo Academicus*. Stanford, Calif.: Stanford University Press.

Bowles, Samuel, and Herbert Gintis. 1976. *Schooling in Capitalist America: Educational Reform and the Contradictions of Economic Life*. New York: Basic Books.

Brubaker, Rogers. 1985. "Rethinking Classical Theory: The Sociological Vision of Pierre Bourdieu." *Theory and Society*, 14, 745–75.

Buscombe, Edward, Christopher Gledhill, Alan Lovell, and Christopher Williams. 1975. "Statement: Psychoanalysis and Film." *Screen*, 16, no. 4, 119–30.

Chambers, Iain, et al. 1977. "Marxism and Culture." *Screen*, 18, no. 4, 109–19.

Clarke, John, Chas Critcher, and Richard Johnson, eds. 1979. *Working-Class Culture: Studies in History and Theory*. London: Hutchinson.

Coward, Rosalind. 1977. "Class, 'Culture' and the Social Formation." *Screen*, 18, no. 1, 75–105.

Crompton, Rosemary. 1993. *Class and Stratification: An Introduction to Current Debates*. London: Polity.

Foley, Barbara. 1993. *Radical Representations: Politics and Form in U.S. Proletarian Fiction, 1929–1941*. Durham, N.C.: Duke University Press.

Hall, Stuart. 1980a. "Cultural Studies and the Centre: Some Problematics and Problems." In Stuart Hall, Dorothy Hobson, Andrew Lowe, and Paul Willis, eds., *Culture, Media, Language*. London: Hutchinson.

———. 1980b. "Recent Developments in Theories of Language and Ideology: A Critical Note." In Stuart Hall, Dorothy Hobson, Andrew Lowe, and Paul Willis, eds., *Culture, Media, Language*. London: Hutchinson.

Hansen, Karen V., and Ilene J. Philipson, eds. 1990. *Women, Class, and the Feminist Imagination: A Socialist-Feminist Reader*. Philadelphia: Temple University Press.

Hansen, Miriam. 1983. "Early Silent Cinema: Whose Public Sphere?" *New German Critique*, no. 29 (Fall), 147–84.

Harris, David. 1992. *From Class Struggle to the Politics of Pleasure: The Effects of Gramscianism on Cultural Studies*. London: Routledge.

Heath, Stephen. 1974. "Lessons from Brecht." *Screen*, 15, no. 3, 103–28.

Jameson, Fredric. 1990. "Class and Allegory in Contemporary Mass Culture:

Dog Day Afternoon as a Political Film." In *Signatures of the Visible*. New York: Routledge.

Johnson, Richard. 1979. "Three Problematics: Elements of a Theory of Working-Class Culture." In John Clarke, Chas Critcher, and Richard Johnson, eds., *Working-Class Culture: Studies in History and Theory*. London: Hutchinson.

Kleinhans, Chuck. 1974. "Contemporary Working Class Film Heroes: *Evel Knievel* and *The Last American Hero*." *Jump Cut*, no. 2 (July-August), 11–14.

Laclau, Ernesto, and Chantal Mouffe. 1985. *Hegemony and Socialist Strategy: Towards a Radical Democratic Politics*. London: Verso.

Lesage, Julia. 1974. "The Human Subject—You, He, or Me?" *Jump Cut*, no. 4 (November-December), 26–27.

Lukács, Georg. 1971. *History and Class Consciousness*, trans. Rodney Livingstone. Cambridge: MIT Press.

Lyotard, Jean-François. 1984. *The Postmodern Condition: A Report on Knowledge*. Minneapolis: University of Minnesota Press.

Mayne, Judith. 1982. "Immigrants and Spectators." *Wide Angle*, 5, no. 2.

Morely, David. 1992 [1980]. *Television, Audiences and Cultural Studies*. London: Routledge.

Nichols, Bill. 1972. "Horatio Alger Goes to Hollywood." *Take One*, 3, no. 11, 11–14.

Przeworski, Adam. 1977. "Proletariat into a Class: The Process of Class Formation from Karl Kautsky's *The Class Struggle* to Recent Controversies." *Politics and Society*, 7, 343–402.

Ross, Steven J. 1991. "Struggles for the Screen: Workers, Radicals, and the Political Uses of Silent Film." *American Historical Review*, 96, 333–67.

Ryan, Jake, and Charles Sackrey. 1984. *Strangers in Paradise: Academics from the Working Class*. Boston: South End.

Ryan, Michael, and Douglas Kellner. 1988. *Camera Politica: The Politics and Ideology of Contemporary Hollywood Film*. Bloomington: Indiana University Press.

Sennet, Richard, and Jonathan Cobb. 1973. *The Hidden Injuries of Class*. New York: Knopf.

Sklar, Robert. 1975. *Movie-Made America: A Cultural History of American Movies*. New York: Random House.

Sklar, Robert, and Charles Musser, eds. 1990. *Resisting Images: Essays on Cinema and History*. Philadelphia: Temple University Press.

Stead, Peter. 1989. *Film and the Working Class: The Feature Film in British and American Society*. London: Routledge.

Thompson, E. P. 1963. *The Making of the English Working-Class*. New York: Knopf.

_____. 1978. *The Poverty of Theory*. London: Merlin.

Traube, Elizabeth. 1992. *Dreaming Identities: Class, Gender, and Generation in 1980s Hollywood Movies*. Boulder, Colo.: Westview.

Tucker, Robert C., ed. 1978. *The Marx-Engels Reader*, 2d ed. New York: Norton.

Wiener, Jon. 1991. *Professors, Politics and Pop*. London: Verso.

Willis, Paul. 1981 [1977]. *Learning to Labor: How Working Class Kids Get Working Class Jobs.* New York: Columbia University Press.

Wood, Ellen Meiksins. 1986. *The Retreat from Class: A New "True" Socialism.* London: Verso.

Wright, Erik Olin. 1979. "Intellectuals and the Class Stucture of Capitalist Society." In Pat Walker, ed., *Between Labor and Capital.* Boston: South End.

———. 1980. "Varieties of Marxist Conceptions of Class Structure." *Politics and Society,* 9, 323–70.

———. 1985. *Classes.* London: Verso.

———. 1989. "Rethinking, Once Again, the Concept of Class Structure." In Erik Olin Wright, ed., *The Debate on Classes.* London: Verso.

Chapter 2

Beyond the Screen: History, Class, and the Movies

Steven J. Ross

Filmmakers were far more concerned with class conflict during the silent era than at any subsequent time in American history. Politically engaged screenwriters and producers turned out movies that examined strikes, lockouts, union organizing, and efforts by socialists and anarchists to overthrow the capitalist system. These class-conscious productions grew so prominent by 1910 that movie reviewers spoke about the emergence of the "labor-capital" film. At first, this new genre depicted class battles from a wide variety of ideological perspectives. Of the thirty-six labor-capital films made in 1914, nearly half offered liberal portrayals of workers, radicals, and their struggles; one-third were conservative, five were radical, two were populist, and two were antiauthoritarian. However, by 1922 the ideological range and political sympathies of filmmakers had changed quite dramatically: nearly two-thirds of the fifteen labor-capital productions of that year were decidedly conservative, only three were liberal, and three were antiauthoritarian; not a single radical or populist film was released.[1]

This pronounced change in political sensibilities raises a number of important questions: Why were silent films so concerned with class conflict and so varied in their ideologies? Why did an industry that started out with strong liberal sympathies toward the struggles of workers, unions, and radicals grow so conservative in later years? What were the forces that shaped the subject matter, politics, and ideology of film? Film scholars unaccustomed to doing historical research face an additional set of questions. How do they begin and where do they look for answers? How far can theory take them? What kinds of empirical sources are likely to help them?

The field of film studies is at yet another crossroads in its development. The myriad theoretical approaches that dominated the field during the past several decades proved valuable in the unraveling of the multiple meanings of films and the various ways in which audiences may have understood them, but theory alone is not enough to explain the actions and motivations of the people who both made and watched movies. To paraphrase Karl Marx, the world of film scholarship must be informed by theory, but its theories must become more worldly. That advice is slowly being heeded. The recent publication of several volumes in the Scribner's History of the American Cinema series and new works by Miriam Hansen, Charles Musser, Douglas Gomery, Thomas Elsaesser, and William Uricchio and Roberta Pearson signal renewed concern for analyzing film within its larger historical context. Yet although film scholars have ventured beyond just theorizing about cinematic images, they have only begun to examine the people and material forces responsible for shaping the ideology of film. Simply utilizing scattered historical examples, as critics of Miriam Hansen's work have suggested, is not the same thing as conducting a systematic analysis of the past. But how is such an examination to be conceived and written? Scholars without Ph.D.s in history are certainly capable of doing historical research, but many wonder how and where to begin.[2]

Using the period between 1914 and 1922 as a microcosm of change, this essay offers scholars a way of thinking about historical problems and a blueprint for unraveling and analyzing the complex forces that shaped the ideological direction of American cinema. My goal here is not to examine the films themselves or the techniques the directors used to visualize their ideological points of view; nor do I offer an extensive analysis of the oppositional filmmakers who challenged industry leaders (I explore both themes in other publications). Rather, my intention is to conceive a way of understanding the historical factors that contributed to the construction and changing nature of visual ideology.[3]

I begin this analysis of labor-capital films by venturing beyond the screen to examine the actual circumstances under which real men and women—not abstract theoretical forces—made these movies. The historical materialist approach used here recognizes the researcher's inability to discover some ultimate truth or the "smoking gun" of causation, but also recognizes the value in examining the conjuction of multiple forces to begin to understand why people and classes do what they do. Writing a materialist history demands that one adopt a mode of analysis in which one begins research in linear fashion, by understanding the history of each key element, but in which one ultimately conceives the subject matter (in this case, the construction of cinematic ideology) in terms of the *simultaneous development and interaction* of several critical forces. Specifically, I propose that we look at five factors that evolved in their own unique ways, but that also, like the circles of a Venn diagram, overlapped at particular points to create common fields of intersection: the movie industry, movie audiences, the general political dynamics of the period, the uses of state power, and labor relations within the movie industry. Each of these factors has its own history, and many of these histories are well documented. Yet it is the less well known interaction of these forces that is of paramount interest here, for the films that audiences saw were, in large part, the products of this interplay.

Ideology and the Emergence of the Movie Industry

The first mandate of materialist history is that we abandon all teleological assumptions about the movie industry and look instead at the specific struggles that shaped the course of its development and the politics of its films. Just because we know how the contemporary movie industry functions, we should not assume it was destined to be that way. The movie industry in the United States began as a relatively small-scale business with hundreds of producers, distributors, and exhibitors scattered throughout the country. The initial decentralized nature of production, the minimal demands of technological expertise, and the relatively modest costs of making films ($400 to $1,000 a reel in many instances) allowed large numbers of diverse individuals and companies to participate in this artisanlike business.[4]

This vast array of producers made it possible for many points of view to reach the screen. Yet the remarkable ideological range of early movies arose not so much because silent filmmakers were inherently more political than their modern counterparts, but because of the material demands imposed upon the industry by the rapid growth of its theaters and changing desires of its patrons. The meteoric expansion of exhibition outlets—from a few hundred in 1905 to fourteen thousand in 1914—generated a vast new demand for films. Producers responded by increasing their output from ten thousand feet of film a week in November 1906 to twenty-eight thousand feet a week in March 1908; but this still did not meet the insatiable hunger for more movies. The demands of production were further complicated by changing audience tastes. As the novelty of watching moving images wore off, patrons asked exhibitors for new and different kinds of films. Hoping to fulfill audience demand and attract new customers, exhibitors began changing their programs daily and sometimes twice daily on weekends. This, in turn, created an even greater demand for new product. Quantity quickly superseded quality as the central concern of producers and exhibitors.[5]

Movies did, however, have to be about something, and decisions concerning the subject matter of films were profoundly influenced by the composition and perceived tastes of the audience. Movie theaters attracted a wide variety of people, but few were as passionately devoted to picture shows as the nation's immigrant and working-class population. Film scholars have debated when middle-class people first started going to the movies, but it is clear that workers and their families constituted the bulk of the movie-going population before World War I. Whether in massive urban centers like New York, where a survey conducted in 1912 found that 95 percent of the audience came from the blue-collar and clerical sectors, or in smaller towns, such as Winona, Minnesota, movies attracted a largely working-class audience. Only with the opening of elegant movie palaces after World War I did middle-class folk attend films in large numbers and on a regular basis.[6]

Given that prewar audiences were overwhelmingly working-class, it is not surprising that films about the dreams and hardships of immigrants and blue-collar workers came to occupy a central position in American cinema. Between "1909 and 1914," writes film distributor and historian Tom Brandon, "far more movies were produced about ordinary people—men, women, and children—as people who engage in work and participate in the productive process of society, than at any comparable length of time since." These working-class films—a classification I use that is based on a film's subject matter rather than its genre—generally fell into one of three categories: innocuous romances, melodramas, comedies, and adventures that used workers and immigrants as their protagonists, but could just as easily have used middle-class or elite characters; films that depicted the general problems of contemporary working-class life; and movies that told highly politicized stories of class struggle. It was this last category that formed the core of labor-capital films.[7]

Filmmakers were not afraid to confront the burning issues of the day, and few burned as brightly or as dangerously as the battles between employers and employees. The rise of monopolies and trusts during the late nineteenth and early twentieth centuries was met by labor and the left with upsurges in strikes and organizing activities. Union membership skyrocketed, from 447,000 in 1897 to 2.1 million in 1904 and 3.5 million in 1917. The moderate American Federation of Labor was the chief beneficiary of this expansion, but radical organizations such as the Western Federation of Miners and Industrial Workers of the World were also winning new recruits. In the political arena, the Socialist Party was making equally impressive gains. Beginning the century with only 10,000 members, the party began capturing local offices around the country and by 1912 its presidential candidate, Eugene V. Debs, succeeded in winning nearly 1 million votes.[8]

The class struggles that frightened so many of the nation's politicians and businessmen provided lively material for movie screens. Whereas most working-class films either shied away from overt political statements or adopted a liberal perspective that, in keeping with the strengths and limitations of Progressive Era politics, portrayed workers as helpless innocents who relied on the paternal actions of outsiders to aid them, labor-capital films placed issues of collective action at the forefront of their stories. Their plots usually dealt with male workers who labored in the nation's most militant and highly organized industries: miners, steelworkers, railroad workers, and skilled industrial workers. In telling these stories, labor-capital productions offered viewers liberal, conservative, radical, populist, and antiauthoritarian perspectives on the everyday dynamics of class conflict.[9]

The significance of these films lay not in their relative number, but in their ability to shape the ways in which millions of Americans *looked at* and perhaps understood class conflict. Between 1908, when labor-capital films began appearing in large numbers, and April 1917, when American entry into World War I dramatically altered the focus and politics of films, at least 228 movies fit this genre. Given the fact that the movie industry was turning out several thousand films a year, 228 may seem like a rather small and perhaps insignificant number, but we should not confuse sheer quantity with qualitative impact. It was by watching these films that many Americans drew their information and perhaps formed their opinions about contemporary class struggles. Indeed, labor-capital films mattered most for people who had little daily contact with unions, radicals, strikes, or mass movements. Certainly no one film was likely to alter a viewer's vision of the world, but the repetition of the same images and political messages over and over again could change the way people thought about class relations—especially as the range of political perspectives grew narrower.

Early filmmakers presented audiences with a wide array of ideological viewpoints, but why did their films assume the ideologies they did? Why was liberalism so pronounced and radicalism allowed such easy access to the screen? A fully developed answer would require far more space than I am permitted here, so let me offer some general ways of responding to these questions. Part of the answer lies in the political character of the age. Today, most Americans talk in terms of two basic political categories, liberal and conservative. But politics at the turn of the century was far more varied in its scope. Populism, socialism, and progressivism engaged the support of hundreds of thousands of citizens. The pervasive liberal character of early movies was fully consistent with the pervasive liberal reformist attitudes of the age. Cinematic ideology, however, was also shaped by the internal politics and economic structure of the film industry itself.

The film industry was a capitalist business, but not all capitalists were alike. The diversity of producers allowed for a contest of ideas and a variety of perspectives unknown in today's film industry. In drawing ideas for tirades against trusts, monopolies, and rapacious capitalists, filmmakers had only had to look in their own backyards. Many producers entered the business by challenging the ten firms that constituted the monopolistic Motion Picture Patents Company (MPPC), popularly known as the Trust. Moreover, a number of these independent mavericks were Eastern European Jews who had suffered repression and hardship in their lives and could never completely shake the antiauthoritarian sentiments of their youth, or the anti-Semitism they encountered in the movie industry itself. Indeed, whereas independents and Trust companies turned out a range of conservative and liberal films, radical and prolabor movies were produced more frequently by independent companies than by the original members of the MPPC.[10]

The liberal sympathies of early films may also have been influenced by the large numbers of women employed in the creative end of the business. Various studies have shown that women maintained more positions of power in the prewar era (as producers, directors, writers, script editors, and heads of script divisions at studios) than at any other time in the industry's history. Although only a few of these women were feminists or radicals, many could not help but recognize the problems of discrimination that plagued society and the movie industry. Alice Guy Blaché, Anita Loos, Lois Weber, Cleo Madison, and others used their positions to make films about problems of particular concern to many female moviegoers: marriage, sexual equality, birth control, earning a living, women's suffrage, raising children, and labor-capital conflicts.[11]

The financial structure of the early industry also afforded producers some leeway in indulging their political sentiments, or those of their directors and writers. "When film companies turned out several short films a month," explains cinema scholar Kay Sloan, "the production of a potentially controversial film was far less of an economic risk than it would be in the later age of the blockbuster."[12] Market demand for films was so great and production costs so low that even if a movie flopped in its first run in major urban markets, it could still make money being shown in neighborhood theaters, small towns, and rural communities.

Filmmakers could also assume liberal attitudes toward strikes and unions because producers faced few major labor problems before 1916. The movie industry did not just depict labor problems, it was also the site of them; however, it was exhibitors, not producers, who first came under fire from organized labor. Militant movie operators' unions were well established by 1910 and engaged in numerous strikes and lockouts with theater owners across the country. On the nation's movie lots, however, unions were slow to organize, and when they did they remained bitterly divided by jurisdictional disputes over who should control production within the industry. Although there were occasional walkouts and threats of more serious actions, studio unions did not launch a single industrywide strike before the war. Organizational efforts by movie actors and actresses were equally ineffective. Thus, it was easy for producers to be tolerant of unions on the screen when they did not have to battle them off the screen.[13]

The relatively low costs of production and high demand for film also allowed a wide variety of groups outside the industry to gain access to the screen. Capitalists, unions, radicals, reformers, women's groups, religious organizations, and government agencies produced their own films or cooperated with established film companies in making films that presented their causes to a mass public. Movies portraying the evils of child labor, the unfair competition caused by the use of prison labor, the hardships faced by widowed mothers, the unsafe conditions of factories and tenements, and the injustices suffered because women were denied the vote helped publicize and facilitate the passage of laws aimed at remedying these problems.[14]

Business and labor groups were especially active in using movies as weapons of class struggle. As big business came under scathing attack from muckraking journalists, liberal filmmakers, and organized labor, the National Association of Manufacturers (NAM), the American Bankers' Association, the New York Central Railroad, and the Ford Motor Company made films aimed at disparaging the claims of their critics and projecting capitalist ideology in a more favorable light. *The Workman's Lesson* (1912) and *The Crime of Carelessness* (1912), both produced by NAM in cooperation with the Edison Company (a firm known for its antiunion policies), are excellent examples of the subtle ways in which capitalists used movies to promote their interests by rewriting history. Produced in the wake of the Triangle Shirtwaist Company fire, which claimed the lives of 146 female garment workers in 1911, these films portrayed employers as deeply concerned with the safety of their employees and shifted blame for workplace accidents to the carelessness and stubbornness of a few bad workers. The success of these and similar films, which, as one scholar notes, "circulated through the nation's movie houses as if they were no different from slapstick comedies, westerns, and historical dramas," led other big businesses to make movies.[15]

Labor and the left were equally successful in using the screen to reach mass audiences with more radical visions of past, present, and future class struggles. Corporate claims of paternal concern for employee welfare and vicious attacks on union selfishness were countered by worker-made films that told of capitalist exploitation, greed, deceit, and lawlessness. *From Dusk to Dawn* (1913) and *What Is to Be Done?* (1914), produced, respectively, by socialists Frank E. Wolfe and Joseph L. Weiss, offered viewers unabashedly radical portrayals of workplace life and the ways in which collective action—depicted in the form of unions and Socialist politics—could transform the world into a more just place for the nation's wage earners. Though adopting a more liberal perspective, *A Martyr to His Cause* (1911), produced by the American Federation of Labor for $2,577, reversed the negative images of antiunion films and portrayed trade unionists, not capitalists, as the true upholders of democratic institutions and purveyors of a better life for all Americans. These movies also played in theaters throughout the country and were seen by far more people than ever turned out for labor or Socialist rallies.[16]

The active participation of these nonindustry groups, the diverse character of industry producers, the constant need for more films, and the low cost of production allowed a wide range of political visions to be seen. These factors also prevented any one group—be it the Trust or its increasingly powerful independent competitors—from maintaining hegemony over the movie industry. But the outbreak of war in Europe soon changed the structure of the industry and, in so doing, made it considerably more difficult for independent and oppositional films to reach the screen.

The Rise of Hollywood and the Reshaping of Cinematic Ideology

World War I marked a turning point not only in domestic and world politics, but in the evolution of the American movie industry and its relations with government, business, and labor. In 1914, the United States produced slightly more than half the world's movies. By 1919, 90 percent of the films exhibited in Europe and 100 percent of those shown in South America were made in the United States. Although European producers slowly resumed production after the war, America remained the center of world film production.[17]

The rapid growth of American production signaled the rise of a new type of film industry and the birth of "Hollywood" as a metaphor to describe it. By 1920, Hollywood was no longer just a place, it was a way of doing business. The large number of modest-sized, geographically scattered producers, distributors, and exhibitors that dominated the prewar era were steadily supplanted by an increasingly oligarchic, vertically integrated studio system based in Los Angeles and New York. These transformations did not happen at once, nor was it inevitable that American filmmakers would continue to dominate the world market. To turn foreign disaster into domestic profit, industry leaders had to change the ways they did business. Studio executives abandoned the haphazard methods of the past in favor of more efficient modern business practices. Cost accounting, not artistic expression, became the new industry bywords. No longer were directors allowed to begin shooting with just a bare outline of a story. Now everything was carefully planned and budgeted before filming began.[18]

Movies were now big business, and as in other big businesses, those who were most successful increased profits and secured greater control over the market by expanding into other areas of the industry. Distributors moved into production, producers into exhibition, and exhibitors into production and distribution. Powerful exhibitors such as Fox, Loew, and the twenty-seven firms that formed the First National Exhibitors' Circuit in 1917 ventured into production by building or buying their own studios, and prominent film companies such as Universal and Goldwyn formed modest theater chains in which to show their products. Industry giant Paramount responded to increased competition by creating its own chain of theaters.[19]

All this ambitious expansion required money, more money than any single individual or company could raise. Some studios tried to expand through a series of mergers, but the most venturesome firms turned to the nation's financial and industrial communities for capital. By the early 1920s, Wall Street firms and major industrial corporations were represented in the boardrooms of virtually every major film company—a development that did not sit well with many company employees. "When we operated on picture money there was a joy in the industry," recounted Cecil B. DeMille, "when we operated on Wall Street money, there was grief in the industry."[20]

Changes in financing and production were paralleled by changes in the nature of films themselves. Multireel films featuring famous movie stars slowly supplanted the modest one- and two-reel movies of past decades. But spiraling star salaries, combined with longer and more lavish productions, quickly drove up the cost of making first-run feature films. In 1909, before the star system took hold, a one-reeler could be made for less than $1,000. Ten years later, five-reel features cost $40,000 to $80,000 to produce, and more elaborate six- to nine-reel "special" productions ran $200,000 or more.[21]

Not all companies built large studios or made expensive films with movie stars. Dozens of modest-sized independents were content to rent space on studio lots and turn out several films a year. Varied audience tastes meant that clever producers would always find a place in the industry. But the power of independents and small studios greatly waned in the wake of increased efforts at industrial consolidation by their larger brethren. Rising production costs quickly reduced the range of nonindustry filmmakers. Suffragists, child labor reformers, birth control advocates, religious groups, and other organizations were forced off the screen as the price of making commercially viable films rose from a few thousand to tens of thousands of dollars.[22]

The increasingly big-business character of Hollywood affected not only the composition of the industry's participants but the politics of its films. Ideological changes, however, were not solely the result of the industry's internal transformation. From April

1917 until the early 1920s, political pressure by federal agencies and state censors, mounting public hysteria over perceived Communist threats, and heightened labor militancy outside and inside the movie industry interacted to reshape the ways in which filmmakers looked at issues of class conflict.

With American entry into World War I, federal involvement with movies and the movie industry assumed unprecedented new dimensions. The forces of the state, long used against labor at the workplace, now extended their powers into the arena of leisure as government officials began exercising greater control over the production, distribution, and ideological focus of American films. On April 14, 1917, President Woodrow Wilson created the Committee on Public Information (CPI) and charged its chairman, former newsman and erstwhile screenwriter George Creel, with using the mass media to "sell the war to the American public." Three months later, the special War Cooperation Board was formed and representatives from the National Association of the Motion Picture Industry (NAMPI) were assigned to virtually every government agency to help produce slides, shorts, and trailers that would publicize their war work.[23]

Initial relations between the movie industry and the government proved cordial as studios discovered there was a great deal of money to be made in making, distributing, and exhibiting government films. But industry magnates soon learned that the government expected a quid pro quo in return for its "favors." Tensions mounted as the CPI pressured studios to promote particular visions of class relations in American society. Determined to counter enemy propaganda that portrayed the United States "as a Nation of dollar-mad materialists," Creel asked studios to produce cheerful films that "presented the wholesome life of America, giving fair ideas of our people and our institutions," and to "keep out of circulation" movies that "gave entirely false impressions of American life and morals."[24] Creel relied on economic incentives and subtle threats to force studios into compliance. With theaters throughout the world clamoring for movies, huge profits could be made by sending American films abroad. In order to reach these markets, however, companies had to secure an export license for every film shipped overseas. CPI censors, who had the sole authority to grant these lucrative licenses, exercised their power by withholding them from films portraying negative aspects of American life—especially class conflict. Movies showing strikes and labor riots, hunger and poverty, or ghetto slum conditions were repeatedly rejected on the grounds that they were a "bad testimonial to the value of democracy."[25]

Industry leaders also discovered that government agencies could control their very ability to carry on business. Although movie personnel initially managed to escape the draft, coal shortages in the winter of 1918 and the need for more soldiers led outraged Americans to demand the closing of movie theaters and the drafting of all eligible industry workers. After months of frantic lobbying, studio bigwigs persuaded the War Industries Board (WIB) to declare the movies an "essential industry" and exempt its employees from the draft. But in return, the WIB imposed a number of conditions that regulated a wide variety of industry practices. The industry's continued "essential" status, the WIB declared, depended upon its willingness to produce "only wholesome films." Indeed, a month earlier, the NAMPI curried government favor by agreeing to follow CPI guidelines governing the kinds of ideological statements acceptable for export. Filmmakers were cautioned against making pictures that contained "mob scenes and riots which might be entirely innocent in themselves but [could be] distorted and used adversely to the interests of the United States."[26]

Producers, distributors, and exhibitors may have privately balked at these efforts to control the subject matter and ideology of their films, but publicly they acceded to government demands and complied with CPI guidelines. Whether motivated by fear or patriotism, industry personnel simply could not risk having their employees drafted, their theaters closed, or their profitable export markets taken away. The growing consolidation of the film industry was another powerful force working on behalf of compliance. With studios now involved in all ends of the business, the ideology of films was less important than securing their widespread distribution. Creel's victory was clear when Adolph Zukor announced in July 1918 that henceforth his company would "produce only plays of a cheerful nature" and "select only such subjects for production as will dictate to the peoples of foreign nations the qualities and spiritual texture which have been developed in American manhood and womanhood by the institutions which we are now striving to preserve."[27]

The end of the war in November 1918 did not signal the end of government efforts to shape the ideological focus of American cinema. The Joint Committee of Motion Picture Activities of the United States Government and Allied Organizations, created after the armistice to monitor federal film activity, saw movies as valuable vehicles for addressing the nation's postwar problems. And of the many problems confronting government leaders, few evoked more concern than the dual threats of Bolshevism and labor militancy.[28] As the flush of victory began to fade, American workers found themselves fighting domestic battles to restore their fallen standard of living. With government agencies doing little to help them, workers pursued justice through strikes and labor organizations. By the end of 1919, 4.1 million Americans belonged to unions (a 49 percent increase since 1916) and more than 4 million men and women had participated in 3,500 workplace stoppages—including a general strike in Seattle and a police strike in Boston. The haunting specter of the Russian Revolution and the subsequent growth of the American-based Communist Party and Communist Labor Party intensified the growing climate of fear and prompted federal and state agencies to adopt policies aimed at suppressing radicalism.[29]

Government agencies also moved to quell Bolshevism and labor militancy by influencing depictions of unions and radicals in Hollywood films. David Niles, head of the Labor Department's Motion Picture Section and chairman of the Joint Committee of Motion Picture Activities, sent a letter to producers in November 1918 requesting that they confer with him "prior to starting productions based on Socialism, labor problems, etc." Portraying a screen villain "as a member of the IWW or the Bolsheviki is positively harmful," he suggested, whereas "portraying the hero as a strong, virile American, a believer of American institutions and ideals, will do much good." Niles's "request" was accompanied by a series of incentives and threats. Those who cooperated with the Labor Department might receive valuable government endorsements; those who did not might open themselves to federal censorship.[30]

Secretary of the Interior Franklin K. Lane pursued an even more aggressive course of action. In December 1919, acting with the approval of Congress, he met with movie industry magnates and secured their pledge to assist the government in using film "to carry on a nation-wide campaign to combat Bolshevism and radicalism" that would "crush the Red movement in America." Within several weeks, the newly constituted "Americanism Committee of the Motion Picture Industry of the United States," comprising the nation's leading production, distribution, and exhibition firms, began circulating suggested scenarios to producers aimed at combating the "revolutionary sentiment so assiduously and insidiously being fomented in this country."[31]

Government officials such as Lane and Niles could ask anything they wanted, but would movie industry leaders do their bidding? Compliance was easy so long as it involved only sending in a few scenarios or turning out a few financially insignificant Americanism films. The more important question was, How would studios deal with problems of unionism and Bolshevism in their own productions? Would they give in to government pressure? Would they resist? The answers to these questions were critical, for with Hollywood now dominating the world market, its visions of radicalism and class relations reigned as the dominant cinematic visions of the postwar world.

It would be a mistake to interpret cinematic ideology of the 1917–22 period simply as the product of an evil government twisting the arm of a reluctant liberal film industry. Changing class relations on the studio lots also played a vital role in altering class relations on the screen. Industry leaders may have resented the pressures placed on them by federal officials, but when it came to dealing with labor issues, government fears of unbridled class conflict found a sympathetic response among many powerful studio executives. Strikes, militant unionism, and Bolshevism were not things that happened only "out there" in society. They also happened on the studio lots.

The antilabor, antileft films of the era were paralleled by the emergence of the movie industry as a major big business and by increased militancy among its workers. The years between 1916 and 1922 saw the first sustained efforts at unionizing virtually all film industry jobs. The studio craft unions founded before the war—stage employees, carpenters, electricians, and building tradesmen—remained the dominant unions after the war. However, increased production and wartime labor shortages prompted new organizations among actors and actresses, movie extras, movie cowboys, scenic artists, cameramen, and film laboratory workers. The strategy of centralization adopted by emerging studios was also used by Hollywood workers, who established the Amusement Federation to represent all industry unions in May 1919. The Motion Picture Producers' Association (MPPA), which represented the industry's leading studios, responded to this upsurge by pledging to maintain the "principle of the open shop upon which the picture studios have hitherto been conducted" and by hiring spies to penetrate unions and report on their activities.[32]

With organizing activities on the rise and the MPPA determined to thwart the spread of unionism, the relative harmony of prewar years gave way to a series of bitter strikes, boycotts, and lockouts. Hollywood experienced its first major strike in August 1918 when 1,100 members of International Alliance of Theatrical and Stage Employees (IATSE) Local 33 walked off their jobs at the twenty-five studios refusing to grant their request for a wage increase. Although IATSE won their demands, antiunion feelings in Hollywood ran so high that negotiations had to be shifted to the studios' financial headquarters in New York City, where cooler heads prevailed. The labor militancy that swept the nation during the next two years was also felt in the movie industry, as studios came under assault from building tradesmen, actors, film lab workers, and cameramen. Movie theater owners also faced scores of strikes by projectionists, musicians, and attendants. Tensions between employers and employees peaked in July 1921, when rival IATSE and Building Trades' unions joined together to launch what became a two-year boycott of the industry's leading studios.[33]

The bitter class conflicts that beset the industry between 1917 and 1922 were accompanied by a pronounced shift in the political sympathies of labor-capital films. During the prewar era, when few strikes plagued producers, 44 percent of all labor-capital productions were liberal and 36 percent were conservative. Yet as industry labor policies grew more conservative, so did the films: 65 percent of the labor-capital films made between April 1917 and 1922 were conservative, and only 27 percent were liberal. Audiences also found themselves exposed to a narrower ideological range of films, as not a single radical movie was made by industry regulars. Not surprisingly, the studios experiencing the most labor trouble—Fox, Vitagraph, Goldwyn, Universal, Famous Players-Lasky—were also the leading producers of antiunion, antiradical films.[34]

Prewar conservative portrayals of unionists as lazy or corrupt were superseded by postwar images of unions and their leaders as the dupes or willing agents of the Bolshevik plot to conquer America. The militant industrial unionism preached by the IWW (and favored, in a milder form, by studio nemesis IATSE) was presented as the typical ideology of organized labor. Sympathetic depictions of radicals completely disappeared from the screen. "When radicals are pictured in the films," observed socialist film critic Louis Gardy, "they are not shown as champions of the people, but as traitors of the deepest dye."[35] The collective message of these conservative films was that honest *American* workers did not need self-serving radical organizations, but could bring their complaints to their employers, man to man. And the employers, of course, would respond favorably to the just grievances of individuals.

I do not wish to be so simplistic as to suggest that what happened on the studio lots was directly translated to the screen. There were other reasons for the proliferation of antileft imagery. Making anti-Bolshevik films, suggested one writer in the *Moving Picture World,* offered opportunities for "reaping a cash reward while serving a further and equally vital purpose of patriotism." Director William deMille attributed the prominence of screen reds to the need for good villains—ones who could make audiences boo, hiss, and cover their eyes in fear: "We had to have villains, and there was that tremendous land, far too busy to protest and containing one hundred and sixty million potential menaces."[36]

The rising costs of filmmaking and heightened fears of box-office failure proved equally crucial in determining the kinds of ideological statements that reached the screen. As films grew longer and production costs higher, studio output dropped from several hundred one- and two-reelers to several dozen feature films a year. Consequently, the financial stakes involved in any one movie grew more significant. Producers repeatedly expressed a desire to please audiences, but deciding what audiences wanted was often a matter of guesswork. Studios did know, however, that ignoring government "suggestions" regarding labor-capital themes meant risking domestic censorship and the loss of profitable foreign markets. Postwar industry leaders also had to contend with local and state censors who operated in a hundred cities and nearly a dozen states by 1926. These boards—especially those in areas plagued by strikes—did more than threaten; they censored films and newsreels that criticized capitalists or offered sympathetic depictions of working-class struggles. Pennsylvania censors, for example, ordered substantial changes in William S. Hart's *The Whistle* (Famous Players-Lasky, 1921), a liberal film that exposed unsafe working conditions in textile mills. State censors also ordered Pathé, Hearst, Gaumont, and Fox to cut scenes of newsreels showing ongoing strikes and labor agitation. Sympathetic footage of coal miners' strikes in Ohio, Pennsylvania, Illinois, and West Virginia never reached the screen.[37]

Studios could, of course, refuse to comply with censors' demands, but doing so would mean delaying, perhaps even canceling, a film's release in any number of states. With the cost of an average feature film spiraling from $12–18,000 in 1918 to $40–80,000 in 1919 to $1–2 million for the star-studded extravaganzas of the early 1920s, the financial risks involved in making provocative labor-capital films were simply too great. Potential losses were heightened for powerful moguls such as Zukor, Loew, Laemmle, and Fox, for whom the delay of a film meant less product and less profit for their distribution and exhibition wings. The stakes were perhaps even greater for struggling smaller companies, where, as Jack Warner later noted, "every nickel counted."[38]

Industry perceptions regarding the changing composition and tastes of audiences also affected the political character of movies. Major studios and exhibition chains strove to increase their profits after the war by building lavish movie palaces that would attract prosperous middle-class patrons while also retaining loyal working-class fans. The people who flocked to these palaces, or so producers and exhibitors believed, wanted to forget about war and social problems and instead celebrate the flowering of peace and prosperity. The diaries, memoirs, and correspondence of industry leaders suggest they truly believed people craved films about money, sex, cars, and clothes—films "in harmony with the life it was leading or, at least, hoped soon to lead."[39]

With the perceived tastes of audiences changing, censors looming over them, and "Wall Street watchdogs"—as Jesse Lasky called them—offering "much unappreciated advice," industry leaders grew more cautious in their choice of productions.[40] Indeed, 69 percent of the labor-capital films made between 1922 and 1929, and 77 percent of the films made after the publication of the industry's internal code in 1924 (created to stem the public hysteria that followed the Roscoe "Fatty" Arbuckle and William Desmond Taylor scandals), took a decidedly conservative point of view. Studios also responded to heightened financial risks by drastically reducing their labor-capital productions. Between 1923 and 1929, when roughly 700 features were released each year, the movie industry (excluding labor film companies) produced only forty-two labor-capital films, an average of six films per year—a sharp drop from the 173 films released between April 1917 and December 1922 (an average of thirty-one films per year).[41]

Not all Hollywood producers were antiunion or anti-Red, nor did the increasingly conservative direction of the movie industry go unopposed. Companies run by Charlie Chaplin, William Hart, Mary Pickford, and Douglas Fairbanks were strong supporters of organized labor and gave preference to union members in hiring. Yet, despite their liberal sympathies, these prounion producers and their films were in the decided minority. Indeed, the greatest challenge to the dominant Hollywood vision of class conflict came from labor and radical groups outside the industry. Beginning in 1918, angry working-class organizations across the country, from the teeming metropolis of New York to the quiet town of Vallejo, California, challenged the ideological domination of Hollywood by forming production, distribution, and exhibition networks that would bring "the aims and hopes of the worker . . . before the masses in a most impressive and lasting manner."[42] Men and women who waged war to make the world safe for democracy now embarked on a crusade to make the screen safe for labor and the left.

The leaders of this renewed labor film movement, like their prewar predecessors, were not filmmakers per se, but working people who used film to offer the public positive portrayals of unionism, socialism, and radicalism. But the dramatic changes that gripped the postwar movie business made their undertakings considerably more complicated than a decade before. Independent producers now had to clear three major hurdles in order to reach the screen. First, they had to raise sufficient funds to finance a film—this now meant raising tens of thousands rather than two or three thousand dollars. Then they had to make movies good enough that people would *pay* to see them. Filmmakers could no longer just pick up a camera, as Frank Wolfe had done in 1913, and shoot a bunch of scenes. Audiences were now accustomed to more elaborate Hollywood films and expected good production values (good acting, costumes, sets, and lighting—all of which cost money). Finally, they had to find distributors and exhibitors outside the increasingly oligopolistic studio system who would handle their products. Class-conscious labor companies faced the additional problem of overcoming the powerful opposition of censors and government agencies. After being warned that worker filmmakers were producing pictures for the "purpose of inciting class feelings" and hatred against employers, J. Edgar Hoover dispatched Bureau of Investigation agents to monitor the efforts of these fledgling companies.[43]

Despite these considerable barriers, labor film companies turned out a number of feature films and newsreels that challenged Hollywood representations of contemporary labor struggles and offered viewers markedly different ways of looking at and solving the problems of class conflict. *The Contrast* (1921), produced by the New York-based socialist Labor Film Services; *The New Disciple* (1921), produced by the Federation Film Corporation—an organization composed of militant trade unionists from the Seattle area; *Labor's Reward* (1925), produced by the AFL; and *The Passaic Textile Strike* (1926), produced by the Communist-led International Workers' Aid, offered, respectively, depictions of miners' strikes, worker cooperatives, efforts to organize women wage earners, and ongoing textile strikes. Though the particular politics of these films varied, their general ideological message was the same: strikes, labor militancy, and unionization drives were not caused by Bolshevik agents or corrupt union leaders, but were the results of ordinary, law-abiding people responding to the unjust actions of employers and their hired thugs.[44]

These movies also challenged dominant industry assumptions regarding the kinds of movies audiences wanted to see. Men and women may well have enjoyed watching escapist fantasies about luxury and the high life. Yet, *when given a choice,* they also went to see serious political films that offered radical critiques of capitalist society. Worker-made films, like their Hollywood counterparts, contained strong doses of fantasy, but they were working-class fantasies that showed men and women winning strikes, defeating employers, and taking greater control over their industries and their lives. These films played in theaters throughout the country and, taken collectively, were seen by millions of enthusiastic viewers.[45]

Unfortunately for their newly won fans, the initial success of these labor film companies proved short-lived. With the exception of the IWA, none of them produced another feature film. Trying to overcome industry opposition to *all* independent filmmakers proved too difficult. Briefly stated, the internal problems of raising the money needed to finance a second production, combined with the external opposition of national distributors who refused to handle their films, theater chains that refused to show them, and state censors who often banned them, frustrated financially pressed labor film companies and led them to abandon the screen in favor of transferring their propaganda efforts to the more accessible and less costly medium of radio.[46]

Technological changes in the late 1920s further restricted the ideological range of movies by making it even more difficult for any small film company to reach the screen. As "talkies" came to replace silent films, production costs soared to a level that few labor or independent producers could afford. Moreover, few of the neighborhood houses that screened labor and independent productions could afford the high costs of wiring for sound—$10,000 to $30,000, depending on the theater's size. With the onset of the Great Depression, many of these politically sympathetic exhibitors either went bankrupt or sold out to theater chains that were loath to show any kind of oppositional film. From the 1930s onward, studios (Warner Brothers in particular) and smaller production companies occasionally made films dealing with class conflict, but they were few in number and occupied a far less radical, or even liberal, position than silent films of the prewar years.[47]

Class struggle is not a subject we usually associate with Hollywood or its films, but that has not always been the case. The history of the movies is the history of struggles by various groups and classes—in and outside of Hollywood—to control the structure of the industry and the politics of its films. The establishment of ideological hegemony, as I have tried to show in this essay, is not an event but a process—and an unpredictable one at that. To understand the changing political focus and ideological range of films, we must first understand the changing historical conditions under which dominant groups and challengers operated. Theoretical assumptions are certainly important for locating the issues and problems we need to study, but they cannot take the place of concrete historical analysis. Simply labeling the movie industry a capitalist culture industry, as Frankfurt school theorists did, tells us very little about its actual evolution. Although capitalism was always the dominant system under which it operated, not all capitalists or industry participants were the same. The movie industry began as an amalgam of relatively small-scale capitalists, each exerting only a modest degree of control over the entire industry. The low costs of production and the relatively easy access to the screen allowed a wide variety of groups (including noncapitalists) to visualize their politics and prevented any one group from dominating the screen. Yet, as the nature of the industry and its key participants changed, so too did the kinds of ideological statements audiences were likely to see.

Ideological hegemony is never total, but is constantly shifting depending on who is challenging whom. Although labor film companies were beaten back, subsequent generations of filmmakers—on the left and right—rose up to resist studio control over the industry. We must be careful, however, not to romanticize or overstate the impact of such resistance. If our primary concern is understanding the ideological control of the screen, then it is the process by which dominant groups maintain their power and beat back their opponents that must ultimately occupy the center stage of analysis. The structure of the movie industry, the nature of internal labor relations, the composition and perceived desires of audiences, the pressures applied by government agencies and other powerful external actors, and the general political climate of a particular era offer starting points for understanding this process.

Identifying these five factors is relatively easy, but analyzing the ways in which they interact is not. And that is precisely the task that confronts any scholar investigating the material bases of cinematic ideology: to explain the interaction among competing forces and begin to show how the everyday struggles of real men and women shaped the kinds of cinematic politics available to viewers.

Notes

I wish to thank Paul Adler, Phil Ethington, Doug Flamming, and Lary May for their helpful comments.

1. Political labeling is an arbitrary act. However, to provide some common understanding, some attempt at definitions is in order. I see conservative films as those that present worker, union, or radical activity in the worst possible light and rarely explain the causes of strikes or employee discontent. Radical films offer unabashedly positive depictions of socialists, radicals, and their struggles, and equally scathing critiques of capitalists and capitalism. Liberal films decry the exploitation of innocent workers, condemn irresponsible capitalists, call for cooperation between labor and capital, and advocate reform, not radicalism, as the best method for solving the nation's industrial ills. Populist films preach a gut-level hatred of monopolists and show how they consistently undermine the well-being of ordinary citizens. Antiauthoritarian movies, though not directly challenging capitalism, mock the authority of those who often give workers the hardest time: foremen, police, judges, and employers. None of these ideological visions is uniform; one can find important political shadings within each category. My list of labor-capital films is gathered from a variety of sources. Labor and radical newspapers contain an invaluable array of movie reviews, audience comments, and discussions about the changing politics of the film industry; most useful are the *New York Call, Los Angeles Citizen, Seattle Union Record, Chicago New Majority*, and *Chicago* and *New York Daily Worker*. Other sources that offer insights into the politics of silent film are *The American Film Institute Catalog of Motion Pictures Produced in the United States*, 6 vols. (Berkeley: University of California Press, 1971–88); Kemp R. Niver, *Early Motion Pictures: The Paper Print Collection in the Library of Congress* (Washington, D.C., 1985); *The George Kleine Collection of Early Motion Pictures in the Library of Congress*, prepared by Rita Horowitz and Harriet Harrison (Washington, D.C., 1980); Richard Fauss, *A Bibliography of Labor History in Newsfilm*, 4 vols. (Morgantown: University of West Virginia, 1980); Writers' Program of the Works Projects Administration Staff, ed., *The Film Index*, 3 vols. (New York: Kraus International, 1985). My analysis of labor-capital films is most heavily informed by my viewing of more than two hundred silent films dealing with working-class life.

2. Charles Musser, *The Emergence of Cinema: The American Screen to 1907*

(New York: Charles Scribner's Sons, 1990); Eileen Bowser, *The Transformation of Cinema 1907–1915* (New York: Charles Scribner's Sons, 1990); Richard Koszarski, *An Evening's Entertainment: The Age of the Silent Feature Picture, 1915–1928* (New York: Charles Scribner's Sons, 1990); Miriam Hansen, *Babel and Babylon: Spectatorship in American Silent Film* (Cambridge: Harvard University Press, 1991); Charles Musser, in collaboration with Carol Nelson, *High-Class Moving Pictures: Lyman H. Howe and the Forgotten Era of Traveling Exhibition, 1880–1920* (Princeton, N.J.: Princeton University Press, 1991); Charles Musser, *Before the Nickelodeon: Edwin S. Porter and the Edison Manufacturing Company* (Berkeley: University of California Press, 1991); Douglas Gomery, *Shared Pleasures: A History of Movie Presentation in the United States* (Madison: University of Wisconsin Press, 1992); Thomas Elsaesser, ed., with Adam Barker, *Early Cinema: Space, Frame, Narrative* (London: BFI, 1990); William Uricchio and Roberta E. Pearson, *Reframing Culture: The Case of the Vitagraph Quality Films* (Princeton, N.J.: Princeton University Press, 1993). For reviews that both praise and criticize Hansen's uses of history, see Lary May's review in *Journal of Social History*, 27 (Fall 1993), 149–52; David Grimsted, "Through the Looking-Glass of Film," *Reviews in American History*, 21 (March 1993), 86–92.

3. For more detailed examinations of labor-capital films, see Steven J. Ross, "Cinema and Class Conflict: Labor, Capital, the State, and American Silent Film," in Robert Sklar and Charles Musser, eds., *Resisting Images: Essays on Cinema and History* (Philadelphia: Temple University Press, 1990), 68–107; Steven J. Ross, "Struggles for the Screen: Workers, Radicals, and the Political Uses of Silent Films," *American Historical Review*, 96 (April 1991), 333–67; Steven J. Ross, *Struggles for the Screen: Politics, Class, and the Rise of the Movies* (Princeton, N.J.: Princeton University Press, forthcoming).

4. The cost of making films and the diversity of producers and production centers are discussed in George Mitchell, "The Consolidation of the American Film Industry 1915–1920," in Ron Burnett, ed., *Explorations in Film Theory: Selected Essays from Cine-Tracts* (Bloomington: Indiana University Press, 1991), 254–72; Terry Ramsaye, *A Million and One Nights* (New York: Simon & Schuster, 1964 [1926]); Benjamin B. Hampton, *A History of the Movies* (New York: Covici-Friede, 1931); Mae D. Huettig, *Economic Control of the Motion Picture Industry: A Study in Industrial Organization* (Philadelphia: University of Pennsylvania Press, 1944); Lewis Jacobs, *The Rise of American Film: A Critical History* (New York: Teachers College Press, 1968); Tino Balio, ed., *The American Film Industry* (Madison: University of Wisconsin Press, 1976); Suzanne Mary Donahue, *American Film Distribution: The Changing Marketplace* (Ann Arbor: UMI Research Press, 1987); Kay Sloan, *Loud Silents: Origins of the Social Problem Film* (Urbana: University of Illinois Press, 1988); Kevin Brownlow, *Behind the Mask of Innocence* (New York: Alfred A. Knopf, 1990).

5. The problems of producing and distributing films are described in Fred Balshofer and Fred C. Miller, *One Reel a Week* (Berkeley: University of California Press, 1967); David Bordwell, Janet Staiger, and Kristin Thompson, *The Classical Hollywood Cinema: Film Style and the Mode of Production to 1960* (New

York: Columbia University Press, 1985); Donahue, *American Film Distribu-tion*. For early exhibition practices, see David Nasaw, *Going Out: The Rise and Fall of Public Amusements* (New York: Basic Books, 1993); Russell Merritt, "Nickelodeon Theaters 1905–1914: Building an Audience for the Movies," in Tino Balio, ed., *The American Film Industry* (Madison: University of Wisconsin Press, 1976), 59–79; Gomery, *Shared Pleasures;* Musser, *The Emergence of Cinema*.

6. David O. Thomas, "From Page to Screen in Smalltown America: Early Motion Picture Exhibition in Winona, Minnesota," *Journal of the University Film Association,* 33 (Summer 1981), 9–10. New York survey results are quoted in Lary May, *Screening Out the Past: The Birth of Mass Culture and the Motion Picture Industry* (New York: Oxford University Press, 1980), 164. May discusses the changing class and gender composition of audiences; see also Merritt, "Nickelodeon Theaters," 59–82; Robert C. Allen, "Motion Picture Exhibition in Manhattan, 1906–1912: Beyond the Nickelodeon," *Cinema Journal,* 18 (Spring 1979), 2–15; Douglas Gomery, "Movie Audiences, Urban Geography, and the History of American Film," *Velvet Light Trap Review of Cinema,* 19 (Spring 1982), 23–29; Garth Jowett, *Film: The Democratic Art* (Boston: Little, Brown, 1976); Roy Rosenzweig, *Eight Hours for What We Will: Workers and Leisure in an Industrial City, 1870–1920* (Cambridge: Cambridge University Press, 1984); Kathy Peiss, *Cheap Amusements: Working Women and Leisure in Turn-of-the-Century New York* (Philadelphia: Temple University Press, 1986); Hansen, *Babel and Babylon*.

7. Thomas Brandon, "Populist Film," ch. 1, p. 17, folder C34, unpublished manuscript, Film Studies Center, Museum of Modern Art, New York. I offer a much fuller analysis of working-class films in *Struggles for the Screen,* chs. 2–3. Secondary works that explore the working-class focus of early film include Musser, *The Emergence of Cinema;* Al Auster, "Mary Pickford (1893–1979): The Star the Working Class Found," *Cineaste,* 9 (Fall 1979), 42–43; Peter Stead, *Film and the Working Class: The Feature Film in British and American Society* (London: Routledge, 1989); Charles Musser, "Work, Ideology, and Chaplin's Tramp," in Robert Sklar and Charles Musser, eds., *Resisting Images: Essays on Cinema and History* (Philadelphia: Temple University Press, 1990), 36–67; Robert Sklar, *Movie-Made America: A Cultural History of American Movies* (New York: Random House, 1975); Jacobs, *The Rise of American Film;* Sloan, *Loud Silents;* Brownlow, *Behind the Mask of Innocence*.

8. These statistics are taken from U.S. Department of Commerce, *Historical Statistics of the United States: Colonial Times to 1970,* 2 vols. (Washington, D.C.: U.S. Government Printing Office, 1975), 1:177; James Weinstein, *The Decline of Socialism in America: 1912–1925* (New Brunswick, N.J.: Rutgers University Press, 1984), 27. For an overview of labor and the left during this era, see Weinstein, *The Decline of Socialism;* James R. Green, *The World of the Worker: Labor in the Twentieth Century* (New York: Hill & Wang, 1980); Melvyn Dubofsky, *We Shall Be All: A History of the IWW* (New York: Quadrangle, 1969); David Montgomery, *The Fall of the House of Labor: The Workplace, the State,*

and American Labor Activism, 1865–1925 (New York: Cambridge University Press, 1987).

9. The politics and plots of working-class films are explored more thoroughly in Ross, *Struggles for the Screen,* ch. 2.

10. The Trust included eight production companies, one film importer, and one manufacturer of raw film stock, all of which joined together to limit film stock and production, distribution, and exhibition of movies solely to Trust members. For histories of the Trust and its competitors, see Neal Gabler, *An Empire of Their Own: How the Jews Invented Hollywood* (New York: Crown, 1988); Upton Sinclair, *Upton Sinclair Presents William Fox* (Los Angeles: private printing, 1933); Ramsaye, *A Million and One Nights;* Jacobs, *The Rise of American Cinema;* Sklar, *Movie-Made America.*

11. The role of women in the silent film industry is discussed in Martin Norden, "Women in the Early Film Industry," *Wide Angle,* 6, no. 3 (1984), 58–67; Anthony Slide, *Early Women Directors* (New York: Da Capo, 1984); Richard Koszarski, *Hollywood Directors 1914–1940* (New York: Oxford University Press, 1976); Karen Ward Mahar, "American Women Filmmakers in the Silent Film Industry," Ph.D. dissertation, University of Southern California, 1995.

12. Sloan, *Loud Silents,* 5.

13. For overviews of labor activities and jurisdictional disputes within the movie industry, see *Combined Convention Proceedings National Alliance of Theatrical Stage Employees and Moving Picture Operators of the United States and Canada: A Record of All Conventions Held since the Inception of the Organization, July 1893* (New York: Musicians' Press, 1926); Robert Osborne Baker, *The International Alliance of Theatrical Stage Employees and Moving Picture Machine Operators of the United States and Canada* (Lawrence, Kans., 1933); Alfred Harding, *Revolt of the Actors* (New York: William Morrow, 1929); Louis B. Perry and Richard Perry, *A History of the Los Angeles Labor Movement, 1911–1941* (Berkeley: University of California Press, 1963); Los Angeles Times, *The Forty Year War for a Free City: A History of the Open Shop Movement in Los Angeles* (Los Angeles: Los Angeles Times, 1929); Murray Ross, *Stars and Strikes: Unionization of Hollywood* (New York: Columbia University Press, 1941); Michael Charles Nielsen, "Motion Picture Craft Workers and Craft Unions in Hollywood: The Studio Era, 1912–1948," Ph.D. Dissertation, University of Illinois at Urbana-Champaign, 1985.

14. Discussions of movies produced by business, labor, radical, reform, religious, and government organizations can be found in Steven J. Ross, "The Unknown Hollywood," *History Today,* 40 (April 1990), 40–46; Sloan, *Loud Silents;* Brownlow, *Behind the Mask of Innocence;* Jacobs, *The Rise of American Film.*

15. Sloan, *Loud Silents,* 4. For a more detailed analysis of the ways in which businesses used movies, see Ross, "Cinema and Class Conflict," 68–107. *The Workman's Lesson* and *The Crime of Carelessness* can be found, respectively, at the Library of Congress and the Museum of Modern Art, New York.

16. The cinematic activities of labor and the left are discussed in Ross, "Cin-

ema and Class Conflict"; Ross, "Struggles for the Screen"; Brownlow, *Behind the Mask of Innocence;* Brandon, "Populist Film."

17. These production figures are taken from Jacobs, *The Rise of American Film;* Donahue, *American Film Distribution.*

18. The rise of the studio system and the transformation of the movie industry during the war and postwar years have been discussed in hundreds of books and articles. Among the best older works are Howard T. Lewis, *The Motion Picture Industry* (New York: D. Van Nostrand, 1933); Ramsaye, *A Million and One Nights;* Hampton, *A History of the Movies;* Jacobs, *The Rise of American Film;* Huettig, *Economic Control of the Motion Picture Industry.* The most useful recent works include Douglas Gomery, *The Hollywood Studio System* (New York; St. Martin's, 1986); Thomas Schatz, *Genius of the System* (New York: Pantheon, 1988); Ethan Mordden, *The Hollywood Studios: House Style in the Golden Age of the Movies* (New York: Simon & Schuster, 1988); Balio, *The American Film Industry;* Bordwell et al., *Classical Hollywood Cinema;* Koszarski, *An Evening's Entertainment;* Gomery, *Shared Pleasures;* May, *Screening Out the Past;* Sklar, *Movie-Made America.*

19. Movie industry expansion during this era is described in Koszarski, *An Evening's Entertainment,* 63–94.

20. Cecil B. DeMille, *The Autobiography of Cecil B. DeMille,* ed. Donald Hayne (Englewood Cliffs, N.J.: Prentice Hall, 1959). For an insider's view of financing operations, see A. H. Giannini, "Financing the Production and Distribution of Motion Pictures," *Annals of the American Academy of Political and Social Science,* 128 (November 1926) 46–49.

21. The rise of the star system and the skyrocketing costs of production are examined in Catherine E. Kerr, "Incorporating the Star: The Intersection of Business and Aesthetic Strategies in Early American Film," *Business History Review,* 64 (Autumn 1990), 383–410; Mitchell, "Consolidation of Film Industry," 254–72.

22. For an analysis of small production companies, see Paul Seale, " 'A Host of Others': Toward a Nonlinear History of Poverty Row and the Coming of Sound," *Wide Angle,* 72 (January 1991), 72–103.

23. Woodrow Wilson, quoted in Craig W. Campbell, *Reel America and World War I* (Jefferson, N.C.: McFarland, 1985), 67. Government and movie industry representatives met weekly as part of the Committee on Motion Picture Activities. The organization of the War Cooperation Board and the initial mandate of the NAMPI are described in *New York Times,* July 29, 1917; "Working Agreement between the Committee on Public Information and the Export Division of the National Association of the Motion Picture Industry," July 12, 1918, Record Group (RG) 63, CPI, Creel Correspondence, 1-A1, box 2, folder 66 (Brady), National Archives, Washington, D.C. (hereafter, NA).

24. [George Creel], *Complete Report of the Chairman of the Committee on Public Information* (Washington, D.C., 1920), 8.7.103.

25. From "Films Rejected for Export," Records of the CPI, RG 63, 30-B3, NA. For movie industry relations with the CPI and related federal agencies, see

Records of the Committee on Public Information, RG 63, NA; [Creel], *Complete Report;* James R. Mock and Cedric Larson, *Words That Won the War: The Story of the Committee on Public Information, 1917–1919* (Princeton, N.J.: Princeton University Press, 1939); Stephen Vaughn, *Holding Fast the Inner Lines: Democracy, Nationalism, and the Committee on Public Information* (Chapel Hill: University of North Carolina Press, 1980); Craig W. Campbell, *Reel America and World War I* (Jefferson, N.C.: McFarland, 1985).

26. WIB agreement, quoted in *New York Times,* August 26, 1919; "Working Agreement between the Committee on Public Information and the Export Division of the National Association of the Motion Picture Industry," July 12, 1918, RG 63, Creel Correspondence, 1-A1, box 2, folder 66, NA.

27. Zukor quoted in *New York Call,* July 11, 1918.

28. The creation and activities of the Joint Committee are discussed in *Variety,* November 29, 1918; *New York Times,* January 5, 1919; Secretary of Labor William B. Wilson to Secretary of the Interior Franklin Lane, January 13, 1919, Records of the Department of the Interior, RG 48, box 304, NA; C. H. Moore to Joseph J. Cotter, February 27, 1919, Department of Interior, RG 48, box 304, NA.

29. For a general overview of labor and radical activities during this period, see Robert K. Murray, *Red Scare: A Study in National Hysteria, 1919–1929* (Minneapolis: University of Minnesota Press, 1955); Paul L. Murphy, *World War I and the Origin of Civil Liberties in the United States* (New York: W. W. Norton, 1985). See also the sources listed in note 8, above.

30. Niles's letter is reprinted in *Variety,* November 29, 1918.

31. *Los Angeles Times,* January 3, 1920; "Look through Lincoln's Eyes," letter circulated by the Americanism Committee, c. January 1920, box 164, NBRMP. For correspondence regarding film scenarios, see Franklin K. Lane to George Kleine, May 19, 1920, and W. A. Ryan "To the Producer," May 19, 1920, box 1, George Kleine Papers, Special Collections, Library of Congress; W. A. Ryan to David Horsley, June 14, 1920, David Horsley Papers, folder 28, Margaret Herrick Library, Academy of Motion Picture Arts and Sciences, Beverly Hills, Calif.

32. W. J. Reynolds to Rolin Film Corporation, August 31, 1918, Motion Picture Producers' Association, folder 3:1920, Hal Roach Collection, Special Collections, University of Southern California (hereafter, MPPA, Roach Papers). Class conflict in the movie industry during this era is discussed in Marion Dixon, "The History of the Los Angeles Central Labor Council," M.A. thesis, University of California, Berkeley, 1929; see also the sources listed in note 13, above. For the activities of MPPA spies, see W. J. Reynolds to Hal Roach, February 13, 1919, MPPA, file 2, Roach Papers; Reynolds to Roach, January 19, March 5, 1920, and Reynolds to W. H. Doane, September 13, 1920, MPPA, file 3, Roach Papers.

33. For firsthand accounts of strikes and boycotts, see W. J. Reynolds to Hal Roach, September 23, 1918, MPPA, file 1, Roach Papers; "Memorandum of Wage Scale and Working Conditions Effective September 15, 1919 and to Remain in Force and Effect until September 15, 1920," in MPPA, file 2, Roach Pa-

pers; *Journal of Electrical Workers*, 19 (November 1919), 206; *Los Angeles Citizen*, August 19, 1921; *New York Call*, December 11, 1921; Los Angeles Times, *The Forty Year War*, 25.

34. Using the sources mentioned in note 1, above, I was able to determine the politics of 153 (88 percent) of the 173 labor-capital films produced during this period.

35. *New York Call*, May 2, 1920.

36. Walter K. Hill, review of "It's 'Everybody's Business' Now," *Moving Picture World*, August 9, 1919; William C. deMille, *Hollywood Saga* (New York: E. P. Dutton, 1939), 134.

37. *New York Call*, August 22, 1921. For censorship of *The Whistle*, see *New York Call*, August 5, 1921; for newsreel censorship, see "In re: Censorship of News Weeklies by State Board of Censorship of Pennsylvania," c. March 1921, and W. D. McGuire to Samuel Gompers, July 12, 1922, in Subject Correspondence (AFL), box 15; General Solicitation Letter by W. D. McGuire, March 16, 1921, and Charles Stelze to Dr. Herbert Gates, March 17, 1921, in Subjects Correspondence (Stelze), box 43, National Board of Review of Motion Pictures Collection, Special Collections Department, New York Public Library; Chicago *Daily Worker*, April 1, 1924.

38. Jack L. Warner with Dean Jennings, *My First Hundred Years in Hollywood* (New York: Random House, 1965), 125. Production costs are taken from Hampton, *A History of the Movies*; *New York Times*, December 13, 1925.

39. Hampton, *A History of the Movies*, 221.

40. Jesse L. Lasky with Don Weldon, *I Blow My Own Horn* (London: Victor Gollancz, 1957), 144.

41. The Arbuckle and Taylor scandals and influence of Will Hays on movie industry politics are discussed in Lasky, *I Blow My Own Horn*, 153–58; Will H. Hays, "Supervision from Within," in John P. Kennedy, ed., *The Story of Films* (Chicago: A. W. Shaw, 1927), 46–50; William Marston Seabury, *The Public and the Motion Picture Industry* (New York: Macmillan, 1926), 143–59.

42. P. H. Peterson to Samuel Gompers, November 12, 1920, reel 30, Records of the American Federation of Labor Convention for 1920, American Federation of Labor Records: The Samuel Gompers Era (microfilm collection). For examples of the prounion leanings of Chaplin, Hart, Pickford, and Fairbanks, see "Minutes of the Meetings of Local 33, IATSE," July 14, September 8, 1918, Local 33 Headquarters, Burbank, Calif.; *Los Angeles Citizen*, February 10, 1922.

43. Robert A. Bowen to J. E. Hoover, January 7, 1921, Investigative Case Files, reel 926 (BS 212657), Bureau of Investigation, National Archives, Washington, D.C. The rising costs of moviemaking in the early 1920s are described in Janet Wasko, *Movies and Money: Financing the American Film Industry* (Norwood, N.J.: Ablex, 1982), 21; *Report of the Proceedings of the 42nd Annual Convention of the American Federation of Labor . . . for 1922* (Washington D.C.: Law Reporter, 1922), 139.

44. Ross, "Struggles for the Screen," 352–61; Ross, "Cinema and Class Conflict," 89–93. Copies of *Labor's Reward* and *The Passaic Textile Strike* can be

found, respectively, at the UCLA Film and Television Archives, Los Angeles, and the Museum of Modern Art, New York.

45. I discuss the exhibition history of these films in Ross, "Struggles for the Screen," 358–60.

46. For a more extended analysis of the decline of labor film companies, see ibid., 361–65; Ross, "Cinema and Class Conflict," 94–96.

47. The high costs of producing talkies and wiring theaters for sound, and their impact on neighborhood houses, are discussed in Douglas Gomery, "The Coming of the Talkies: Invention, Innovation, and Diffusion," in Tino Balio, ed., *The American Film Industry* (Madison: University of Wisconsin Press, 1976), 193–211; Lizabeth Cohen, *Making a New Deal: Industrial Workers in Chicago, 1919–1939* (New York: Cambridge University Press, 1990), 127–28; Jowett, *Film,* 190–97, 260; Hampton, *A History of Movies,* 383.

Chapter 3

The Melos in Marxist Theory

Jane Gaines

Is Marx's three-volume *Capital* a melodrama? Literary critic Wylie Sypher asserts as much in "Aesthetic of Revolution," a now-forgotten essay that needs to be dusted off in the light of new feminist work on film and television melodrama. However, it is not as though Sypher represents the discovery of new theoretical treasure linking revolutionary moments with popular forms. For Sypher, the "melos" in Marxist theory is somewhat of an embarrassment. Not surprisingly, he holds melodrama in low esteem and argues that its old schematic (the virtuous besieged by the corrupt) is deeply Victorian and no longer relevant to the twentieth century. More than anything, it is the sharpness of the oppositions, the "oversimplication" of the forces at work, and the very stasis of the culminating tableaux that constitute for Sypher the "melodramatic fallacy." Strange as it may seem, he goes on, this most undialectical aesthetic, this dichotomous worldview, this "mentality of crisis," had its influence on Marx himself, who unfortunately succumbed to the temptation to represent the revolution as drama!

Nearly half a century since Sypher's essay was first published, melodrama is enjoying a new critical reputation, particularly in film and television studies, where feminism has been responsible for the restitution of melodrama as a genre, a mode, and a historical worldview. In the 1970s, when feminist film theory was more avowedly materialist than it is today, film as melodrama was

56

picked up by British critics who have left us a legacy of Marxist aesthetic theory that warrants reconsideration. Some of the terms of this aesthetic theory bridge the contemporary reconsideration of silent film melodrama, women's films, television soap opera, and materialist aesthetic theory in the 1940s, including not only Sypher's provocative essay but Eisenstein's film theory from the same decade.

I want to single out one particular concept, at once scientific and sensational, that has received relatively little theoretical attention in relation to its use in aesthetic theory. In comparison with other basic Marxist concepts such as commodity fetishism and ideology, which have been submitted to exhaustive critiques of their use in cultural theory, this concept has been quietly used, with little fanfare. One could argue that it is a lesser term with a supporting role, particularly in its function as a key to understanding Marxist dialectics. And yet it does meet a basic test—it is one of Marx's elastic and generalizable terms that shows up on multiple levels of the social formation. Playing its part in the economic base as well as in superstructural realms, this concept describes a structural condition specific to societies organized around capitalist economic relations. And finally it is one of those features that theoretically disappear when the capitalist mode of production is abolished.

My reader will think from these last remarks that perhaps I am referring to class struggle, as well I might be. Although it is often argued that this structural condition, which always requires a historically specific manifestation for it to be *seen* as such, is evidenced in class struggle. Mao Tse-tung went even further; he liked to use this concept as synonymous with class struggle.[1] But although this condition takes on the movement and the intensity of class struggle, the relationship between the two is also reciprocal. To class struggle, this concept contributes dignity and the cool head of analysis. To this concept (which I have yet to identify), class struggle contributes movement. But in the final analysis, I think, this concept is more apocalyptic and grand than class struggle, accounting, as it does, for so much more.

As you may have already guessed, only Marx's theory of contradiction (properly dialectical contradiction) is able to do quite so much in so dramatic a way.[2] Sometimes it is small, boring away in the commodity form (as the crucial difference between labor and exchange value). Sometimes it is significantly larger, as it comprehends the tensions between production and consumption, capitalism and socialism, labor and capital. However, I use the word *tension* here only to avoid tautology. The "tension" in each instance above is a "contradiction," with all of the implications of inconsistency, for Marx was always interested in making a point of irrationalities wherever he found them, especially when they arose in the face of the assumption that things are perfectly consistent. Recall that it was the brutal inconsistency of the aristocratic family inheritance laws defended by Hegel (*Philosophy of Right*) that first drew Marx's attention to problems in the Hegelian philosophical system. Entailed landed property, the practice of inheritance favoring the eldest son, was at odds with the ideal of the family bound together by love (Marx, *Critique* 99). We might then say that dialectical materialism sprung from a perception of familial injustice, however significantly this philosophical system later came to apply to the great class rupture.

Still there in the materialist theory of class contradiction is recognition of the sting of such injustice and the heartlessness of such inequity, but above all the inconsistency of the justification for exclusion—"in the name of love." Turning this observation about family feeling into the materialist theory of contradiction removes some of the sentiment and offers hope in the form of a theory of inevitable change. With a sense of restitution, the cause of its own undoing is ingeniously located *within* the offending institution, whether that institution is capitalism or the patriarchial family. More than anything, it is this *within* aspect of the theory of contradiction, this turning of the revered institution back on itself, showing how it is against itself, and then wresting change out of it, that appeals to the melodramatic sensibility.[3]

The theory of contradiction produces the "melos" in *Capital*. To demonstrate this, let me start where I should, that is, with the contradiction between labor and capital. Again and again, commentators cite this antithesis as the most compelling contradiction in materialist theory. Althusser, in his important "Contradiction and Overdetermination," cites the "simplicity of the Labor/Capital 'beautiful' contradiction [that] has answered to certain subjective necessities of mobilization of . . . masses" (104). In the same essay he calls the labor/capital conflict the "purest" form of contradiction (98). Does he mean by this that other contradictions are still reducible to something else, or that the whole theory could be generated out of these two positions, labor and capital? However, if the labor/capital antagonism is able to "mobilize" masses (as the production/consumption dichotomy, for instance, cannot), then there must be something else going on, and I would suggest that it is more than just theoretical embodiment.

The labor/capital dichotomy suggests characters acting out a scenario. Wylie Sypher reminds us that *Capital* is rife with personifications of economic concepts, his examples being "our friend moneybags" and "dead labor, vampire-like" (265–66). The author of *Capital* admits as much and encourages our seeing economic theory as human drama (among other things) when he says that "the characters who appear on the economic stage are merely personifications of economic relations" (179). This particular literary strategy makes complete sense when one recalls that *Capital* is all about the interchangeability of persons and things. Also, the fact that some of the passages in *Capital* are Dickensesque are to its credit. Describing the *dramatis personae* in terms of the "physiognomy" of the capitalist and the worker, in a typical passage, Marx animates lifeless categories: "The one smirks self-importantly and is intent on business; the other is timid and holds back, like someone who has brought his own hide to market and now has nothing else to expect but—a tanning" (280). Why not bring these concepts to life? These economic categories are not exactly empty; they are always full ones functioning as a theory of social upheaval as well as the reversal of circumstances of the same real historical persons after whom labor and capital as concepts have been modeled. How else to suggest that these weighty theories have life-and-death consequences than to introduce the image of the puffed-up capitalist and the cowering worker? Sypher is absolutely right that this aspect of Capital renders class struggle as a nineteenth-century dualistic tableau.

But extreme times call for extreme forms, as it is often said. Theatrical melodrama has historically been the preferred form of revolutionary periods for precisely its capacity to dichotomize swiftly, to identify targets, to encapsulate conflict, and to instill the kind of pride that can swell the ranks of malcontents. Revolutionary melodrama can be depended upon to narrate intolerable historical conditions in such a way that audiences wish to see wrongs "righted," are even moved to act upon their reaffirmed convictions, to act against tyranny and for "the people." Recent historical work on the origins of theatrical melodrama refers us again and again to the first melodramas performed around 1789, during the French Revolution, and goes on to show how 1917 Russian revivals tried to keep French revolutionary melodrama alive (Gerould, "Revolution"). Certainly some of the same aesthetic conventions that separated these popular performed works from classical drama are to be found in *Capital*: personifications of the economic, the revolution dramatized. But more important, there appears in both *Capital* and revolutionary melodrama a kind of rhythm, a calculated alternation between the fate of the oppressor and that of the oppressed. And so we come to yet another way in which Sypher sees *Capital* as governed by the aesthetics of melodrama. It has, he says, a "rhythmic stress of an iconic injustice committed against the masses" (163). He is again quite right. In melodrama, the rhythmic alternation works in such a way that the destinies of oppressor and victim are connected (although neither can see this connection and both continue to believe in their separateness). We, the readers of *Capital*, like the melodrama audience, see the pattern of injustice laid out before us, and we are appalled. In Marxist theory this dramatic parallel has its equivalent in the way the capitalist requires the worker to reproduce capital itself while the worker unknowingly is supplying the very labor that is one and the same as capital. Neither (in Marx) is the capitalist exactly aware of his own connectedness, for, although he might appear to understand the source of surplus value, exchange value is as mystifying to him as it is to the worker, who continually thinks that value is in the commodity.

The difficult question is whether labor and capital can be conceived of as a Victorian dualism and still function as a properly dialectical contradiction. I am not going to conclude, as Sypher does, that the melodramatic aesthetic has "damaged" the dialectic, but neither do I want to argue too strenuously that melodrama is compatible with dialectical materialism. For one reason, such a position would seem to put me in conflict with the master of materialist aesthetics who worked through these same questions in a

lifetime of theoretical writing and especially in his classic essay on
D. W. Griffith.[4] Eisenstein's Griffith essay, written in the same decade as Sypher's "Aesthetic of Revolution," has similar points to
make, although, to my knowledge, the similarity between the two
essays has never before been explored in print. The main correspondences, on which I want to touch only briefly, have to do with
the critique of melodrama as a dualistic and therefore insufficiently dialectical form. Both Sypher and Eisenstein attribute the
shortcomings of melodrama to its hopelessly bourgeois alle-
giances, although Eisenstein goes much further in his demonstration of this through his analysis of D. W. Griffith's debt to Dickens.
For Eisenstein, as most who are familiar with this essay will know,
the real concern is to articulate (yet again) the ways in which his
own use of montage, although inspired by Griffith's *Intolerance*
(1916) and other films, takes parallel editing in a radically political
direction.

Seeing Eisenstein's *Strike* as Melodrama

But here I want to turn this around. Instead of confirming Eisenstein's difference from Griffith (a popular exercise in film studies),
I want to look for the remnants of a melodramatic structure in
Eisenstein. Perhaps I will have the most success going against the
critical tradition here if I start with *Strike*. I am not the first to
nominate *Strike* as perhaps the most Griffithesque of Eisenstein's
features. The ending (Part VI, Liquidation) seems to have been
singled out most often as high drama—the mounted Cossacks attacking the strikers and their families and following them to the
forge; the scenes cross-cutting the shots of workers brutally
slaughtered with shots of cows butchered for their meat. For Jay
Leyda, the battle between workers and mounted soldiers is reminiscent of the industrial conflict scenes that open *Intolerance*, and
even the uses of "babies and other soft young animals" he thinks is
Griffithesque (184). Gerald Mast finds the influence of Griffith in
Eisenstein's cross-cutting of the stockholders' cocktail hour with
shots of starving and dying workers (162). Presumably, such re-
semblances also lead Noel Burch to declare that the slaughter-
house sequence in *Strike* is, in its arrangement of space and time,
still consistent with Griffith's "linearity," another way of saying,

Figure 3.1. Fat-cat capitalist (*Strike*, directed by Sergei Eisenstein, 1924)

despite Eisenstein's protests, that strong parallelism is at work in his own films (90).

The question again becomes one of whether or not, as Sypher would ask, dualism is compatible with dialectical materialism. A full consideration of the philosophical problem raised here is beyond the scope of this particular essay. The dialectical method is predicated on the need for the contradiction to play out the consequences of its own internal inconsistencies. One could say that contradiction generates consequential scenarios, the accumulated effects of its causes, and here it is particularly noted for resolving itself into another set of contradictions that only give rise to yet another set. However, no matter how many times new contradictions present themselves, in materialist theory the goal is to do away with the contradiction.[5] And in this "doing away with contradiction," we catch a glimpse of the utopian future that continues to compel us and to renew our interest in Marxist theory. Adorno had an unusual way of putting this that, although it does not suggest much optimism, contains something of the promise: "Dialectics is the ontology of the wrong state of things. The right state of things would be free of it: neither a system nor a contradiction."

Even in this statement, the dualism (the right or the wrong state of things) lurks, although corrected by reference to the contradiction. We have as well the faint intimation of the requisite social transformation in the difference between the right and the wrong state. But if the dialectic (whether as philosophical system or cinematic theory) always seems to involve a laying out of a crisis, a dualism, or a stark conflict at some level, it could be said to involve a *stage* in which it is susceptible to melodramatization. Although the dialectic may not require this stage at all in its philosophical form, in the form of dramatic entertainment, any attempt to represent dialectically related forces may slip into dichotomization. Even Eisenstein's dialectics, after all, theorizes not only abstract nonrepresentational conflict *within* and *between* shots, sequences, and graphic shapes, but conflict *between* representational characterizations of economic forces that seem reminiscent of another mode. And at times these latter conflicts do protrude as dualisms. I would not, however, want to argue that when represented as static and simple (a tableau), the contradiction between labor and capital is a dualism, and when it moves and has analytic complexity it is dialectical. This seems to me to be a dualistic and insufficiently dialectical argument if there ever was one. Perhaps the question is not whether we are in the presence of one philosophical mode or another, but more precisely, in what way is a work divided (sometimes against itself)? Sypher, for instance, argues that *Capital* is philosophically dialectical but aesthetically a melodrama.

Bill Nichols, in chapter 4 of this volume, actually sets the stage for seeing the aesthetics of *Strike* as melodramatic excess. His most important goal is to reclaim the film for a new concept of documentary (now available by embracing reenactment), and in making this claim Nichols shifts Eisenstein's film onto a border between documentary and fiction. In this new classification, *Strike* is "not the documentary record of a real strike, or the true story of an imaginary one." It is both powerful as fiction and impressive as documentary achievement. The surprise is that Nichols arrives at this doubleness by moving backward from the effect of the film to the question of generic and aesthetic classification. The film's reality effect (and its affiliation with documentary), in this argument, has to do with its capacity to change the historical real. But more remarkably, as Nichols understands montage here, its very aesthetic excesses are linked with social change as seen in this passage: the "remarkably sensuous montage of attractions . . . rich with that potential for excess that could be called . . . reality-transforming." Excess, no longer posing the subverting threat to the economy of narrative fiction that it does in bourgeois cinema, is free in socialist cinema to reach the viewer, as Nichols suggests, materially—that is, "viscerally" (110). Dialectical thinking comes closer and closer to Eisenstein's concept of the "affective structure" of inner speech that he calls "sensual thinking" (250–51). So we come around to the conclusion that the film's capacity to move us, to touch affective chords, has everything to do with the political effectivity of *Strike*. Reality effect, aesthetic excess, and social transformation are not mutually exclusive. And we are not far from Eisenstein's completely original usage of "pathos," which to him is always a politically directed swelling and upsurge of feeling.[6]

One would think, considering the terms Nichols gives us—excess, sensuality, viscerality—that we were talking about the melodramatic sensibility. But the value for us in Nichols's discussion has less to do with actually finding melodramatic structures in *Strike* than with establishing something uncommon in materialist political theory but prevalent in Eisenstein—the compatibility between intellect and affect. This expectation that the intellectual is part of *Strike*'s sensuous cinematic texture, however, only suggests to me that the film is open to the kind of excess that can also feed the melodramatic imagination and nurture its worldview. The fact that the film ultimately is not melodrama, however, would suggest that something intervenes at every point.

Perhaps the most productive way to approach *Strike* would be to suggest where it is that the melodramatic sensibility swells up and where its schematic asserts itself, but also where it is thwarted. Melodramatic elements seem to float, unattached to the kind of narrative scheme that could mold them into a moral pattern, the kind of pattern that would demonstrate the inevitable outcome of moral choices.[7] For example, consider the contained pathos of the

Figure 3.2. Suicide of the worker (*Strike,* directed by Sergei Eisenstein, 1924)

suicide of the worker wrongfully accused by the czar's foremen of stealing the missing micrometer. The manager confronts the worker in a scene punctuated by the intertitle "Thief." We are next told that the worker loses three weeks' wages working for the czar. In the subsequent representation of the worker's suicide, the dangling body is juxtaposed with a close-up of the suicide note, which reads "Not guilty." This is a dramatic moment in the film that could conceivably deepen the characters' existing hostility toward the czars because of their unjust treatment of workers. Rather than extracting the pathos from this particular incident, however, the film quickly moves on. The suicide incident seems to function only to trigger the first strike. Finally, heroic lighting, tools tossed to the floor in close-up, the camera tracking back as the masses run from the factory, and the title "Blow the Whistles" all signify the swelling buildup of the workers' resistance.

Recent feminist work on melodrama has emphasized the way the form has historically appealed to the powerless and the disinherited, if only by offering moral patterns in which the wronged are vindicated and the oppressed are morally elevated (Vicinus; Gaines, *Scar of Shame*). *Strike* bypasses an opportunity to appeal to the oppressed psyche by quickly shifting from the powerlessness of the dangling worker to the power of collective protest. Domestic melodrama, in contrast, requires the image of powerlessness for its effect and can even be seen to produce a tearful reaction in the viewer by arranging events in such a way that the irreversibility of time works to the advantage of the production of pathos. Franco Moretti's discussion of "moving literature" suggests that such tears of futility are produced when the chain of causality sets down irrevocable deeds and irreversible actions. Our tearful expressions of powerlessness in the face of such irreversibility testify to a particular understanding of causality. (The suicide death of the worker is caused by management, which has falsely accused him and unjustly penalized him by forcing him to pay what he cannot afford for a tool he did not steal.) Moretti says that crying is the consequence of the perception that causality cannot be controlled. This conclusion relies as well on a presupposition of two competing premises: that things as they are should be changed, and that such change is totally impossible (162).

This analysis would suggest that although one of the goals of Eisenstein's dialectic may be pathos, he is faced with the problem of how to produce this response without dipping into the affective resources and narrative devices of traditional melodrama at too great a price—the identification of his audience with powerlessness. Although he would solve this problem to a degree by modernist disruptions of the mise-en-scene, the melos still flickers through his abstract analysis. In the end, *Strike* does give us at least three pitiable victims—a baby held up by a soldier and dropped to the ground, a mother trying to rescue her child who has innocently walked between the legs of mounted soldiers' horses, and a strike leader repeatedly beaten by policemen who are urged on by a fancy woman riding in a car with a rich capitalist. But these moments function more like accumulations, as in Althusser's notion derived from Engels of the "accumulation of effective determinations" or circumstances that preface the revolutionary act (113). One might say that we have in these moments the cinematic orchestration of the consequences of the festering contradiction. As Nichols reminds us, *Strike* ends with the direct challenge to the viewer: "Remember!" To remember is to keep class antagonism alive until such time as the whole of society can be transformed.

What we do *not* have in this ending is the recognition of wrongs or the negotiation of positions that would give an impression that class injustice can be ameliorated.

Despite the bourgeois traps in the melodramatic aesthetic that would make it unsuitable as a revolutionary vehicle, a number of other Russians in this critical period saw a connection between melodrama and revolutionary ideals. Gorky, once he had resigned himself to the revolution, sponsored a melodrama playwriting contest for workers because he thought that of all genres, melodrama could best embody the "titanic nature" of the civil war. It had the swift pace and strong characters he thought were needed in such crucial times, and, says critic Daniel Gerould, Gorky and others were interested in the didactic possibilities of melodrama ("Gorky" 36). Gerould has also translated parts of the work of at least three Soviet dramatic theorists from the period, one of whom produced what is probably the most exhaustive analysis of the structure of melodrama attempted to date. Sergei Balukhatyi's *Poetics of Melodrama* also emphasizes the didactic achievements of the genre. In Gerould's summary of Balukhatyi: "Melodrama teaches, consoles, punishes, and rewards; it submits the phenomena of life and human conduct to the immutable laws of justice and offers reflections upon men's actions and feelings" ("Russian Formalist" 123). What would be different about socialist melodrama would be the substitution of "materialist" for "immutable." In place of the repugnant local moralism and religiosity of the traditional form, Eisenstein substituted higher values—consciousness change and class struggle.

Contradiction and Reconciliation

Returning to Eisenstein's essay on Griffith, note that he faults Griffith's parallel montage because of its carryover of such Victorian dualisms as the "rich" and the "poor," the classes whose different positions are conceivably reconcilable in bourgeois melodrama (234–35). Indeed, it has been often remarked that in nineteenth-century American melodrama, where capitalists, through a change of heart, can come to see the "errors of their ways," the rich can become poor and the poor can become rich. Consider all of the ideological work done by the platitude "rich in spirit." These

American dramas, of course, are about conflicts between older Christian values of worldly renunciation and new secular worldly aspirations, especially the desire for financial success (Cawelti 39). Popular melodrama undoubtedly did the nineteenth-century work of symbolic resolution of the uncomfortable relation between selflessness and material acquisition, and one of the ways the inconsistency could be wished away would be by such a theatrical sleight of hand—the gentleman in the gutter changes clothes with the lucky tramp.

Eisenstein, again translating economic theory translated into cinematic form, compares Griffith's drama of contrasts with his own montage, where contradiction is not only *within* and *between* shots, but "[threaded] throughout the whole system of planes" (235). Griffith's montage, the very model of his worldview, in Eisenstein's words, "[runs] in two parallel lines of poor and rich towards some hypothetical 'reconciliation' where . . . the parallel lines would cross, that is, in that infinity, just as inaccessible as that 'reconciliation' " (235). So it would seem that for Eisenstein the materialist "reality" of class contradiction assures that Griffith's reconciliation is illusory, like the parallel lines that only appear to meet in infinity. The resolution of class contradiction is associated with a never-never time and a mathematical impossibility.

In materialist theory, the contradiction between labor and capital, made concrete in class struggle, might as well be an "irreconcilable contradiction," yet another way of distinguishing the Marxian contradiction from the contradiction of Hegelian dialectics, where synthesis resolves things by dissolving one antagonistic position into another.[8] Materialist dialectics keeps antagonism alive, must keep it alive in order that change may be generated from contradiction itself, making change not only inherent in it but contingent on contradiction. So this notion of irreconcilability works to express how thoroughly at odds the parties are in the labor/capital contradiction, where the virtual function of the one class is to exploit the other. But this irreconcilability that further describes the conditions of class struggle, while contributing to theoretical precision, also contributes something to the dialectic that enhances its dramatic effect. If the theory of contradiction is the source of the melos in *Capital*, the notion of irreconcilability supplies the germ of a narrative.

Even in the dry and emotionally barren economic realm, the irreconcilable contradiction faintly suggests a story of extremity.[9] Two warring parties are deadlocked; two stories do not match. There is deceit on one side and innocent trust on the other; one party has been wronged and the other denies responsibility. Things are hopeless. The scene is a factory, then the manager's office; the humble home, then the banquet hall, and finally Newgate prison. This visual scenario could be generated from Althusser's "beautiful" contradiction, the contradiction that could conceivably move the masses to act. Never let it be denied that the empathetic appeal could also move the masses to tears.

Notes

1. See "On Contradiction" and "On the Correct Handling of Contradictions among the People," in *Four Essays on Philosophy*.

2. To give one example of the sweeping sense, consider Marx in *The Grundrisse:* "The growing incompatability between the productive development of society and its hitherto existing relations of production expresses itself in bitter contradictions, crisis, spasms" (Tucker 291–2). Marx and Engels of course developed their theory of dialectical contradiction from Hegel, whose theory is predated by the notion of internal contradiction from classical logic. For more, see Hegel's *The Science of Logic;* for an overview, see Inwood (63–65).

3. For a discussion of the significance of *within* and *between* in the Marxist theory of contradiction, see Godelier.

4. For an important contemporary analysis of "Dickens, Griffith, and the Film Today," see Altman; another discussion and further historical background appear in my "Revolutionary Theory, Pre-Revolutionary Melodrama."

5. This obliteration of the contradiction is found in classical philosophy as well as in Hegel, who understood logical thought as progressively overcoming contradictions.

6. For a comprehensive discussion of pathos in Eisenstein, see Aumont.

7. The basic foundational text for new work in literary and film melodrama is Brooks; see Cawelti for discussion of the "moral pattern."

8. Lukács speaks of the "irreconcilable antagonism between ideology and the economic base" (64). Some of the most recent rethinking of the Marxian contradiction has been that of Laclau, who argues that capitalist relations of production are not "intrinsically antagonistic" but that antagonism (not necessarily a contradiction) is seen when a worker resists the process of surplus labor extraction (8–9).

9. In a longer version of this article, I discuss the Marxist theory of contradiction in relation to the uses to which it appears to have been put in feminist film theory and early work on film melodrama. This includes a discussion of melodrama's happy ending, which, as Laura Mulvey has argued, raises like "dust . . .

along the road, a cloud of over-determined irreconcilables which put up a resistance to being neatly settled in the last five minutes" (54). Invariably this returns me to the earliest use of the Althusserian notion of contradiction in literary criticism, to Macherey's "Lenin, Critic of Tolstoy."

Works Cited

Adorno, Theodor W. *Negative Dialectics,* trans. E. B. Ashton New York: Continuum, 1973.

Althusser, Louis. *For Marx.* London: Allen Lane, 1969.

Altman, Rick. "Dickens, Griffith, and Film Theory Today." In *Classical Hollywood Narrative: The Paradigm Wars,* ed. Jane Gaines. Durham: Duke University Press, 1992.

Aumont, Jacques. *Montage Eisenstein,* trans. Lee Hildreth, Constance Penley, and Andrew Ross. Bloomington: Indiana University Press, 1987.

Brooks, Peter. *The Melodramatic Imagination: Balzac, Henry James, and the Mode of Excess.* New Haven, Conn.: Yale University Press, 1976.

Burch, Noel. "Film's Institutional Mode of Representation and the Soviet Response." *October* 11 (Winter 1979): 77–96.

Cawelti, John. "The Evolution of Social Melodrama." In *Imitations of Life: A Reader on Film and Television Melodrama,* ed. Marcia Landy. Detroit: Wayne State University Press, 1991.

Eisenstein, S. E. "Dickens, Griffith, and the Film Today." In *Film Form,* trans. Jay Leyda. New York: Harcourt Brace, 1977.

Gaines, Jane. "*Scar of Shame*: Skin Color and Caste in Black Silent Melodrama." In *Imitations of Life: A Reader on Film and Television Melodrama,* ed. Marcia Landy. Detroit: Wayne State University Press, 1991.

_____. "Revolutionary Theory, Pre-Revolutionary Melodrama." *Discourse* 17 (Spring 1995): 101–18.

Gerould, Daniel. "Gorky, Melodrama, and the Development of Early Soviet Theatre." *Yale/Theatre* 7 (Winter 1976): 33–44.

_____. "Revolution and Melodrama." In *Melodrama: Stage/Picture/Screen,* ed. Jacky Bratton, Jim Cook, and Christine Gledhill. London: British Film Institute, 1994.

_____. "Russian Formalist Theories of Melodrama." In *Imitations of Life: A Reader on Film and Television Melodrama,* ed. Marcia Landy. Detroit: Wayne State University Press, 1991.

Godelier, Maurice. "Structure and Contradiction in *Capital*." In *Ideology in Social Science,* ed. Robin Blackburn. London: Fontana, 1972.

Hegel, G. W. F. *The Philosophy of Right,* trans. T. M. Knox. Oxford: Clarendon, 1942.

_____. *The Science of Logic,* trans. A. V. Miller. London: Allen & Unwin, 1969.

Inwood, Michael. *A Hegel Dictionary.* London: Blackwell, 1992.

Laclau, Ernesto. *New Reflections on the Revolution of Our Time.* London: Verso, 1990.

Leyda, Jay. *Kino: A History of the Russian and Soviet Film.* Princeton, N.J.: Princeton University Press, 1960.

Lukács, Georg. *History and Class Consciousness,* trans. Rodney Livingstone. Cambridge: MIT Press, 1971.

Macherey, Pierre. *A Theory of Literary Production,* trans. Geoffrey Wall. London: Routledge & Kegan Paul, 1978.

Mao Tse-tung. *Four Essays on Philosophy.* Peking: Four Languages Press, 1968.

Marx, Karl. *Capital,* vol. 1 (1867), trans. Ben Fowkes. New York: Vintage, 1977.

_____. *Critique of Hegel's Philosophy of Right* (1843), trans. Annette Jolin and Joseph O'Malley. New York: Vintage, 1977.

Mast, Gerald. *A Short History of the Movies.* New York: Macmillan, 1992.

Moretti, Franco. *Signs Taken for Wonders.* New York: Verso, 1983.

Mulvey, Laura. "Notes on Douglas Sirk and Melodrama." *Movie 25* (Winter 1977–78): 53–56. Reprinted in *Home Is Where the Heart Is,* ed. Christine Gledhill. London: British Film Institute, 1987.

Nichols, Bill. *Blurred Boundaries: Questions of Meaning in Contemporary Cinema.* Bloomington: Indiana University Press, 1994.

Sypher, Wylie. "Aesthetic of Revolution: The Marxist Melodrama." In *Tragedy: Vision and Form,* ed. Robert Corrigan, San Francisco: Chandler, 1965.

Tucker, Robert C., ed. *The Marx-Engels Reader,* 2d ed. New York: W. W. Norton, 1978.

Vicinus, Martha. "Helpless and Unfriended: Nineteenth-Century Domestic Melodrama." *New Literary History* 13 (Autumn 1981).

Chapter 4

Strike and the Question of Class

Bill Nichols

A Film Is Born

I have structured this discussion of *Strike* as though the film had been recently released in order to heighten the sense of its continuing importance. Class and history—the remembrance of struggle, the preservation of icons and moments—always risks ossification, a wedge in the heart of historical consciousness. The crucial sense of linkage between what has gone before and what is yet to come may buckle beneath the weight of an official history of momentous events or treasured artifacts that sets out to preserve itself rather than to transform the present. To the extent that *Strike* now occupies a place of privilege in the pantheon of cinematic achievement, and that most writing devotes itself to the relative merits of this achievement compared with others, its most crucial lessons, which have much less to do with film history than social struggle, may be lost to us. This essay therefore takes the form of a dialogue between the text, written as if *Strike* were a contemporary release, and the notes, in which I address the historiographic tradition surrounding Eisenstein and *Strike*. It is in the notes, which would clutter a "review," that the familiar names in Eisenstein scholarship appear.

Strike presents vivid evidence of the ways in which boundaries between fiction and nonfiction, narrative and nonnarrative have blurred. *Strike,* seen from this retrospective angle, is as fully part of the genealogy of documentary filmmaking as those Soviet films that were described as precursors and foundations in earlier historical periods when the very conception of documentary was distinct from what it is today.

Documentary lacks fixed meaning; it is set both in relation to other, distinct practices, and in relation to a historical context of past conventions, norms, and expectations. It cannot be collapsed into fiction, for any definition of fiction that would engulf and obliterate documentary would also engulf and obliterate other forms, like poetry or essays, that require distinction and exhibit histories of their own. Documentary's failure to achieve a privileged relation to a preexisting reality, its failure to escape the marks of narrative or the accretions of form and structure, does not reduce it to a fiction like any other.

Documentary takes shape as a result of how a community of practitioners, an institutional matrix, a set of textual conventions, and an array of viewer expectations arise, coalesce, and change, in historically specific ways, to constitute the domain that becomes known retroactively as documentary (Nichols 1991, especially ch. 1). (It is the historicality of what defines documentary that distinguishes it from a mere tautology.)

But how do we avoid reifying the historical trace of documentary lineage? Once a pattern of distinct practitioners, institutions, textual strategies, and viewer expectations takes shape, are we obliged not only to describe and assess its profile but to accept it as a given? This is a question that could take up the issues of a tradition or canon and its preservation or subversion. More to the immediate point, documentary tradition can also be posed as a question for an alternative practice of genealogy. A slight rewriting of Judith Butler's (1990) description of a feminist genealogy of the category of women captures the process I want to invoke here. Butler notes:

> To trace the political operations that produce and conceal what qualifies as the juridical subject of feminism is precisely the task of *a feminist genealogy* of the category of women. (5)

Rephrased, the challenge becomes:

To trace the political operations that produce and conceal what qualifies as the subject of documentary criticism is precisely the task of a genealogy of the category of documentary.

And in particular, in that period *before* practitioners, institutions, norms, conventions, and audience expectations congealed into a discernible pattern, where do we look to find examples, models, prototypes, or precursors? How do we restore the polyvalent potential of films that were not yet fully inscribed within any one tradition? A genealogy of documentary criticism must question how tradition has both *produced and concealed* the subject of its own operation. What works affirm the potential of the documentary gesture? How can we remove the encrustations that have led us to see them otherwise? How does the issue of genealogy, like the concept of metahistory, facilitate an understanding of historical processes that conceal as well as reveal?[1] How can our current understanding of documentary help us resee and revise a past that we cannot afford to cede to the force of tradition?

In treating *Strike* as if it were a new release, I want to try to explore how it might well be received within a frame other than the one to which we are accustomed. This essay, therefore, is about Eisenstein and class, but not about Eisenstein's place within the development of the narrative film tradition, however oppositional that place may be. We already have our Museum of Film History with its room devoted to the Eisenstein exhibit. My intention is not to enlarge that room so much as punch a few holes in the walls, move things around, and perhaps even question the permanence and stability of the museum itself.

Breaking New Ground

The question of class inevitably raises the question of audience. To what extent are we, as viewers, drawn into an arena of interpretive struggle where issues of class and historical consciousness fight it out with their transcendental, ahistorical alternatives? Questions of the representation of class and the urge to "get it right" are only a portion of the problem of reception and interpretation. Accuracy, authenticity, fidelity figure into representations that may re-

main caught within a system of narrative realism that proves incapable of representing what has yet to come into being. Realism and
its vicissitudes may leave us trapped within a realm of verisimilitude (mimesis), where manifestations of dialectical consciousness
remain partial, incomplete, or encased within the conventions of
narrative agency that identify character with action, thereby making class into an abstraction without agency.

How are we, as audience, drawn into an alternative space where
the lineaments of class action and historical consciousness manifest themselves, restoring concreteness to what individual consciousness can understand only abstractly? This means not only
developing a strategy to give textual figuration to the collectivity
of class but also finding the means to bring into being a viewer
whose own position escapes the bounds of an individuated consciousness. My contention is that Sergei Eisenstein's remarkable
first film, *Strike*, does precisely this.

By making the abstract incarnate, *Strike* (1925) gives renewed
vitality to the most impressive aspects of documentary today. In
recent films, abstractions like class struggle or racism become
more than categories of debate; they enter the realm of lived experience. They engage us body and soul. As *Shoah* (1985) discovers
the incarnation of past experience in present behavior, as *The Thin
Blue Line* (1987) reveals how memory shapes past events to serve
present needs, as *Tongues Untied* (1989) gives embodiment to subjectivity and a politics of experience, *Strike* makes dialectical consciousness incarnate. Here is a political, and documentary, style of
filmmaking that blurs our received notions of where the bounds of
social representation lie.

Eisenstein clearly deserves the accolades he has quickly gained
for innovation, even if this praise often recruits him to a formal-
ized history of cinema rather than treating him as a key combatant
within the arena of social interpretation. More than any other active filmmaker, Eisenstein has discovered ways to represent not
simply the external appearance of class struggle but its conceptual
foundations as well: historical, class consciousness, and the materialist dialectic. He does so with particular regard for the distinctive space between us, the movie screen, and the surrounding
world. This is the space that Eisenstein infuses with dialectical consciousness; such space subsumes and transforms us. It reconfigures

who we are and makes this new person incarnate, available to consciousness, disposed to action. It is as though Eisenstein chose to respond to Benjamin's (1969) challenge "to articulate the past historically [by seizing] hold of a memory as it flashes up at a moment of danger" (255) by devising his own form of writing in lightning.[2]

As an exercise in rendering the abstract concrete, *Strike* could be considered as the first chapter in Eisenstein's long-promised adaptation of Marx's *Das Kapital* for the screen. It is, in fact, the first of a projected series of films on events leading up to the October Revolution, but this is a misleadingly limited goal for what Eisenstein has actually accomplished.[3] He has not told yet another story of individual conscience and collective struggle, in the same mold as other socially conscious narratives such as *Chapeyev* (1934), *The Molly Maguires* (1970), *Norma Rae* (1979), or even *The Battle of Algiers* (1965), where *individual* characters and their consciousness serve a classic identificatory function.

Eisenstein has not presented a didactic truth or moral message that characters announce or spectators carry away like apples in a lunch pail. Instead, Eisenstein has fulfilled his own goal for what film can do in the representation of class, history, and revolution: *"to teach the worker how to think dialectically. To show the method of the dialectic."*[4] In commenting on this notation, made by Eisenstein in preparation for filming *Das Kapital*, Jacques Aumont (1987) astutely notes, "Finally, and contrary to what one might expect from what has gone before, the object privileged [by Eisenstein] in Marx's work is not the theoretical one, like any of the key concepts from *Capital*. It is at another level entirely that Eisenstein selects his true object—the Marxist method itself" (163).

> Our conception is that a person first of all researches the material, and then poses the question of how to give form to the material.
>   Besides, material can be presented with or without a story. Storyless films still have a plot.
> —Victor Shklovsky (in Tretyakov et al., "Symposium," 33–34)[5]

Strike gives figurative embodiment to more than just a strike; it is not the documentary record of a real strike, or the true story of an imaginary one. *Strike* is not a fictional story realm within which class struggle finds itself constrained by the formal demands of psychological realism and narrative closure. Powerful as a fiction, *Strike* is also the most impressive achievement in documentary representation since *Who Killed Vincent Chin?* (1988).[6]

> When a fact is taken as a brick for a construction of another sort, the pure newsreel disappears. It is all a matter of montage.
> —Sergei Tretyakov (in Tretyakov et al., "Symposium," 29)

Strike, in other words, does not teach us that strikes arise because of exploitative work conditions, the alienation of labor power, or the inhuman attitude of factory owners—although it makes no effort to deny these lessons either. Factual litanies of woes, authenticated catalogs of abuse, detailed chronicles of union struggle with their moments of success and loss, and biographic homage to those who personify defiance in the face of adversity—*Strike* exhibits none of these familiar, limited (but fully understandable) traits so abundant in documentaries on the working class.

Likewise, *Strike* exhibits none of the proclivities of the fiction film that Eisenstein vowed to analyze but not to imitate.[7] It does not present an idealized leader upon whom leadership devolves; it does not present events in strictly causal sequence or embellish them with scrupulous attention to historical details; it eschews the parallel plotting of romantic courtship with social adventure; it lacks those identificatory mechanisms that join viewer to characters with singular precision (psychological complexity, expressive acting styles, point-of-view editing); and, finally, the story world of the characters lacks the coherence or continuity customary to realist, and even expressionist, fiction. *Strike* remains poised to move in whatever direction, as fiction or as documentary, that suits its larger purpose.

Warning: Dialectics at Work

Strike makes incarnate the space between. This is the space between spectator and screen, between social actors and individual consciousness, between ideology and actual conditions, between bourgeois consciousness and its social situation. *Strike* constructs between us and it a historical consciousness and a social subjectivity capable of carrying us beyond the film itself. It does so in the act of viewing. *Strike* engages us in the process of bringing into being a world where this very action prompts us to experience, *materially, viscerally,* the transformative potential of dialectical thinking. We enter a realm in which we actively coalesce an array of fragments to bring into imaginative being a world that does not yet have historical existence and is therefore incapable of empirical documentation. This is a Marxist form of modernist collage, or what Eisenstein himself termed "dialectical montage."

If the final effect of a sign is to dispose us toward action modified as a result of the experience of that sign, as Charles Peirce has suggested, *Strike* may be among the first films to render such an effect dialectically. The rhythms and evocations; the surveillance and subterfuge of the bosses, the resistance of the workers; the reverberations of what has come before within the context of what comes later; and the qualitative transformations wrought by a remarkably sensuous montage of attractions present a temporality that is neither linear in arrangement nor teleological in progression, but contingent and transformative, rich with that potential for excess that could be called *aufhebung,* or reality transforming.

Temporality itself is up for grabs. Eisenstein has, for example, imbued his male workers with a communitarian spirit that may even seem prelapsarian. They cavort and gambol, they frolic on the waterfront, conspire among abandoned locomotive wheels, draw up strike demands while picnicking in the woods. Eric Rhode (1976) takes exception to this treatment, reading the portrayal of the workers as fully realist but wrong: "His workers are boyish, bloody-minded and never seen to work. . . . At home among the machines, these workers swing from girders like monkeys and seem hardly different from the police informers whom Eisenstein protractedly compares to various beasts of prey" (95).[8] Rhode, like most film historians, completely misses Eisenstein's point, which is not to represent workers and their struggles within a realist, fictional, or even historically correct, frame, but to find a way to represent them precisely for what they have yet to be recognized: as a class capable of becoming more than workers.

Eisenstein has overcome the persistent handicap of those who exhort workers to unite: Why should workers join together as workers when it is *as workers* that they experience alienation and exploitation? Frank Lentricchia (1983) makes this point memorably in his discussion of Kenneth Burke's 1935 address to the American Writers' Congress:

> In effect Burke asks Marxists . . . whether or not it is their ambition to become workers. . . . You can't expect, [Burke] says, in effect, to his progressive friends, on the one hand, to keep painting these riveting portraits of workers under capitalism, of degradation and alienation—you can't expect people to accept these portraits as the truth, which is your rhetorical desire, after all, and then, on the other hand, at the same time, expect people to want to identify with workers, or become workers, or even enlist their energies of intellect or feeling on behalf of workers. . . . You must, as Marx would urge, rethink your representation of workers. . . . [You must] make sure that their fate and ours are bound up with each other. (25–26)

This is precisely what Eisenstein has done. It is only when the workers are not workers that some small taste of a better life becomes possible (illusory, if they are ultimately still workers). These workers give suggestive embodiment to this alternative way of being in a world not yet fully of their own devising.

Eisenstein fully grasps the challenge Burke poses to traditional representations of workers, if not their class: if it is not our ambition to *become* workers, then we must represent workers in the process of becoming more than they have been without becoming the bourgeois subjects they oppose. Their representation requires a multiple valency, and Eisenstein has provided one. The spies act furtively, constantly striving to pass as only workers, hiding their intentions and desires, remaining fully, and dangerously, closeted. Eisenstein's workers, however, gambol exuberantly. Their zest and vitality, their defiance and wile, construct a fraternity of men (men largely without women, and without the splintered remains of broken families as clichéd image of their immiseration, either).

The representation of *Strike*'s workers is not the same as, but is nonetheless similar to, the iconography of a gay community. The homoerotic exuberance here, like the homoerotic languor of the *Potemkin*'s sailors in their hammocks, makes these men workers who are more than workers, even as their transformative potential awaits full realization.

Astonishingly, the workers' gay abandon remains unrecognized. No history book refers to it. Almost no criticism identifies it. Neither Vito Russo's *The Celluloid Closet* nor Richard Dyer's *Now You See It* refers to *Strike* at all.[9] Gayness remains a representation with a vivid referent (a set of real social practices) but without a corresponding signified that would mark it as a recognizable sign of community yet to be brought into social existence. The effects of signification have not yet risen to the level of conscious apprehension; the dialectic awaits completion. This blindness to Eisenstein's strategy suggests that we still need a gay genealogy that will address how political operations have produced *and concealed* the gay subject in film.

Knowledge Incarnate

Strike attains that form of embodied knowledge that is so crucial to innovative work in documentary today. Eisenstein resorts to reenactment not to give us a pseudoauthentic impression of what events were really like, but to give substantive form to the political unconscious and radical subjectivity itself. What is it like to share in a communitarian consciousness, and what is it like to leave a film wanting to complete it, in fact, now? *Strike* gives us the closest thing we have to an answer.

In refusing to offer history lessons so much as transformative remembrance, Eisenstein aligns himself with the cinema of exile, diaspora, and dislocation. He breaks with the expository tradition and its classic problem/solution structure. Travel and movement remain restricted, just as social revolution remains beyond the immediate horizon of these workers, under these conditions. The workers are the constant target of surveillance; documentary images, realist *trompe l'oeil,* hidden cameras all serve the interests of the managers. Space and its representation are not yet their own. "Life caught unawares," in Vertov's phrase, is life betrayed. *Strike* refuses to offer an indexical pathway back to the past as the visible ruins of a congealed consciousness and meaning. Documentary authenticity and historical reconstruction necessarily fail to fulfill the need not to change the past but the future we may make from it.

Like those luxuriating, hammock-held bodies of soon-to-be-leaders of rebellion that fill the frame in the opening movement of *Battleship Potemkin* (1925), the workers in *Strike* constantly exude the potential energy of subjects whose very identity stems from their being-in-action. None of that sterile posing that freezes people into mythic icons,[10] none of that studied iconography of desire that renders actors into stars, none of that condensation of action and agency into the individuated figure of psychological realism that defines bourgeois narratives of fiction and documentary alike. Acrobatic, resourceful, determined, these workers remember, and are to be remembered, with open eyes and alert bodies, ready to spring into action with the collective force of five hundred mice.[11]

What we can see, when we see, as Eisenstein allows us, dialectically, is how what was now serves as the ground for what will be. *Strike* makes this dialectical process its final referent as it constitutes its subject both as theme (historical consciousness) and viewer (we are the subjects in which this abstraction becomes an active process).[12] Rather than forging a path back to the historical record through indexical linkages, *Strike*'s path is toward what it brings into being between itself and the viewer: a historical consciousness made manifest by form itself.[13] Along with the constructivists, Eisenstein developed a kinetic art not as an aesthetic experiment or exciting spectacle of interest in itself, but from a "passionate desire to incite the spectator to action" (Lawder 1975, 65). This is a cinema of attractions that transforms itself by means of our apprehension that the whole lies beyond the sum of its parts.[14]

Final Things

When Eisenstein ends—but does not conclude—his final image is a pair of eyes that spring open and urge us, as though with a suddenly dawning consciousness, to "Remember!" This act exceeds indexical reference, allegorical meaning, or bland analogy. His ending, of eyes snapping open, also contrasts radically with Buñuel and Dali's beginning, of an eye cut by a razor blade wielded by Buñuel in *Un Chien Andalou* (1928). *Strike* does not assault but awaken; it does not associate the camera's view with violence, but with re-vision.[15]

Eisenstein's workers no longer make commodities for those who steal their labor. They make themselves. They make themselves over, using material that is not "out there," but is instead the stuff of materialist consciousness itself. They are not only touched but constituted by the production of signs for which the signified is not a history lesson or external referent but a will to transform that brings into being the utopian moment hitherto repressed in the political unconscious.[16]

"Eisenstein's workers" are us. It is we who remember what they have experienced. It is we who act, who continue and complete what they have begun, who exceed that form of consciousness contained by narrative or expository form.

The means to transform "the end" are at hand. They involve the reconfiguration of what has now been figured: they involve the praxis of negating the negation. As Walter Benjamin (1969) puts it, speaking of fashion, where fashion could stand for the standardized flow of novelty and repetition that defines the conventional bounds of both fiction and nonfiction cinema:

> Fashion has a flair for the topical, no matter where it stirs in the thickets of long ago; it is a tiger's leap into the past. This jump, however, takes place in an arena where the ruling class gives the commands. The same leap in the open air of history is the dialectical one, which is how Marx understood the revolution. (261)

The blur of boundaries inaugurated by Eisenstein comes, in part, from the act of leaping itself. To be-in-action is to blur all notions of a subject who is before she leaps. Such is the aim of the genealogy proposed here.

Notes

I presented earlier versions of this essay as a paper at the "Visible Evidence" documentary conference at Duke University, September 8–12, 1993, and the Fourth Annual Berkeley Film Conference, November 6, 1993. I am indebted to Nahum Chandler and Terrence Turner for specific suggestions and comments at the Duke conference that I have tried to incorporate. A different version of this essay, "Eisenstein's *Strike* and the Genealogy of Documentary," also forms a chapter in my book *Blurred Boundaries* (Bloomington: Indiana University Press, 1994).

1. The term *metahistory* refers to Hayden White's seminal work, *Metahistory: The Historical Imagination in Nineteenth-Century Europe*. (1973). His preface sketches out a theory of historical investigation that insists on a deep structure that is essentially precritical and prefigurative. This deep structure involves a poetics of language and provides the necessary precondition for any "exploratory affect" (x). White's goal is to reveal the linguistic basis of historiography, including its impression of realism. Like the idea of genealogy proposed here (which can be traced back to Nietzsche's *The Genealogy of Morals* [1887] 1964), metahistory seeks less to debate the meaning of history than to examine how written histories come to produce the meanings and explanations they usually claim to have found within the historical domain itself. White's schema is somewhat more formal and descriptive than, say, Butler's, who adopts a more pointedly political perspective and takes as strong an interest in concealment as production. Both the concealment of the constructed and arbitrary nature of documentary and the production of the worker as a primarily empirical category are of central concern here. Alternative conceptions of both documentary and the worker take the place of a thoroughgoing theory of representation, a task far beyond the scope of this essay.

2. "Writing with lightning" is a phrase attributed to President Wilson in responding to D. W. Griffith's epic feature *Birth of a Nation* (1915) after a special White House screening of the film.

3. Standish Lawder's (1975) account has useful information on the social context in which *Strike* was made.

4. Sergei Eisenstein, "Notes on *Capital*," quoted in Jacques Aumont (1987, 161).

5. Shklovsky is referring here to "story" as the overall, coherent account one would render of a particular tale and "plot" as the actual successive arrangement of situations and events as read or seen. Both documentary and fiction would have plots in this sense; fiction's plot would resolve into a story, and documentary's into a representation or argument about the historical world.

6. Eisenstein's concern with narrative form in his published writings has led critics to assign him to the ranks of fiction filmmakers, especially with Dziga Vertov setting forth an agenda for what we would call documentary that clearly excludes his work. The disputes between Dziga Vertov and Eisenstein that have been so widely reported in the West present a false temptation: consign Eisenstein to the dustbin filled with that bourgeois opiate, fiction, and elevate Vertov to the rank of *kino* pioneer.

Neither Vertov nor Eisenstein, however, is so readily corralled. The square-peg Eisenstein cannot be fit into the round hole of fiction. Just as Meyer Shapiro's trenchant attack on Freud's psychoanalytic reading of Leonardo banished psychoanalysis from the disciplinary domain of what counts as good art history, so Dziga Vertov and all the film historians who have followed have banished Eisenstein from the domain of what counts as good documentary (see Dziga Vertov 1984; Shapiro 1956).

They have done so, in part, by creating a doxa that insists on a difference between documentary and fiction in the first place, despite their shared use of narrative form, and then pushing Eisenstein over to one side of the line and Vertov to the other. Gerald Mast (1986), for example, in an entry typical of film history books, describes Eisenstein in relation to the larger picture of the development of narrative film even as he also acknowledges that "the Eisenstein films break all the rules of narrative construction. They lack a protagonist and focal characters; they lack a linear plot of the rising or falling fortunes of a single person" (159). In *A History of Narrative Film*, David Cook (1981) also treats Eisenstein as though he were a part of the evolution of a film language that becomes, virtually by default, narrative film language. Calling *Strike* a "non-narrative chronicle" (147), Cook nonetheless contextualizes it in relation to the other narrative films like Chaplin's *The Gold Rush* (1924) or Murnau's *Der letzte Mann* (1924) and the rise of the classic period of silent Soviet cinema. Film historians repeatedly acknowledge Eisenstein's elusiveness and then proceed to incorporate his work into what is finally a narrative fiction film tradition.

Standish Lawder (1975) makes almost an identical point while placing Eisenstein in relation to constructivism: "On the one hand, its bold rejection of almost every traditional element of commercial feature film (no stars, no hero, no happy ending, no sub-plot, not even a plot really, but merely a single incident); its profusion of imaginative camera tricks and clever devices (weird dissolves and superimpositions, spinning titles which dissolve into machinery, the shots through glass, through the tiny spy camera, shots reflected in convex mirrors); its intensely charged sense of realism (the documentary-like photography of real setting in factory and elsewhere)—and, on the other, the film is *so* loaded with wild experimentation that it seems today like an exercise in excess" (69). Lawder's description reads perfectly until we reach his concluding evaluation. What seems to Lawder like "excess" in relation to the positivist tendencies of observational documentary or the realist tendencies of fiction now arrives before us as realism of the sort Brecht had in mind when he rejected dramatic theater and its realism in favor of discovering the underlying mechanisms that such realism conceals.

In a history of documentary comparable to Mast's history of narrative film, Jack Ellis (1989) describes how "Vertov's aesthetic position demanded anti-narrative, anti-fictional forms. His iconoclasm was intended to free film from bourgeois obfuscations of story and the effete pleasure of theatrical performance in order to arrive at the truths of the actual world" (31). Though an accurate rendition of Vertov's polemics, the effect of such accounts is to erect an artificial barrier precisely where boundaries blur in remarkable ways.

7. See Eisenstein's essay "About Myself and My Films" (1970, 13–14). Written in 1945, the essay retrospectively assigns the motivation Eisenstein remembered himself having had back in the 1920s. "Fictitiousness" disturbs him greatly. The emotions spectators feel at a play are real, but they derive from identifying with a fictitious situation. "Thus art . . . enables man through co-experience *fic-*

titiously to perform heroic actions, *fictitiously* to experience great emotions. . . . Why strive for reality, if for a small sum of money you can satisfy yourself in your imagination without moving from your comfortable theatre seat?" (13). Constructivism, however, called for an end to this mirroring without reality, and Eisenstein vowed:

> First master art.
> Then destroy it.
> Penetrate into the mysteries of art.
> Unveil them.
> Master art.
> And then snatch off its mask, expose it, destroy it! (14)

We clearly recruit Eisenstein to the history of the growth and development of narrative fiction at considerable peril.

8. Regarding *Strike* as a combination of newsreel and circus, and within the context of feature filmmaking, Rhode (1976) finds the film wanting in relation to the contemporary realities it presumably portrays. The present essay takes a different tack, asserting that *Strike* belongs squarely with other innovative documentaries that break with empiricism, realism, and the chronicle to approximate the distinct reality of the Marxist dialectic itself through the particularities of form.

9. Eric Rhode's (1976) history condemns Eisenstein's portrayal of the workers and spies as "species of beast" and misreads an iconography of (unspoken) desire as boyish frolic (95).

Roland Barthes constantly approaches the significance of the homoerotic, but just as constantly fails to name it, in his essay "The Third Meaning" (1977). Barthes likens the third or obtuse meaning to "pun, buffoonery, useless expenditure," and says, "It is on the side of the carnival" (55). Barthes also sees a correspondence to disguise but does not connect it to suppression and the homosexual closet: "The characteristic of this third meaning is indeed—at least in [Eisenstein]—to blur the limit separating expression from disguise, but also to allow that oscillation succinct demonstration—an elliptic emphasis, if one can put it like that, a complex and extremely artful disposition" (57). Barthes insists that the third meaning is a "signifier without a signified" (61) because "it does not copy anything" (61). A stranger case of blindness and insight than Barthes's could hardly be imagined.

A singular exception to this myopia is Thomas Waugh's (1977) essay on Eisenstein, in which he pointedly identifies the unseen homoerotic elements of Eisenstein's films.

10. The only exception is in the representation of women, who are primarily presented, when presented at all, in subordinate roles and in poses of suffering or death. Eisenstein does not escape convention in this regard even if he does include a few shots of women as active participants in the strike.

11. This is a reference to *Born in Flames* (Lizzie Borden, 1983), specifically to

a scene in which mentor-radical Zella Wylie states her preference to see five hundred mice on the attack rather than one big lion. "Five hundred mice can do a lot of damage," she notes.

12. This argument parallels, but in a more specifically dialectical vein, Hayden White's argument regarding narrative and time. He asserts that to understand historical acts we must "grasp together" the acts, their motivations, and their consequences, which it is the work of plot to do and which, I argue, it is the work of Eisenstein's modernist collage to do dialectically. If, as White reasons, supporting Ricoeur, narrative has as its " 'ultimate referent' nothing other than 'temporality' itself," then Eisenstein's dialectical referent finds embodiment in a plot constructed dialectically, by the viewer as much as the filmmaker. See White's essay "The Question of Narrative in Contemporary Historical Theory," in *The Content of the Form* (1987, 50–53).

13. Though common sense calls for historical authenticity according to fixed protocols of verification and validation, Eisenstein astutely recognizes the problem this poses for film. Authenticity will be in the eye of the beholder as much as in the images themselves (the image cannot authenticate itself). Validation hinges on the spectator's ability, first, to determine when an image's indexical link to the profilmic event (what happened in front of the camera) can be justifiably equated with a historical event (rather than fiction or other types of events that occur only because of the presence of the camera) and then, second, to interpret this event within the spectator's own social arena in an appropriate manner. This mode of authentication traps us at the level of factual accuracy, a level more proper to the domain of the chronicle, rather than pitching the issue at the level of narrative form itself. To the extent that Eisenstein occupies a blurred zone between fiction and documentary, he need not be held to the factual accuracy appropriate to documentary, nor excused from historical reference altogether.

The form of interpretation preferred by Eisenstein sacrifices specificities of the sort Vertov documented in favor of "the Marxist method itself," rendered no longer as an abstraction but, in keeping with the First Thesis on Feuerbach, as the fullest embodiment of sensuous experience.

As a further distinction, Vertov's conception of consciousness functions more entirely within a reflexive rather than a dialectical frame. As Annette Michelson (1975) puts it, admiringly, "[*The Man with a Movie Camera*] renders insistently concrete, as in another dialectical icon, that philosophical phantasm of the reflexive consciousness, the eye seeing, apprehending itself through its constitution of the world's visibility" (98). The trace of tautology here amounts to the absence of a *materialist* dialectic: the eye apprehends *itself* through its constitution of the world's visibility. This is revolutionary in its own right but radically distinct from the transformative constitution of a subject who has not yet come into being. Althusser ([1965] 1970) clarifies the difference effectively when he argues that *"there is no dialectic of consciousness"* in and of itself, that there is "no dialectic of consciousness which could reach reality itself by virtue of its own contradictions: in short, there can be no 'phenomenology' in the Hegelian sense: for consciousness does not accede to the real through its own internal development, but by the radical discovery of what is *other than itself"* (143).

What we discover (or "Remember!") in *Strike* is an arrested reality that seems "indifferent and strange," undialectical in its incapacity to imagine anything other than what is. This world is the realm of the factory managers, the lumpen proletarians, the spies, henchmen, and Cossacks who are radically other than that consciousness we and the slaughtered workers bring into being. The tension of one with the other, the space between, is precisely where the dialectic arises as something in excess of either reflexive or individual consciousness.

14. The historical importance of the present moment is often lost in historiography and documentary that effaces that moment with the techniques of realism and zero-degree style (style that feigns a near transparency to what it represents). Eisenstein and Vertov, like many modernist, and contemporary, filmmakers, make use of montage, or collage, to establish a vivid sense of tension between a represented past and an experiential present.

What is at issue is whether or not a film, as performance, constitutes its subject (the one out there, the topic, to which it refers as well as the one in here, the viewer, that attends to it) while giving the appearance of finding both subjects already made, in need of little more than discovery and description, or address and (mis)recognition. For both novelistic and historiographical realism "the principal purpose . . . was to substitute surreptitiously a conceptual content (a signified) for a referent that it pretended to describe" (White 1987, 37).

15. The same contrast can be made with the opening of *Peeping Tom* (1960), in which an arrow flies to the center of a bull's-eye in one shot and a human eye opens in the next. The assaultive gaze and the dynamics of sadomasochism are here joined together in unmistakable form. Eisenstein shares much more with the camera eye of Dziga Vertov, in which the figure of the filmmaker himself is reflected (in *The Man with the Movie Camera*), except that Eisenstein eschews this type of open reflexivity to allow his camera to reflect on history more obliquely through the style and plot with which he organizes events.

16. Francis Ford Coppola retains the parallel editing but eviscerates its meaning in his *Apocalypse Now* (1979). Coppola merely negates, or represses, the horror, the stench, the dark underbelly of capitalist logic when he cross-cuts Willard's execution of Kurtz with the ritual slaughter of a bull. The relations between the two men are abstracted outside the realm of class conflict into the realm of ritual practices, individual dementia, and self-purification. Eisenstein has done away with this form of self and its quest for an authenticity denied by its social conditions at the very same moment as they hold it forth as an ideal.

Coppola neglects what Eisenstein teaches. He has shaped a morality tale by restoring an apparent solidity to the very terrain of individual and melodramatic consciousness that Eisenstein bursts asunder. Coppola may well identify with Kurtz, the lone, misunderstood maverick, creator of his own universe of hierarchy, order, and pleasure, who is consequently marked for termination by the hegemonic order. Eisenstein has none of these illusions about his social position or individual ego. His identification is with the masses, who become mere decoration in the negative space of Coppola's mise-en-scène. As Stan Brakhage (1982) says: "What did Eisenstein have to start with, to celebrate? Heroics! He was confronted by a mass of people, which for most of the history of the world is a pretty ugly apparition in any form when it occurs. He made *this* the hero. He strung people out in the most incredible patterns, across vast landscapes and around city streets, in order to create an image of the heroic mass" (171–72).

Brakhage still shares some of the romantic sensibility of a Coppola, seeing in this achievement a mythic representation that would congeal history into formal patterns; Eisenstein's effort also poses an acute contradiction between the individual artist and the collective goals of the nation-state. At least Brakhage recognizes that Eisenstein's achievement lies in giving realization to contradiction, or dialectics, whereas Coppola simply scavenges techniques.

Works Cited

Althusser, Louis. "The 'Piccolo Teatro': Bertolazzi and Brecht." In *For Marx*. New York: Vintage Books, 1970 [1965].

Aumont, Jacques. *Montage Eisenstein*. Bloomington: Indiana University Press, 1987.

Barthes, Roland. "The Third Meaning." In *Image/Music/Text*. New York: Hill & Wang, 1977.

Benjamin, Walter. "Theses on the Philosophy of History." In *Illuminations*. Ed. Hannah Arendt. New York: Schocken, 1969.

Brakhage, Stan. *Brakhage Scrapbook: Collected Writings 1964–1980*. New Palz, N.Y.: Documentext, 1982.

Butler, Judith. *Gender Trouble: Feminism and the Subversion of Identity*. New York: Routledge, 1990.

Cook, David. *A History of Narrative Film*. New York: Norton, 1981.

Dziga Vertov. *Kino-Eye: The Writings of Dziga Vertov*. Ed. Annette Michelson. Berkeley: University of California Press, 1984.

Eisenstein, Sergei. "About Myself and My Films." In *Notes of a Film Director*. New York: Dover, 1970.

Ellis, Jack. *The Documentary Idea*. Englewood Cliffs, N.J.: Prentice Hall, 1989.

Lawder, Standish. "Eisenstein and Constructivism." In *The Essential Cinema*, vol. 1. Ed. P. Adams Sitney. New York: New York University Press, 1975.

Lentricchia, Frank. *Criticism and Social Change*. Chicago: University of Chicago Press, 1983.

Mast, Gerald. *A Short History of the Movies*, 4th ed. New York: Macmillan, 1986.

Michelson, Annette. "From Magician to Epistemologist: Vertov's *The Man with a Movie Camera*." In *The Essential Cinema*, vol. 1. Ed. P. Adams Sitney. New York: New York University Press, 1975.

Nichols, Bill. *Representing Reality: Issues and Concepts in Documentary*. Bloomington: Indiana University Press, 1991.

Nietzsche, Friedrich Wilhelm. *The Genealogy of Morals*. New York: Russell & Russell, 1964 [1887].

Rhode, Eric. *A History of the Cinema.* New York: Hill & Wang, 1976.

Shapiro, Meyer. "Leonardo and Freud: An Art-Historical Study." *Journal of the History of Ideas* 17, no. 2 (1956).

Tretyakov, Sergei, Victor Shklovsky, Esther Shub, and Otto Brik. "Symposium on Soviet Documentary." In *The Documentary Tradition,* 2d ed. Ed. Louis Jacobs. New York: Norton, 1979. (Also translated as "*Lef* and Film." *Screen* 12, no. 4 [1971–72]: 74-80 [from *New Lef* 11–12 (1927)].)

Waugh, Tom. "A Fag-Spotter's Guide to Eisenstein." *Body Politic* 35 (July-August, 1977).

White, Hayden. *The Content of the Form.* Baltimore: Johns Hopkins University Press, 1987.

_____. *Metahistory: The Historical Imagination in Nineteenth-Century Europe.* Baltimore: Johns Hopkins University Press, 1973.

Chapter 5

The Gun in the Briefcase; or,
The Inscription of Class in Film Noir

Paul Arthur

The image of success and its individuated psychology are the
most lively aspects of popular culture and the greatest diversion
from politics.　　　　　—C. Wright Mills, *White Collar*

The image is a fleeting one: in a darkened motel room on the out-
skirts of a border town, a man in a business suit wrestles open a
briefcase, previously entrusted to his new bride, only to discover
that important legal papers and his government-issue revolver are
missing. Without another shred of information concerning narrative context or patterning, this shot might already augur the volatile collision of social and psychosexual themes underpinning our
long-standing fascination with film noir. Add to this scenic description the sole fact that the man in question is a Mexican nar-
cotics agent played by Charlton Heston in olive makeup and we
sense *critical mass* on the horizon. Arriving as it does at the historical end of the noir universe, *Touch of Evil* (1958) is a film in
which practically every discernible signifier can be made to register
with cataclysmic impact.

The empty briefcase is stationed a considerable distance from
the (literal) time bomb that sets Orson Welles's funereal text in
motion—and it is more than a decade removed from the 1945
blast that helped usher in a period of intensified noir production.
Nonetheless, its admittedly minor place in a sequence of dizzying

character inversions and abnegations should remind us of the emblematic role conferred by noir criticism on moments of loss.[1] The apocalyptic language employed here is scarcely arbitrary and cuts in several directions at once. For nearly twenty-five years, this rather small sample of Hollywood crime films—by the most liberal estimates, fewer than two hundred releases—has served as a test case, a ground zero in the swirling interpretive debates proceeding from the 1970s influx of new theoretical paradigms for film studies.[2]

The long and heavily congested critical highway—to mine yet another endemic trope—constructed around the noir series follows from an especially generative, if highly problematic, assumption: that among competing Hollywood genres and series (e.g., domestic melodrama, the musical), noir bears a privileged relation to historically specific "anxieties" through which, at a number of discursive levels, the American postwar climate has been defined. What count as relevant terms in film noir's engagement with social conflict, the thrust of its ideological address, and the best means by which to make that address visible have of course been subject to constant branching and revision. However, two major, and in many instances compatible, pathways have emerged as dominant; interestingly, both are anticipated in critical positions taken on noir during the late 1940s by depth psychological and sociological commentators (see Kracauer; Wolfenstein and Leites).

For feminist psychoanalytic accounts of film noir, the core of its social particularity can be located in the elaboration of sexual difference and gender roles—in the ordering of dramatic and narrational agency, the metonymies of sexual and juridical enigmas, and the successful or aborted recuperation of patriarchal self-interest. A second approach starts with roughly the same catalyst, the ambivalent male protagonist in the throes of a legal-domestic crisis, and works outward, as it were, rather than inward to develop the ideological contours of paranoia and unstable authority (criminal conspiracy, personal betrayal) as expressions of Cold War liberal politics, encompassing at times the internal dynamics of the Hollywood industry. A shared, perhaps even an enabling, strategy of both practices is the displacement of realist conventions, the surfaces of social reality inscribed in narrative and visual desiderata, onto "repressed" sanctums of meaning about which commercial cinema must either remain silent or present in highly mediated form.

To put it another way, in either approach the empty briefcase in the scene cited above would attain significance precisely because of what is absent from it: the revolver or government briefs as symbolic indices of, say, castration fears or doubts about the efficacy of legally sanctioned power. Although such insights are often illuminating and useful—despite their overly simplistic treatment here—there is a lurking suspicion that sometimes a briefcase is just a briefcase. Or is there something to be said about the narrative, iconographic, and formal trajectories in which that object figures as part of a broader representation of concrete, quotidian social identities? Without pretending to redirect attention to the "thing itself" as opposed to a chain of abstract associations—the chain I will propose is neither more nor less *present*—it pays to sketch out certain connections routinely made by film noir between the dire criminal predicaments of its characters and the network of social referents within which and against which transgressive impulses are enacted. Through this process the category of work as a determinant of social status, of role expectations and class identification, and the circulation of these issues alongside familiar noir themes, can be retrieved as an important mechanism in the creation of meaning.

To be sure, the critical omission of class as legible discourse, or as a site of intersection with the regulatory functions of sexual difference and legal authority, is not surprising, nor is it evidence of a criminal conspiracy.[3] As Dwight Macdonald has remarked, the subject of work and its social ambit is for Hollywood "like the dark side of moon"; only the job descriptions of cowboys and detectives—and, one might add, thieves—are shown in any detail (quoted in Stead 243). Further, to the extent that social significance was ever mappable through elements of plot and characterization, the repeal in the late 1940s of the "problem film" was intended, in the wake of the blacklist, to inoculate the industry against charges of subversion.[4] Yet it is undeniable that a large measure of film noir's critical and box-office cachet was attributable to an often well-advertised fidelity to the real, and it *is* curious that analogical codes have received so little concerted attention.

Aside from the conspicuous display of location shooting, noir sought product differentiation through references to topical events and issues (e.g., the bomb, spy trials, the Senate investigation into organized crime), with a far greater proportion of its literary sources being drawn from newspaper and magazine stories than from, say, hard-boiled fiction. Firmly rooted in the landscapes of actual cities visualized through their signature monuments and industries—in contradistinction to the generic or dimly realized locales of 1930s gangster films—noir protagonists for the most part occupy jobs and engage in social processes immediately accessible to the mass audiences at which they were aimed. It is to this "daytime" world of ordinary relations and discontents that we turn in order to understand better how they are projected onto the nocturnal, dreamlike eruptions of violence and sexuality for which noir is justly celebrated.

The focus of the following discussion will be on specific social positions delineated *before* the narrative Fall and the imbrication of those positions in liminal investigative activities undertaken by the hero in an (often failed) effort to restore markers of personal identity and collective stability. After establishing a framework in which the series mobilizes a semiotics of class and status, I shift to an examination of, in particular, the rhetoric of popular social science tracts of the 1950s in their sublation of class difference as a tool of analysis and potential praxis. Only through the charting of the convergences and frictions between film noir's allegories of "demotion" and the postwar ideology of social "homogenization" will the force of noir's exposure and unsettled crossing of class boundaries become evident. Unlike Oedipal fixations or the oppressive nature of the Cold War security state, class antagonism may constitute a textual feature less unspeakable than it is unheard.

Day and Night

A useful starting point in a capsule account of salient aspects of noir narrativity is the occupational profiles and attendant skills displayed by its roster of protagonists.[5] Job-related tensions, in conjunction with and often in advance of romantic or domestic struggles, provide a trigger for criminal or criminal/investigative impulses in more than half the films. Contrary to the cliché-ridden model of marginalized private eye, noir heroes tend to be salaried employees in the service sector, professionals, or middle-echelon members of law enforcement. For obvious dramatic reasons, they operate under semiautonomous working conditions, without constant supervision but responsible to older male figures in some institutional hierarchy.[6] When characters are shown as self-employed, the designation of authority figure is often vested in members of a criminal conspiracy. The point is that rarely are noir protagonists exempt from some existing structure of economic-social power directly inflecting the course of their exploits. Typical occupations include *Double Indemnity*'s (1944) salesman, *D.O.A.*'s (1950) accountant, *Force of Evil*'s (1948) lawyer, and the doctor in *Where Danger Lives* (1950). Placed within roughly the same social matrix but minus their white-collar trappings are a mail carrier in *Side Street* (1950), a cab driver in *99 River Street* (1953), and a factory worker in *Kiss of Death* (1947).

For a few scattered drifters, such as the temporary chauffeur in *The Chase* (1946), no fixed vocation is indicated, and thus they appear relatively detached from the mesh of stable social relations engulfing most noir characters at the outset of their adventures. The secure order that is unbalanced by the enactment of a task or forbidden desire is an axiom of narrativity in general, but the world usurped in film noir is never that of perfect stasis. Rather, it is already fraught with uncertainty over personal identity, with only a thin membrane of material relations and moral attitudes separating it from the utter alienation of the underworld. Many stories begin with the hero facing prospective changes in work status—a new assignment, dismissal, promotion—and these changes are frequently paralleled and amplified by imminent domestic transitions (e.g., a marriage proposal, childbirth, a solitary vacation).[7] Mutually limiting to the fulfillment of economic and erotic desires, job and home are depicted as mutually determinant in the eventual formation of criminal or quasi-criminal (in the case of rogue cops and undercover agents) pursuits. For example, the pressures of a tyranical boss and a souring marriage together propel the hero of *The Big Clock* (1948) into an outcast domain of illicit and inverted social roles. Similar correspondences are at work in the otherwise quite divergent plots of *Detour* (1945), *Fear in the Night* (1947), and *Panic in the Streets* (1950). In *The Big*

Heat (1953), a police detective, in allowing job frustrations—both financial and ethical in nature—to disrupt the harmony of his family, winds up placing both in such jeopardy that his only recourse is to assume the guise of lawless vigilante.

The petty-bourgeois discontents of the noir hero limn the gap between expectations of social equilibrium and privilege and their inadequate realization under a system in which real power—variously configured as criminal/legal knowledge, ostentatious wealth, possession of a desired woman—is exercised by either off-screen forces or malevolent "doubles." Constrained by ideological burdens of normality, conformity, marriage, friendship, and loyalty (to lawful or criminal codes of vocational conduct), the narrative course of the protagonist is to attempt, consciously or unconsciously, to escape expectations that constitute his social regime. Minor transitions in work and/or domesticity become openings through which alternative actions and identities are envisioned and subsequently mobilized as either voluntary effects (e.g., as a means of "advancement" or the solving of a criminal enigma) or the machinations of "fate." In nearly all situations, new identities are in retrospect perceived—if not by the character himself—as desiderata, as being the product of latent contradictions attached to his initial positioning.

The distinction, then, between the voice-over lament of a crime-magazine editor in *The Big Clock*, "Thirty-six hours ago I was a decent, law-abiding citizen with a wife and a kid and a big job," and the complaint of a burned-out insurance investigator in *The Pitfall* (1948), "I don't want to be an average American," is reducible "merely" to the angle at which a particular textual system chooses to frame its protagonist in relation to a set of social circumstances. Regardless of the places from which they depart, however, the American dreams they entertain are strikingly modest or ill defined (admittedly, government undercover agents out to save the social fabric from the depredations of counterfeiters or communist spies operate from different motives, even though they wind up in roughly the same boat as their more transgressive kinsmen). In this, they are quite far from the aggressively acquisitive egotists of 1930s gangster films such as *Little Caesar* or *The Public Enemy,* for whom the journey up the social ladder from working-class immigrant background to leadership role in a criminal network is predicated on an ultimately deceptive projection of wealth and power mirroring that of "legitimate" corporate-political interests. In film noir, progress is calibrated as a deepening estrangement from, leading to a perverse renegotiation with, the signifiers of the "decent and respectable."

Take as an example the film that many consider the *locus classicus* of the series, *Double Indemnity*. The lure of criminal activity is for Walter Neff indigenous to the job of selling insurance and evaluating claims. Tutored by a paternalistic older man—Keyes, the head claims investigator and Neff's nominal superior—in the stratagems of fraud, Neff confesses he has spent sleepless nights figuring a way to "crook the house," cheat his company and thus extricate himself from the oppressive atmosphere of a dead-end job. The suggestion that he quit his salesman's job to become Keyes's assistant, an even more suffocating and unremunerative post, coincides with an erotic encounter between Neff and a dangerous married woman. Here, as in *The Pitfall* and other films, the femme fatale serves as a catalyst, albeit a powerful and psychologically complex one, for discontents rooted in the space of daily routine.

Typical of the forms in which the quotidian is addressed in film noir, Neff's job is not only the vehicle (literally, in that it entails the use of an automobile) for murder and adultery, it returns following the crime to mock, in several registers, his presumption of social privilege through economic gain. The other, no less vexed, presumption entails Neff's seizing the prerogatives of father in an established family order. His habit of meticulously logging sales calls, his knowledge of the Los Angeles street grid and familiarity with the "angles" of fraudulent claims are all worked into the murder scheme.[8] Back at his desk after the completion of the deed, Neff is approached by Keyes, who tries to enlist his vocational talents to examine the death claim for which Neff himself is accountable. But such recuperation is impossible; for better or worse, Neff is a person transformed—"I couldn't hear my own footsteps. It was the walk of a dead man." He has exchanged identities (again both literally and figuratively) with his ostensibly more settled and affluent victim, but the order of loss he experiences is more than just metaphysical (or psychic).

When we first see Neff in the present-tense prologue, prior to the onset of narrated flashbacks, he is entering his workplace at night. Instead of fellow salesmen, company executives, and clerical workers, the building's only occupants are a night watchman (who complains in the elevator that he cannot obtain an insurance policy because of his bad heart!) and the traces of a janitorial staff. Despite his ruse, Neff is clearly not there doing "overtime." The nocturnal world he has accessed is a ghostly version of the commercial middle-class bustle abandoned as the day closes, and it is redolent of a social category all but suppressed by the narrative[9]—indeed by the larger institution, at least in its representational practices, of which that narrative is exemplary. Endeavoring to rise in station, or at least to erase the coordinates of a fixed and dreary social location, Neff discovers the "lower depths." And, given the confusions created by his myriad role infractions, it hardly seems stretching the point to conclude that symbolic slippage in the characterization of class is a signal consequence of Neff's criminal passage.

Setting their sights on what transpires in the dark, movements of the unconscious, and the social relations they enforce, psychoanalytic commentators on noir too easily bypass another kind of narrative "history" made in the glare of the workday, of which there are several further ramifications.[10] As protagonists near the threshold of criminal identity, a battery of visual tropes may signal the abrogation of bourgeois order and the encroachment of a liminal space in which formerly fixed roles become fluid. Nightfall is often conjoined with the appearance of water (rain, fog, harbor locations), a bridge or tunnel or claustrophobic enclosure (automobile interior, telephone booth). Along the physical axis of flight/ pursuit, characters migrate to a new city or a new quarter of the same city, and this almost always entails a shift from stable urban center (signified by residential or business or governmental architectures) to social margins (including deserted industrial sites, waterfront areas, and red-light districts).

The hero may be required to change clothing, adopt a disguise, or assume a different name. The altering of identity betokened by environmental degradation, associations with filth and decay, is invariably consolidated (or at times anticipated) by a scene in which the character loses consciousness. Sleep, beatings, alcoholic stupor, amnesia, and the administration of drugs are common indices of mental *depaysement*. Stigmata appear: blood, bandages, sweat, rent garments. Looking and acting only fitfully sentient, they offer verbal confirmation of their impaired states—"I couldn't hear my own footsteps"—by declaring an inability to "feel," an annulment of previously validated emotions such as romantic love or friendship. The iconography of noir hero-as-automaton draws sustenance from several cinematic discourses of male alienation: combat soldiers and disoriented vets, horror-film monsters, sci-fi alien possession (a generic motif that surfaces late in the noir cycle).[11]

To cross into the netherworld is to court symbolic death, and noir is replete with thanatopic previews. The downward spiral frequently carries images of burial (a motif that absorbs much of the visual and verbal energy of the last section of *Night and the City* [1950]). The epithet "dead man" is applied to the living in at least ten films. Yet the conventional invocation in noir of a living death takes on a specific resonance requiring a bit more fleshing out. Associations between the city depicted as a dark, criminalized labyrinth and the lower classes has a long literary tradition (see Williams 144–48). Bourgeois humanism of the homegrown variety idealizes the capacity to experience and express emotional states bound to the maintenance of the romantic couple, nuclear family, and social network while attributing the absence of sentiment to an alienation fostered by either a lack of material-social security or its surfeit. In this mythology, only the rich and the poor are "exempt" from the burdens of validating social ideals and are thus endowed with a ruthlessness and "amorality" appropriate to the violations manifest in noir narratives.

Unlike generic structures in, say, domestic melodrama, film noir must punish and *enrich* its discontented figures through fantasies of transformation in which they are first divested of a secure social identity only to be reinvested with the qualities of a disavowed class.[12] Voluntarily abandoning or forced by job or other circumstances to leave behind an "organic community" primed to absorb or minimize difference, the noir hero slides into an abject identification whose consequences include ostracization, debility, and death. He is, however, rewarded for this change to the extent that it sanctions transgressive sexual and legal behavior, allowing him to enact radical individualist solutions to anxieties fostered by entrapment and powerlessness. In the anarchy of social expectations and sexual roles unleashed by his demotion, the protagonist recognizes an agency denied him in his previous position. But this ambivalent potency can do little more than cause the destruction of an antagonist, who in many instances is configured as a projection of the protagonist's own desires and self-doubts.

Assessed as bourgeois cautionary tales, film noir manages to subsume any contradictions it raises concerning class society under issues of individual deviance and guilt. Society may be sterile and repressive, but all attempts at change result in something worse than the original ills.[13] And certainly, the fantasization of a class "below" as a violent, sexualized, yet benumbed Other offers scant challenge to the liberal ideology of the time. Nonetheless, in a historical period of intense economic globalization dictated by American geopolitical preeminence—among whose effects was a decisive shift from an industrial to a service-based domestic economy[14]—a popular rhetoric of class homogenization, the vaunted "bourgeoisfication" of the worker (see Marcuse 10–18; also Poulantzas 58–61), can be resituated in film noir through scenarios of middle-class subjects confronted with their potential "proletarianization."

Film noir narrative's notorious hesitancy at, or lack of conviction in, the final restoration of a dominant order stems in part from the difficulty of reintegrating its heroes into a structure intent on denying the existence of class society.[15] But the failure to reconvene a "natural" stability of social roles has a corollary in the representation of urban settings. Even if a protagonist solves a criminal enigma, cleansing his "name" of legal culpability, the terrain on which his adventure was realized remains intact. Its authenticity has, in many instances, been guaranteed by the visual system (reinforced by voice-over narration, title cards, and other devices). That is, in contrast to other Hollywood narratives of the period, the domain of underworld adventure is not veiled by historical distance (e.g., the western), geography (e.g., the spy film), or the supernatural (e.g., sci-fi). Although in moments of intense action the city may appear to be an expressionistic reflection of a character's inner state, in general whether the physical environment is a product of psychic forces or vice versa remains an open question. The noir city is at once oneiric and actual, highly stylized—in its lighting, composition, editing construction, and so on—yet distinctly real. Buildings, streets, and objects bristle with metaphoric valence, but their deployment anchors a realist agenda and is surprisingly consonant with a public discourse around urban sociology in postwar American culture.

Indebted to earlier analyses by Lewis Mumford and the Chicago school (Robert Park, Louis Wirth, and others), popular journalism—abetted by dystopian novels such as Orwell's *1984*—extended a venerable strain of antiurbanism in addressing the plight of America's cities. Two interrelated forms of this address are relevant here: the demonization of urban society in contrast to the promise of suburbia and the imagination of nuclear disaster. Film noir narrativizes an obsessive concern with the breakup of old neighborhoods, increasing separation of home and workplace, and the decline of "primary" communities of affiliation. The city it reveals is already a product of middle-class flight, a deracinated zone of violent crime and sexual license. Characters do not so much *reside* in the city as nervously circulate through it, adopting temporary or surrogate dwellings in sleazy rooming houses *(Side Street)*, abandoned buildings *(The Window* [1949]), lofts *(The Dark City* [1950]), and even automobiles *(Cry of the City* [1948]).[16] Their transience is matched only by their disorientation, with noir's formal codes dissolving spatial boundaries that separate interior from exterior architectures (e.g., the use of fire escapes and constricted alleyways framed as if they were part of interior structures).

The haunted nighttime tableaux of deserted streets, empty buildings, and decaying factories and warehouses stipulate another image in the arsenal of postwar urban representations. In the wake of Hiroshima/Nagasaki, large industrial cities emerged as the imagined targets of future wartime destruction. Detailed speculative accounts of nuclear attacks, accompanied by maps and illustrations, flooded newspapers and magazines in the late 1940s and early 1950s. A discourse of apocalyptic obsolescence fed the economically motivated development of suburban tracts and can be understood as both an adjunct to serious discussions on urban renovation—in the sense that planners tried to envision ways of rebuilding cities to make them less vulnerable to attack—and a displacement of that issue. For our purposes, it is tempting to assign the currency achieved by talk of urban disaster in part to a wider postwar campaign to discourage reactivation of a class consciousness identified with urban labor movements of the 1930s; indeed, the anticipation of urban cataclysm might be taken as a form of symbolic obliteration of that consciousness. Appositely, the portrayal of urban social relations in film noir brings together two thematic strands of middle-class anxiety, "mobility" and "entrapment," preoccupying social science discourses of the 1950s.

The Smell of Success

Unlike other hustlers and social strivers in the ranks of film noir, Joe Morse, the ambitious mob lawyer of *Force of Evil*, has no interest in obscuring his working-class roots; thus the arc of his descent is somewhat atypical. In order to salvage the "business" of his estranged bookie brother from hostile takeover by a numbers conglomerate, Morse ventures from the protective confines of a Wall Street law firm to reengage with the immigrant neighborhood in which he was raised. A key dialogue motif expounds the wisdom that "business is theft," and the film intertwines three distinct levels of corporate activity as propped up by exploitation, graft, and violence. As director Abraham Polonsky phrased it, "Gangsterism is like capitalism, or the other way around" (quoted in Sherman and Rubin 10). The story is in essence an indictment of blind assimilation into mainstream society and of the human toll exacted by organizational imperatives of loyalty and conformity.

Given the unusual bluntness of its critique, it is not surprising that *Force of Evil* was written and directed by a prominent member of the Hollywood left who was blacklisted shortly after the film was released. What remains consistent with the majority of noir is an attitude about the repressiveness of centralized authority, regardless of whether it is vested in the elites of big business, government agencies, or criminal syndicates (or, for that matter, the communist underground). In setting up a strict dichotomy between individual agency and shadowy bureaucratic control, noir equates virtually all forms of "corporatism." Isomorphic patterns in imagery and narrative function consign disparate representatives of detached, abstract organs of power to either grossly malign

or, in the case of government officials, inflexible roles in the pre-
cipitation of events.

The pressures exerted on Hollywood in the period of *Force of
Evil* to revise a conventional, sentimental animus toward big business are glimpsed in a pamphlet written Ayn Rand and distributed
to movie exhibitors and the press, "Don't Smear the Free Enterprise System": "Don't tell people that man is a helpless, twisted,
drooling, snivelling, neurotic weakling" (quoted in Sayre 50).
Rand could have had in mind the brand of impaired individualism
rampant in film noir. With production increasingly mired in a climate of political reaction, the series maintained a mistrust of corporate ideology even as the dominant occupational profile of its
heroes gradually shifts from the private sector to government employment. *Force of Evil* is a clear example of what Manny Farber
called "social significance gone sour," generic products with progressive elements infected by despair (82). Yet, whatever else film
noir can be accused of, it never quite succumbs to the prevalent
"mythology of success" (Kleinhans 12) in which Hollywood routinely couches the dynamics of class difference.

By 1950, the apogee of film noir's popularity, American social
science was in headlong retreat from "partisan" analyses of social inequality and injustice. What C. Wright Mills would later
chastize as "the metaphysic of labor" had to be jettisoned in favor
of a focus on the "inner man" (xx). For Daniel Bell, to understand
contemporary social relations one had to address the issue of in-
trapsychic identity through concepts of "self and status" (*End of
Ideology* 13). For David Riesman, this task recommended an approach based upon "socially oriented psychoanalytic characterol-
ogy" (xxvi). At the risk of flattening a diverse and nuanced body of
theory to fit the outlines of noir storytelling, there is a marked con-
vergence of assumptions in a group of texts otherwise at variance
in their conclusions and ideological perspectives. A common
stance was a self-validating break with reigning modes of social
analysis necessitated by dramatic historical transformations. And
despite a basic adherence to the discursive conventions of an academic field, the "new sociology" attained unprecedented popular
reception through its dissemination in mass-culture magazine and
paperback book markets.

One assumption central to the work of sociologists, social psychologists, historians, and political scientists is that "standard explanations of American political behavior [had become] inadequate" due to circumstances of class mobility and homogenization (Bell, "Preface" ix). Moreover, both the "liberal ethos" and Marxist categories inherited from the 1930s were now "inadequate" (Mills xx). In the view of Seymour Martin Lipset, this was because "class politics" is applicable only under conditions of economic depression, whereas "status politics" predominates in periods of prosperity (308–9). Thus, in the context of what Richard Hofstadter refers to as "pseudo-conservatism," the managed effects of the Cold War and McCarthyism, "ideology" was granted a privileged stake in political behavior above "economics" ("Pseudo-Conservatism Revisited" 98). Arguing that material conflicts over wages, job safety, or union representation no longer fueled the consciousness of the American worker, the most pressing problems were those of "conformity, adaptation, and adjustment" (Riesman xxvi).

Taking into account the "structural" change in the economy governing the rise of the "new middle class," the Organization Man and his white-collar colleagues become the implicit engine of American social welfare. With this preeminent role came certain reflexive dilemmas. As a concomitant of economic transformation, massive geographic mobility nurtured the spread of suburbia, and with it an intensifying concern over status:

> Instead of a fixed or known status, symbolized by dress or title, each person assumes a multiplicity of roles and constantly has to prove himself in a succession of new situations. Because of all this, the individual loses a coherent sense of self. His anxieties increase. (Bell, *End of Ideology* 22)

The conversion from "an age of production to an age of consumption" (Riesman 6) was discussed as an underlying cause of heretofore unsounded insecurities that threatened the ideological tenets of individualism. According to Mills:

> The material hardship of nineteenth-century industrial workers finds its parallel on the psychological level among twentieth-century white-collar employees. The new Little

Man seems to have no firm roots, no sure loyalties to
sustain his life and give it a center. (xvi)[17]

What W. H. Auden in 1946 dubbed the "Age of Anxiety"
evolved into a heuristic framework for social analysis. In the political sphere, a suspicious and fearful petty bourgeoisie harbored
the belief that despite their illusion of automony, "those who hold
real power have often come to exercise it in hidden ways. . . . In
the amorphous twentieth-century world, where manipulation re-
places authority, the victim does not recognize his status" (Mills
110; see also Hofstadter, "Pseudo-Conservative Revolt" 78; Riesman 205). This was the foundation of Hofstadter's "paranoid
style," a "projective politics" obsessed with conspiratorial designs
and the impotence of individual action ("Pseudo-Conservatism
Revisited" 100; see also Fromm 22–26). The aura of secrecy and
increasing government centralization emblematic of the Cold
War security state became a mirror image for the accelerating con-
glomeration of private capital. As the perception of once-stable
boundaries between public and private, government and corporation, began to disappear, the middle-class "Little Man" found himself caught in a contradiction between demands for absolute loyalty (and conformity) and an overriding mistrust of institutional
power.

The result was deemed a "dense and massive irrationality"
(Hofstadter, Pseudo-Conservativism Revisited 81) manifest in the
superimposed thematics of anticommunist hysteria and status confusion. Under conditions of expanding affluence and its attendant
myths of social mobility, the theoretical postulate of "identity crisis" served as an explanatory model for the coexistence of virulent
political reaction and widespread apathy. William H. Whyte criticizes the "Social Ethic"—"a body of thought that makes morally
legitimate the pressures of society against the individual" (*Organization Man* 5)—insofar as it creates the false unity of "belong-
ingness" and stigmatizes the desire for change. The beleaguered individualist, Riesman's "inner-directed personality" (14), unable to
balance role expectations and divided loyalties, is labeled "deviant." Or to frame this designation in the political language of Mc-
Carthyism, resistance to the moral-legal authority of corporatism
is tantamount to criminal behavior.[18]

Social theory of the 1950s returns us to the moment in which the leitmotif of class homogenization and its anxieties gained ascendency. The products of mass culture, especially film and television, were important in the formulation of sociological analyses to the degree that they purportedly reflected the promotion of conformist and quietist values (see Riesman 156; also Whyte, "Literature" 65; Podhoretz 89–90). Mills suggests that Hollywood clung to outmoded fables of social achievement even as the public ideal of success grew "less widespread as fact, more confused as image, often dubious as motive, and soured as a way of life" (259). Leslie Fiedler takes a similar tack in scoring the tendency of mass culture "to suppress violent or fearful experiences." Discovering no 1950s equivalent to the stories of the brothers Grimm or Hans Christian Andersen, he remarks: "Everywhere the fear of fear is endemic, the fear of the very names of fear" (543).

If nothing else, film noir delivers a group of parables worthy of the fear animated by Cold War society. The relation of these films to the branch of social thought discussed above is at once complex and perhaps reciprocal. On one hand, noir's discontented, anxiety-riddled heroes forecast the emergent sociological emphasis on uncertain identity in a world of bourgeois constriction. The noir protagonist struggles with the difficulty of achieving knowledge, much less agency, in the face of immiscible desires for advancement and transgression. His only recourse is to assume the position of criminal subject and submerge himself in a violent ordeal of (self-) incrimination and investigation. Nonetheless, he is unmistakably a *dis-organization man,* acting out of personal motives of greed, lust, revenge—and this is so even when he is given the mantle of legal representative. Moreover, his journey through the lower depths can be reconfigured as a slippage in class identification, unmasking in a gesture of ambivalence a stratification suppressed by post-World War II social theory in the name of historical rupture and renewal.

McCarthyism was once defined by its namesake, in a Whitmanesque turn of phrase, as "Americanism with its sleeves rolled." The working-class drift of this phrase is hardly accidental. Although it would eventually be revealed as a canard, the senator from Wisconsin addressed his national following as "the little people," urban and rural blue-collar ethnic Americans. As was

Figure 5.1. The empty briefcase.

hinted at the time, McCarthy appears to have fashioned for himself a movie-made "character" mixing bits of Capra, John Wayne, and the private detective.[19] With a two-day stubble of beard and rumpled suit, a bottle in his desk drawer, this "vulgarian by method" (Rovere 48) worked deep into the night. When regular channels of intimidation failed to obtain a desired effect, he could resort to physical threat and even violence. An archaic bastion of rugged individualism, his dogged investigative pursuit of "subversives" was, in his personal mythology, challenged at every step by the conspiratorial corruption of government bureaucracy.

McCarthy's media image, in its inferred debt to the protagonists of film noir, was given an odd and affecting spin by Orson Welles, who completed initial production on *Touch of Evil* in the spring of 1957, on the eve of McCarthy's death. Welles's Hank Quinlan is a rogue cop who thinks his pursuit of criminals places him above the law—a heavyset, hard-drinking Irish-American with a bum leg (McCarthy falsely claimed his limp was the result of a wartime bombing mission) who plants evidence against those he intuits are guilty. Quinlan stalks the murderer of a prominent businessman blown to pieces by a car bomb, but his real target is Charlton

Figure 5.2. Rogue cop and government bureaucrat.

Heston's meddling government official. Mike Vargas is in turn a spokesman for corporate-liberal ideals and possesses an abiding faith in the state's legal and political apparatus: "In a free country, the policeman is supposed to enforce the law, which protects the guilty as well as the innocent."

The philosophical antagonists engage in an ongoing argument about the role of the police. Quinlan admits he has a "dirty job," but "there are plenty of soldiers who don't like war." Vargas counters that a "policeman's job is only easy in a police state." He accuses Quinlan of "abuse of power," momentarily recruiting the sheriff's superiors in local government to curb his methods of interrogation. Forced to confront the contradiction lurking in his accusation, "Who's the boss, the cop or the law?" Vargas winds up adopting some of the same brutal tactics as his nemesis. In order to clear his name and that of his wife of false charges, Vargas follows Quinlan into the underworld, retracing the latter's well-worn path through sleazy bars, cheap motels, and brothels. In keeping with the trajectory of other noir characters, Vargas is by the end transformed from a middle-echelon bureaucrat to a wounded, confused, and disheveled lout. Fortunately for him, he is able to have

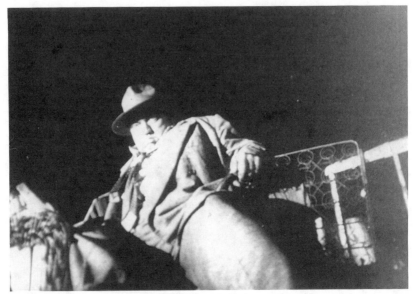

Figure 5.3. Quinlan/McCarthy on the garbage heap of history.

the last word, convincing Quinlan's faithful assistant to wear a wire and extract a confession of guilt. Quinlan dies in a garbage heap and Vargas drives off in a new convertible—but, as always, the stench of decaying values lingers on.

Touch of Evil's master conceit of "border crossing"—a palimpsest of legal, psychosexual, national, racial, and class transversals—may at first glance seem devoid of historical specificity, but it can briefly be reopened for the incursion of a personal itinerary. Welles had been an active member of Hollywood's liberal left during the 1930s. He campaigned for FDR's fourth term and supported the continuation of New Deal social policies as a newspaper columnist for the *New York Post*. As early as 1945, he decried the "phony fear of communism . . . smokescreening the real menace of renascent Fascism" (Naremore, *Welles* 136–42). He was the object of long-term FBI surveillance, yet avoided blacklisting mainly because he was already ostracized for purported financial profligacy.[20] In a later interview he expressed resentment that the circle of Hollywood progressives "demolished itself, ceding to a new generation of Nihilists" (Rubio, Cobos, and Pruneda 545). Quinlan is Welles's version of McCarthy, but McCarthy is also, in the symbolic logic of the film, Welles himself—an individualist "betrayed" by a corporate system that had used him to do its "dirty job." Welles's battles with white-collar executives and his sense of abandonment by former allies on the left are engraved like a tombstone on this final gasp in the noir series.

Notes

1. The briefcase turns out to be a less anomalous image than it might seem. In a bizarre bit of dialogue from *The Pitfall* (1948), an insurance investigator confesses to his prospective lover, "I'm a little unsure of myself when I crawl out of my briefcase." The equation of business accoutrement and personal identity is at least implicit in several other films, and the strange leather satchel that contains fissionable material in *Kiss Me Deadly* (1955) is a close iconographic kin to the Organization Man's favorite symbol.

2. I discuss in some detail the genesis of the film noir topos in my forthcoming book, *On the Brink: Film Noir and Cold War America, 1945–1958*. Far from an "innocent" or entirely textually motivated choice, analytic schemata have tended to mask at least two psychohistorical factors: first, that these films emanate from the childhood or adolescent viewing contexts of many of their most ardent commentators; and second, that their pervasive alienation and paranoid regard for authority are loosely consistent with political attitudes fostered by the upheavals of the late 1960s, the same period in which noir was "rediscovered" by Anglo-American film studies.

3. George Lipsitz (175–80) is practically the only writer to acknowledge class as a determining category in film noir. However, I find his contention that on a "covert" level, noir "reflected many of the working issues raised by postwar labor unrest" (see 179–81), and his reading of *Detour* (1945) as a wildcat strike, at best idiosyncratic.

4. The tenuous claim that following World War II Hollywood broached, then abandoned, concrete engagement with issues such as racism and anti-Semitism, with film noir often figured as a symptom of retrenchment, is propped up by loose statistical studies (see, for example, the table "Changes in the Content of Hollywood Motion Pictures, 1947–1954," reproduced in Cogley 282; Sayre [48] cites similar findings published in *Variety*).

5. My sample consists of eighty-eight films made between 1942 and 1958. Of these, thirty-seven feature characters connected in some way with private sector, mostly service economy, jobs, whereas another thirty-one are municipal or government investigators (with the former dominant before 1950 and the latter after 1950). The remaining films involve professional criminals (ten), private eyes (five), and a "hybrid" category of journalists (five). Unlike most analysts of noir, I believe that overarching narrative and thematic patterns bind protagonists stationed at disparate points on the legal-social compass (cops as well as professional criminals and middle-class adventurers).

6. Anthropologist Geoffrey Gorer, writing at the height of noir popularity,

asserts that such a job profile, with its implicit rejection of unambiguous positions of social and economic authority, is integral to the mythology of the American middle-class virtue (27–31).

7. In nineteen of forty-nine noir produced prior to 1950, the protagonist's passage from one signifier of social identity to another is underscored by his designation as a recent war vet, a status that often plays into narrative tropes such as amnesia and iconographic tropes of (shell-shocked) somnambulism.

8. In a similar way, the cab driver in 99 *River Street* and the postal worker in *Side Street* employ knowledge of the city gained in legitimate jobs during their nighttime rounds of quasi-criminal investigation. For rogue cops and vigilante cops, the conversion of job skills for criminal ends is demonstrated as a seamless process. Even anomalous figures such as a professor in *The Woman in the Window* (1945) and a Hollywood screenwriter in *In a Lonely Place* (1950) find uses for their specialized skills while they are undergoing criminal ordeals.

9. As with other minor players encountered by Neff at night, the blue-collar status of a black parking attendant is "dramatized," in the Freudian sense, by placement in an *underground* garage. The revisiting of deserted work areas previously shown during the day (e.g., *D.O.A.*, *Follow Me Quietly* [1949], *Scene of the Crime* [1949]) and the revelation of concealed or subterranean spaces below sites of job activity (e.g., *T-Men* [1948], *Union Station* [1950], *He Walked By Night* [1948]) are fairly prominent motifs that connect with the broader pattern of staging climactic chase sequences at multilevel industrial or commercial locales (in approximately two dozen films).

10. A possible reason psychoanalytic critics have been unable to accommodate a perspective on class issues is that their interpretive evidence tends to be drawn from noir's narrative codes and structures, whereas much of the discourse on social class resides in iconographic cues.

11. In their trancelike bearing, protagonists shoulder the legacy of the somnambulistic killer in *The Cabinet of Dr. Caligari*. Noel Carroll's explication of the "interstitial" status of monsters (31–34) provides a useful correlative to noir's upending of social categories (cop/killer, father/son, living/dead). The narrative and visual linkages between noir and 1950s science fiction are, unfortunately, beyond the scope of this essay, but the citation of two film titles will suggest the overlap: *I Married a Communist* (1949; aka *Woman on Pier 13*) and *I Married a Monster from Outer Space* (1958).

12. See Thomas Elsaesser's astute analysis of relations between noir and domestic melodrama.

13. Ronnie Scheib argues this point in relation to Hitchcock's seminoir *Shadow of a Doubt* (1943), and I have adapted several of her excellent insights here.

14. By 1956, white-collar workers outnumbered blue-collar employees for the first time in history; from 1947 to 1957, factory jobs fell 4 percent while clerical jobs rose 23 percent and the "salaried middle class" increased by 61 percent (Leuchtenburg 79).

15. This hesitancy is, to be sure, imbricated with problems of sexual difference and the patriarchal "voice" as instantiated by the textual system's unsettling

dispersion of subjectivity and authoritative knowledge. The imputed disruption of classical effects of narrative authority, coherence, and continuity has generated considerable critical controversy. For opposing views of film noir's narrative "deviance," see Gledhill (10–16) and Bordwell (74–77).

16. In the quirkily titled *Private Hell 36* (1954), the infernal region turns out *not* to be the city, but a mobile home rented by a rogue cop as a place to stash illicit funds. Like the ghost town hideout in *The Prowler* (1951) and the "model home" in *Shield for Murder* (1954), the cramped trailer perfectly expresses the impossibility in noir of fixed habitation.

17. Mills cites as symptomatic a speech by a character in Orwell's *Coming Up for Air:* "There's a lot of rot talked about the sufferings of the working class. I'm not sorry for the proles myself. . . . The prole suffers physically but he's a free man when he isn't working" (xi). Riesman as well discusses the "envy" of factory work by the "other-directed" personality (268). The notion here is that, unlike other forms of labor, white-collar work entails pressures that insinuate themselves into the fabric of all social relations, including family life.

18. Pop psychologist Robert Linder capitalized on the discursive linkages among psychic disorder, criminality, and the "un-American" in his best-selling volume of case histories, *The Fifty-Minute Hour.*

19. Richard Rovere, in his study of McCarthy, provides considerable evidence of self-conscious image construction. He also cites newspaper accounts by Joseph and Stewart Alsop in which they commented that a visit to the senator's office was "like being transported to the set of one of Hollywood's minor thrillers" (144).

20. On FBI surveillance of Welles, see Naremore ("The Trial"). Welles's handling of the themes of state abuse of the legal system and juridical instability of course predate *Touch of Evil.* One example is an episode of *Orson Welles' Sketchbook,* a series of six short television programs made for the BBC in 1955, in which the issue of police abuse of power is rehearsed in nearly the same rhetorical pitch evident in the feature film.

Works Cited

Bell, Daniel. *The End of Ideology.* New York: Free Press, 1960.
———. "Preface." In *The Radical Right*, rev. ed. Ed. Daniel Bell. Garden City, N.Y.: Anchor, 1963.
Bordwell, David. "The Classical Hollywood Style, 1917–60." In David Bordwell, Janet Staiger, and Kristin Thompson, *The Classical Hollywood Cinema.* New York: Columbia University, 1985. 1–84.
Carroll, Noel. *The Philosophy of Horror.* New York: Routledge, 1990.
Cogley, John. *Report on Blacklisting: I. Movies.* N.p.: Fund for the Republic, 1956.
Elsaesser, Thomas. "Tales of Sound and Fury: Observations on the Family Melodrama." In *Movies and Methods II.* Ed. Bill Nichols. Berkeley: University of California Press, 1985. 165–89.
Farber, Manny. *Movies.* New York: Hillstone, 1971.

Fiedler, Leslie A. "The Middle against Both Ends." In *Mass Culture*. Ed. Bernard Rosenberg and David Manning White. New York: Free Press, 1957. 537–47.

Fromm, Erich. *May Man Prevail?* Garden City, N.Y.: Doubleday, 1961.

Gledhill, Christine. "*Klute*: Contemporary Film Noir and Feminist Criticism." In *Women in Film Noir*. Ed. E. Ann Kaplan. London: British Film Institute, 1978. 6–21.

Gorer, Geoffrey. *The Americans: A Study in National Character*. London: Cresset, 1948.

Hofstadter, Richard. "The Pseudo-conservative Revolt." In *The Radical Right*, rev. ed. Ed. Daniel Bell. Garden City, N.Y.: Anchor, 1963. 75–95.

_____. "Pseudo-conservatism Revisited." In *The Radical Right*, rev. ed. Ed. Daniel Bell. Garden City, N.Y.: Anchor, 1963. 97–103.

Kleinhans, Chuck. "Contemporary Working Class Film Heroes: *Evel Knievel* and *The Last American Hero*." *Jump Cut* no. 2 (July-August 1974). 11–14.

Kracauer, Siegfried. "Hollywood's Terror Films." *Commentary* 2 (August 1946). 132–36.

Leuchtenburg, William E. *A Troubled Feast*. Boston: Little, Brown, 1973.

Lindner, Robert. *The Fifty-Minute Hour*. New York: Bantam, 1954.

Lipset, Seymour Martin. "The Sources of the 'Radical Right.' " In *The Radical Right*, rev. ed. Ed. Daniel Bell. Garden City, N.Y.: Anchor, 1963. 307–72.

Lipsitz, George. *Class and Culture in Cold War America*. South Hadley, Mass.: J. F. Bergin, 1982.

Marcuse, Herbert. *One-Dimensional Man*. Boston: Beacon, 1964.

Mills, C. Wright. *White Collar: The American Middle Classes*. New York: Oxford University Press, 1951.

Naremore, James. *The Magic World of Orson Welles*. New York: Oxford University Press, 1978.

_____. "The Trial: The FBI vs. Orson Welles." *Film Comment* 27 (January-February 1991). 22–27.

Podhoretz, Norman. "Our Changing Ideals, as Seen on TV." In *The Popular Arts*. Ed. Irving Deer and Harriet A. Deer. New York: Charles Scribner's Sons, 1967. 76–91.

Poulantzas, Nicos. *Political Power and Social Class*. London: New Left, 1973.

Riesman, David, with Nathan Glazer and Reuel Denney. *The Lonely Crowd: A Study of the Changing American Character*. New Haven, Conn.: Yale University Press, 1961.

Rovere, Richard H. *Senator Joe McCarthy*. New York: Harper & Row, 1973.

Rubio, Miguel, Juan Cobos, and Jose Antonio Pruneda. "Orson Welles." In *Interviews with Film Directors*. Ed. Andrew Sarris. New York: Avon, 1967. 528–57.

Sayre, Nora. *Running Time*. New York: Dial, 1982.

Scheib, Ronnie. "Charlie's Uncle." *Film Comment* 12 (March-April 1976). 55–64.

Sherman, Eric, and Martin Rubin. *The Director's Event*. New York: Atheneum, 1969.

Stead, Peter. *Film and the Working Class*. New York: Routledge, 1991.

Whyte, William H., Jr. *The Organization Man.* New York: Simon & Schuster, 1956.

_____. "Literature in an Organization Society." In *The Popular Arts.* Ed. Irving Deer and Harriet A. Deer. New York: Charles Scribner's Sons, 1967. 50–75.

Williams, Raymond. *The Country and the City.* New York: Oxford University Press, 1973.

Wolfenstein, Martha, and Nathan Leites. *Movies: A Psychological Study.* Glencoe, Ill.: Free Press, 1950.

Chapter 6

"No Sin in Lookin' Prosperous": Gender, Race, and the Class Formations of Middlebrow Taste in Douglas Sirk's *Imitation of Life*

Marianne Conroy

Early in *Imitation of Life* (1959), there occurs a scene that illustrates just how volatile class categories become in American film after the Second World War. At a late-night rendezvous in his office, theatrical agent Allen Loomis proposes how the film's protagonist, Lora Meredith, might realize one part of her ambition for theatrical stardom—her wish to be "important," that is, not her desire to act. He offers her the material accoutrements of stardom and social rank—an expensive wardrobe and a celebrity's social life—on the condition that she "eat and sleep" with him and with whomever else might advance her career. Lora responds with predictable moral outrage: she refuses Loomis's bargain and questions whether his proposition has anything "to do with acting." *Pace* Annie Johnson, Lora's black live-in maid, who has assured Lora only moments before in the film that there is "no sin in lookin' prosperous," Loomis's explicit sexual overtures outline a future for Lora in which the act of "lookin' prosperous" will in fact directly entail "sin."

In a fashion perhaps typical for 1950s Hollywood melodrama, this scene shapes audience identification with Lora through a conspicuous appeal to moral categories: it at once outlines the ethical limits that Lora refuses to transgress in her rise to theatrical success and delineates in fine cautionary style the moral dangers that women court when they enter the public sphere. Yet, in this instance, such high Hollywood moralism does not entirely erase the class relations at work in the film. Loomis's bargain has in fact everything to do with the kind of "class act" Lora herself presents. After all, Lora first meets Loomis by impersonating a wealthy Hollywood actress so convincingly that she fools his secretary. In that sense, Loomis's offer to make Lora look the part of an important actress does nothing more than extend her habit of assuming a class style above her actual economic station. In effect, the scene delineates a class formation in which material signs of class identity have become radically unreliable. For Lora and Loomis alike, competence in fashion and taste translates into actual class mobility, as if social status were only a matter of "lookin' prosperous," and social rank were as easily assumed as the full-length mink coat that Loomis proffers to Lora as the proper costume for a "big party" with "lots of important people." In that sense, the moral categories so pointedly deployed in the scene work to reanchor floating commodity signifiers of status—"prosperous" looks—to a determinate class identity.

What is at stake in the rendezvous scene is not simply how *Imitation of Life* represents a priori class categories, but, more important, how the film itself dramatizes the volatility and complexity of class categories in the United States after World War II, a period when prevailing concepts and practices of class differentiation undergo a radical transformation. Two events especially orient this change: first, the rise of 1950s "middlebrow" taste, that peculiar hybrid of high and mass cultural style whose heterogeneous cultural, aesthetic, symbolic, and economic aspirations were roundly demonized by the Cold War intellectual elite;[1] and second, one popular experience of this middlebrow heterogeneity, namely, a widespread anxiety over whether class identity is determined by economic status alone, a condition that postwar American sociologists dub "status panic."[2] I want to argue that these two developments—status panic and middlebrow taste—define the historical constellation of ideas that *Imitation of Life* engages in its address to its contemporary audiences. As such, *Imitation* typifies a larger cultural dynamic at work in postwar American film and popular culture, a dynamic that informs the rise of Method acting, the stardom of Dorothy Dandridge, and the social problem films of Stanley Kramer, among other examples (Conroy 253–58). Such phenomena invite audiences to identify with middlebrow culture itself as an empowering agency that exploits a historically specific class instability in American society. As one allegory of the class aspirations described by status panic and middlebrow taste, *Imitation of Life* speaks to the indeterminate nature of American class identities, especially in relation to gender and race. Through its highly self-conscious meditations on middlebrow taste, *Imitation of Life* enacts a dialectical reading of the postwar American class/taste matrix, thematizing both its feminist promise of cultural empowerment and its racial double binds.

As an enactment of the class, gender, and racial complexities of middlebrow taste in an age of status panic, *Imitation of Life* reminds us that in the United States, the class that we call uniformly "middle" and whose ideology we assume unproblematically hegemonic was itself quite economically and culturally diverse throughout various historical phases of capitalism. As such, the film demonstrates that we need to remember how for a variety of reasons—racial, economic, and ideological—large sectors of the postwar American middle class lived out a disproportion between their economic class and their taste class—that is, their structural position in the economy and their standard of living—such that their relation to culture often displayed the sort of misrecognitions of established cultural value attacked by postwar intellectuals in their policing of middlebrow taste, suggesting why Pierre Bourdieu labels the middlebrow audience the most "objectively and subjectively 'unhappy' " of cultural consumers (327). A reading of the film in relation to middlebrow taste should remind us that the social determinations of taste—and the understandings and misunderstandings of social distinction elicited by different strata of taste—require thorough historical analysis if we want to come to terms with how audiences might have actually used the vocabularies of class identity that mass culture provides. In that sense, the ultimate historical referent of Sirk's *Imitation* lies in its reflection on what it actually means to "look prosperous"—that is, to look through the frames of taste, class, race, and cultural capital operating in an age of status panic.

Status Panic and the New Middle Class

In the rendezvous scene, *Imitation of Life* alludes to a central issue in the postwar history of American class formations: the disintegration of traditional economic class rankings and the reconfiguration of class identity along lines of cultural status. Lora's choice turns precisely on the question of *which* status signifers will give her the class identity she desires: the material signifiers that Loomis can purchase for her or the cultural signifiers that she herself can acquire as an actress. In effect, her moral dilemma speaks to a social formation in which *taste* enforces class identification. Moreover, as a 1950s film, *Imitation of Life* operates in a historical context where what it means to *have* a class identity has changed radically. This period witnessed what C. Wright Mills, with uncharacteristic hyperbole, has called the "most decisive occupational shift in the twentieth century," when a "new middle class" of salaried managers and professionals displaced the "old middle class" of independent entrepreneurs associated with nineteenth-century liberal capitalism ("Stratification" 308).[3] To read *Imitation of Life* in relation to the occupational chances and values of the new middle class is to underscore how the centrality of cultural work to Sirk's narrative makes this a distinctively 1950s film.

In *White Collar*, his 1951 study of the American middle classes, Mills analyzes this structural transformation in the American economy and its cultural consequences. He contends that the rise of the new middle class brings with it a widespread "malaise," a result of the erosion of the traditional economic and ideological bases of class identity (xvi). A key symptom of this malaise is "status panic"—a deeply felt unease over the expression and recognition of prestige claims that becomes for Mills the constitutive feature of new-middle-class experience. In Mills's analysis, the salaried new middle class has little prestige except what it "borrows" from its entrepreneurial predecessors or achieves through consumption (*White Collar* 242). Moreover, the tenuousness of these status claims evinces the general sense of uncertainty about status that obtains in postwar American culture, where taste and consumption have become unmoored from a stable, class-determined system of social stratification. For Mills, status panic designates a cultural paradox in which commodity marks of status become more important in enforcing class identification at the same time that the class signification of commodities becomes radically less reliable (*White Collar* 256–57).

Imitation of Life is wholly implicated in the postwar economic and cultural milieu that Mills describes in *White Collar*. Sirk's film reconfigures the paradigms of economic success operative in both Fannie Hurst's original novel and John Stahl's 1934 film adaptation along distinctively new-middle-class lines. Unlike Hurst's novel and Stahl's film, which both focus on the working life of a female entrepreneur, Sirk's version features as its protagonist an actress who is explicitly defined as a salaried employee: when Lora receives her first call to audition on Broadway, her agent emphasizes not the physical type or acting talent that the role requires, but rather the "two-fifty a week" that the part pays. This emphasis on salary prefigures how Lora's success as an actress will be defined in Sirk's film in prototypically new-middle-class fashion: not by the expansion of her property, but rather by her ascension *within* an already established professional hierarchy (*White Collar* 262), a point emphasized by the formulaic structure of Sirk's success montage, in which each succeeding year brings Lora more prominent billing on the theater marquee.

It is with respect to cultural production and consumption that claims to prestige are most explicitly exercised in the film and that the instability of middle-class identity is most acutely registered. Indeed, the entire film testifies to the stratification of 1950s taste: almost every object and action depicted onscreen relates to a precisely calibrated scale of cultural capital, ranging from lowbrow to middlebrow to highbrow. Consider the character of David Edwards, who is introduced to Lora (and to the film audience) not simply as a playwright, but more specifically as a "prizewinning playwright." That introduction speaks to a world that not only organizes human expression into different cultural strata, but even takes the calibration of cachet *within* a given cultural stratum quite seriously. The references to real-life cultural figures and events sprinkled liberally throughout the film reinforce this pervasive sense of cultural stratification: the screenplay alludes to the Museum of Modern Art, to *New York Times* theater critic Brooks Atkinson, to a "blockbuster" play by Tennessee Williams for which Lora hopes to audition, and to Italian film director "Amerigo Fellucci," a fictional character whose name quite obviously trades on the celebrity of the real-life Federico Fellini. Taken together, these appeals to high cultural prestige index the precarious status situation of the new middle class in several different ways. Within the film's narrative, these references function as instances of status panic: characters invoke these names to call forth the imprimatur of the cultural elite to which they themselves aspire. In a broader sense, these allusions authenticate the film's representation of its contemporary cultural moment, for they generate "reality effects" by evoking the entire cultural prestige economy of the 1950s. And perhaps most important, such allusions operate by way of product tie-in, to elicit the patronage of culturally knowledgeable consumers, the audience that expects and wants its moviegoing experience to come with its status bona fides in place.

The irony, of course, is that these appeals to cultural prestige are wholly undercut by their clumsiness—indeed, their sheer desperation. The references to Tennessee Williams provide a key case in point. The possibility that Lora might audition for a Williams play is no sooner proffered than it is dropped. The play is "all cast" before she even appears in Loomis's office; the film does not entertain what might have happened were Lora to have read for the Williams play that was actually being cast in 1947, *A Streetcar Named Desire*. In fact, the specific play is largely beside the point of the reference; indeed, Williams himself matters only insofar as he is arguably the one American playwright a mass audience in 1959 would have recognized as a serious writer of "blockbuster" plays. From an elite perspective, the allusion to Williams seems almost laughably camp: in it, we see a gesture of cultural legitimation invoked on the slightest of pretexts and in the most tangential fashion that turns out to be the most transparent of mistakes.

Yet it is precisely as a mistake that the reference invites critical consideration. In its very tenuousness, the citation to Williams delineates the cultural situation of the new-middle-class audience, for whom recognition of what counts as legitimate culture outpaces actual knowledge of the forms so designated. Pierre Bourdieu has suggested that the peculiar combination of motives that we see dramatized in *Imitation of Life*—bare nodding acquaintance with legitimate culture accompanied by desperate citation—actually typifies how the middle classes experience culture in relation to their own precarious place in the social totality:

This undifferentiated reverence [for legitimate culture], in

which avidity combines with anxiety, leads the petit
bourgeois to take . . . an "imitation" for the genuine
article, and to find in this at once worried and over-assured
false recognition the source of a satisfaction that still owes
something to the sense of distinction. (323)

The dialectic that Bourdieu describes here has clear relevance to
the postwar phenomenon that American sociologists called status
panic. On the one hand, Bourdieu acknowledges the real appeal of
this reverence for culture: it marks status distinctions in such a way
as to satisfy deeply felt needs for prestige and for identity among a
devalued and highly variegated class. At the same time, the empti-
ness of such reverence demonstrates why status claims give rise to
panic: the spurious basis on which prestige claims bring satisfaction seems always on the verge of exposure.

Through the various covert and overt signals of status panic
that *Imitation of Life* displays in its treatment of its own contemporary cultural milieu, the film participates in the postwar crisis in
class identification. Furthermore, the historical complex of status
motives that we see condensed in *Imitation of Life*'s cultural ci-
tations—the dialectic between avid status overreaching and abject
status anxiety—has distinctively gendered resonances, for the film
delineates the postwar crisis of belief in middle-class identity in
ways that underscore middlebrow taste's ambiguous function
within mass-produced fantasies of class and cultural empowerment addressed to female audiences.

Middlebrow Taste and New-Middle-Class Femininity

When C. Wright Mills casts about in *White Collar* for symbols in
the American cultural imaginary that give expression to the status
panic among the postwar middle classes, he most frequently returns to images of women from prewar popular fiction: white-
collar girls such as the titular heroines of Booth Tarkington's *Alice
Adams* and Christopher Morley's *Kitty Foyle* (*White Collar* xi and
passim). That choice reveals a significant, though often deeply hidden theme within 1950s American sociology: how the postwar replacement of class by status hierarchy affects gender roles. Admittedly, gender issues are largely confined to the subtext of 1950s
taste stratification studies in this era in which, as Betty Friedan has

memorably observed, the social unease of white middle-class women had no given public name (20 and passim). A close reading of this subtext, however, demonstrates how American sociology represented status panic as a problem typified in the *normative* working and consuming lives of middle-class women. As a historical phenomenon, status panic especially pertained to the life chances of middle-class women insofar as such women participated in two far-reaching postwar social transformations: the retooling of the American economy toward the production of consumer goods and the reprivatization of everyday life. As we shall see, this understanding of status panic also decisively inflects the representation of women's working and consuming lives in *Imitation of Life*.

In popular memory, as in much cultural criticism, the expansion of the consumer economy is associated with the oppressive conformity and political quietism of 1950s middle-class life, as embodied in the gingham-and-graham-cracker domesticity of Donna Reed and her various television sitcom avatars. For American sociologists of the period, however, consumerism involved altogether more ideologically inchoate consequences, insofar as that development exacerbated the postwar crisis in class identification. Thus, for example, in *The Status Seekers*, a best-selling popular survey of stratification studies published in 1959, Vance Packard suggests that the postwar expansion of the consumer economy actually increased the relevance of status panic across various social divides. He notes that the postwar period witnessed a radical redefinition of market shares, as goods previously marketed exclusively to class elites were promoted across class and racial lines through status appeals, in further testimony to the class ambiguity of taste signifiers occasioned by postwar prosperity (307–19).

Many postwar social observers identify women as the primary focus of the status panic engendered by this transformation in the American economy. Sociologists observe that women become especially susceptible to the status panic prompted by consumer capitalism because their social agency is largely confined—in cultural representation if not in actual practice—to the domestic sphere of consumption rather than the productive sphere of work. Speculating on the consequences of the move of women back into the home for what he called "the American character,"

David Riesman notes with doubtless unintentional understate-
ment that women consigned to the domestic sphere experience
"competence" in consumption as a "problem." He further suggests that their anxiety over whether they display competence in
their choices of consumer goods is magnified insofar as women are
"compulsory" consumers whose *only* significant social agency is
exercised in the marketplace (332). Along similar lines, Betty
Friedan argues in *The Feminine Mystique* that postwar advertisements specially target women for status appeals, on the assumption that middle-class women feel the instability of their class identity more intensely than do men and find in consumption a way of
publicly affirming their class position (219). These sociological accounts describe a social formation in which middle-class women's
behavior as consumers uniquely indexes the instability of class
identity in the postwar American economy. Equally important,
however, such accounts also suggest that, as it pertains to women,
status panic names a distinctively gendered contradiction between
the reality of a privatized social existence and the desire for public
cultural empowerment.

This historically specific configuration of gender roles, class
misrecognitions, and status anxieties would thus seem to support
the strong feminist critique of *Imitation of Life,* a critique that fo-
cuses on the film's representations of women's working lives. Marina Heung has argued, for example, that the film amounts to a
polemic for the same ideology of sexually separate spheres of influence that supported the postwar return of women to the home.
In her analysis, *Imitation of Life* wholly discredits Lora's work
outside the home by associating her success in the theater with bad
mothering and inauthentic personhood, while at the same time the
film renders Annie's labor within the home invisible as work, thus
normalizing her domestic servitude (28). Along similar lines,
Jackie Byars contends that *Imitation* conforms to "the dominant
ideology that refuses the compatibility of female independence in
the public sphere with heterosexual romance (and mothering),
privileging the latter as the only appropriate—even if unconvincing—closure" (261). One might thus extend these analyses of
Imitation of Life to argue that the film actively *promotes* status
panic as a feminine condition, insofar as such representations re-

affirm the private sphere as the proper place for women to exercise their agency in society.

Such a critique of *Imitation of Life* radically simplifies the complicated dynamic that authorizes the postwar understanding of status panic as a woman's problem, however. What gets lost in the argument that the film's representations of work exclude women from the public sphere is the more ambiguous form of female identification with public empowerment expressed within postwar paradigms of status panic: the collective identification with the process of cultural legitimation that drives status-panicked consumption. An analysis of *Imitation of Life* in light of this gendered problematic suggests that the feminist significance of the film lies not only in its mystified representations of women's work, but also in its more ideologically inchoate evocations of women's *cultural* agency. This alternative notion of the cultural sphere as a space in which women's private expressions of taste lead to their public cultural empowerment is condensed in the film's theme of theatricality.

Critics have long noted that *Imitation of Life*'s narrative focus on the theater bears heavily on the whole complex of gender, class, and racial ideologies operating in the film. Indeed, in a 1972 interview, Sirk himself explained his film's most significant revision of Hurst's original story—the transfer of the story from the business world to the New York theater milieu—by arguing that the change gives the scenario more historical verisimilitude in its representation of social arrangements:

In Stahl's treatment of the story, the white and the Negro women are co-owners of a thriving pancake business—which took all of the social significance out of the Negro mother's situation. Maybe it would have been all right for Stahl's time, but nowadays a Negro woman who got rich *could* buy a house, and wouldn't be dependent to such a degree on the white woman. . . . So I had to change the axis of the film and make the Negro woman just the typical Negro, a servant, without much she could call her own but the friendship, love, and charity of a white mistress. This whole oppressive and kind of uncertain situation accounts much more for the daughter's attitude. (in Halliday 129)

Sirk here draws attention to the intensified dynamics of class and racial differentiation that result from the change. He notes that by making Annie Lora's servant rather than her business "partner," his version dramatically emphasizes the disparate social positions of the Johnson and Meredith families. Moreover, he suggests that the change also inflects the actions of Annie's daughter, Sarah Jane—her attempts to "pass" across racial lines—with a specific resentment over the uncertainty of her class position (Heung 29–30; Selig 16). Of course, these references to class consciousness are muted if not undermined by the film's presentation of domestic labor as "help" offered in a context of "friendship," as Marina Heung has shown and as Sirk's own rhetoric concerning "the friendship, love, and charity of a white mistress" attests (Heung 28). Sirk's comments thus suggest that his film's revisions of the original entrepreneurial scenario ultimately objectify a "whole oppressive" structure of class and racial relations.

A number of feminist critics have pointed out, moreover, that by replacing the business world of Hurst's novel with a theatrical setting, the 1959 version of *Imitation* not only reinforces such reified class and racial dynamics, but further underscores the patriarchal dimension of such dynamics. Lauren Berlant thus asserts that Lora's stage career exemplifies how mass culture addressed to women elaborates a false public sphere to which women gain entry by the commodification of their bodies rather than their participation as citizens (132). Other critics have likewise suggested that the film's portrayal of the theater symbolizes the diminished public role of postwar American women. The theatrical setting of *Imitation* comes freighted with residual popular prejudices against acting, centering mostly on the frivolity of the profession and its dubious propriety. Such associations undermine Lora's authority to function independently in the public sphere—a point that is underlined by the vast difference between the social worth popularly attached to the managerial skills possessed by Hurst's Bea Pullman and the more dubious artistic talents of Sirk's Lora (Byars 245; Fischer 15). For these critics, then, the film's theatrical setting symbolizes the most ideologically regressive elements that characterize the woman's picture as a genre, insofar as that setting determines a conservative denouement that locates the authentic place of the film's female characters in the domestic sphere.

But although such arguments reveal how the film configures Lora's character so that her theater career connotes the postwar ideological animus against working women, none addresses the specific kind of intervention into the public sphere that her chosen profession—stage acting—represents. What makes this critical omission particularly troubling is that it leads to a situation in which the feminist critique of the film ends up sharing the film's own heavily moralistic position on acting. In the film, acting is discredited by its association with imitation—that is, with a self that is "not real," as Steve Archer tells Lora. By the same token, in the feminist critique of the film, acting is discredited by its association with an inauthentic style of public identity that is particularly injurious to women—a style epitomized by the "glamour queens" produced by the Hollywood star system, like Lana Turner herself (Dyer 47–52). But Lora chooses the Broadway theater and *not* Hollywood as the setting for her rise to power—a distinction that is fraught with historical resonances that we must recover. A consideration of theatrical acting as a particular kind of public cultural work suggests a more ambivalent reading of *Imitation of Life*'s perspective on the role of women in the public sphere. The choice of a theatrical career for the film's protagonist is neither an explicitly antifeminist move nor a merely incidental choice. Rather, the whole point of the choice lies in the specific cultural legacy of status panic that the theater would bear for postwar audiences, as opposed to what other forms of acting—such as Hollywood stardom—might connote. Lora's career in the theater needs to be read in relation to the problematic cultural stature of the postwar American theater, a context that associates her character with the same ideological contradictions between publicity and privacy that lent status panic its special force as a description of the social existence of new-middle-class women.

Through its theatrical setting, the 1959 *Imitation of Life* conjures up a whole context of debate on taste, class, and national identity—a debate focused on the much-maligned level of taste that postwar intellectuals termed middlebrow. For 1950s intellectuals, the Broadway theater epitomized middlebrow culture as almost no other medium could, largely because of its heterogeneous cultural positioning: as a cultural institution, Broadway combines the commercial impulse associated with "lowbrow" forms of mass culture with the claims to cultural importance characteristic of "highbrow" or elite culture (Macdonald, "Theory" 64–65; Kronenberger). Lora's career path in *Imitation of Life* shows a similar cultural heterogeneity: in moving from regional theater to Broadway, from drawing-room comedy to problem drama, or from Broadway theater to "foreign" film, Lora always seeks both financial success and cultural distinction. Through the emphatically middlebrow trajectory of Lora's career, moreover, the film evokes another aspect of this critique of Broadway as the epitome of middlebrow taste: its patriarchal content. The antifeminist connotations of the postwar intellectual attack on middlebrow culture do not consist in any simple rejection of public roles for women; rather, as Janice Radway suggests, such connotations register in polemical strategies troped in gendered ways ("Mail-Order" 523–24). In the particular case of Broadway, that antimiddlebrow polemic becomes directed against a cultural imaginary significantly associated with female audiences (Fiedler 541–43). For many postwar critics, the middlebrow style in American theater is typified by narratives that, in high sentimental fashion, transpose public social problems into domestic situations (Macdonald, "Masscult" 38–46). As we shall see, such a cultural imaginary figures crucially in Lora's empowerment within the theatrical world.

To read *Imitation of Life*'s theatrical setting in relation to the disputes over middlebrow taste is to recover the struggles over cultural and social distinction enacted in the film. Admittedly, the film's narrative itself seems at times to sanction the postwar intellectual critique of the middlebrow tendencies in the American theater. In one particularly noteworthy scene, David Edwards argues with Lora over her decision to appear in a prototypically middlebrow "problem" drama called *No Greater Glory*. When Edwards criticizes the play for the "colored angle in it," which he terms "absolutely controversial," and presses Lora to explain what she "know[s] about controversy," Lora responds by asserting the limits to her knowledge of the social problems that the play portrays:

> Nothing! And I don't want to know. I only know it's a good script, and they're not easy to find. Besides, I . . . feel I need something different . . . a new experience.

Judith Butler contends that this scene denies any possible link between Lora's choice of "socially problematic" theater projects and "her own sense of political commitment" (8–9). Indeed, Lora here retreats from express political commitment entirely: she offers *only* an aesthetic rationale to support her choice of projects. Her exchange with Edwards thus seems to support the negative characterization of middlebrow taste as a cultural stratum of suspect cultural worth and shallow political intentions. Indeed, one might argue that the scene actually *grants* postwar intellectuals' strongest arguments against the middlebrow. When Lora demurs from knowledge of public controversy, her apparent disingenuousness suggests that the highly circumscribed and superficial politics associated with the middlebrow theater remains fundamentally incompatible with genuine art.

In the context of the paradigms of gender and taste associated with postwar status panic, however, the scene demands another reading. It must be pointed out that when Lora justifies her decision to appear in a problem drama on the basis of the quality of the script rather than its ideological content, she does not *simply* demur from the expression of her own political commitments. Equally important, she also resists the purely cynical view of political commitment that Edwards expresses: the view in which public controversy matters only to the extent that it provides fresh dramatic "angles" capable of commercial exploitation. It is Edwards and not Lora, in other words, whose logic conforms to the facile understanding of politics that made the American theater "middlebrow" in the specific pejorative sense used by postwar intellectuals. In his satiric description of the problem drama as a genre in which a "dull social worker with high dreams and low heels" would have the status of a heroine, Edwards reflects the standard highbrow assumption that the problem drama portrays the world and the home as separate, albeit homologous, spheres, such that the "controversy" registered in the former can be easily transposed into the latter for dramatic resolution.

In Lora's defense of the dramatic potential of *No Greater Glory,* by contrast, the relations among the private sphere, the public sphere, and the stage are configured in more complex ways than Edwards's logic allows. What is significant about her argument is the status vocabulary—the rhetoric of cultural capital—that she uses to justify her choice of theatrical material. From Lora's perspective, that vocabulary does not simply characterize her next theater project in aesthetic terms, as Butler suggests; rather, that status vocabulary allows Lora to associate the middlebrow genre of the problem drama with opportunities for *both* personal transformation (as "a new experience") and public cultural recognition (as an occasion for "good acting"). In her argument with Edwards, in other words, Lora exploits the vocabulary associated with status panic in order to assert her own independent agency within the cultural sphere. That point is underscored by the way Lora's argument with Edwards over the "controversial" content of *No Greater Glory* resonates with an earlier dispute between the two characters: the audition in which Lora refuses to play a scene for the "delicate reactions" that Edwards wants because she contends that the scene is too badly written to support a high-comedy technique. Significantly enough, in both scenes, Lora asserts that she understands what counts as a "good" play better than Edwards does. Insofar as her judgments of quality are not overturned, these incidents establish her cultural capital—her authority in matters of taste and status. And equally to the point, through its exploitation of such status judgments, the film imagines for her a position of cultural empowerment from which she might resist the aesthetic, sexual, and financial proprietorship that Edwards would exercise over her public career. *Imitation of Life* thus shapes Lora's theatrical career in ways that speak directly to the complex dynamics attending the emergence of new-middle-class women in the postwar social totality. In effect, Lora's success story develops a status vocabulary for female cultural empowerment that at once exploits and resolves status panic.

The further point must be made, however, that even as this reconfiguration of success through a vocabulary of cultural empowerment might have benefited new-middle-class women, such a revision of Hurst's original success scenario also reveals the ideological limits implicit in the postwar conceptualization of status panic as a woman's problem. The limits that I have in mind here are not strictly those involved in the judgment that the film's narrative renders on Lora's maternal inadequacy. The film offers a far more ruthless critique of the vocabulary of female cultural empowerment by juxtaposing Lora's success story to a parallel narrative of life in the cultural sphere, embodied in the person of Annie Johnson's mulatto daughter, Sarah Jane.

Status Panic and Racial Double Binds

Where Hurst's novel develops a plot in which the lives of two women of different races are paralleled on the basis of their shared generational identity as mothers, Sirk's film instead contrasts two women of different races and generations who share a professional identity as performers. An extensive set of visual and narrative similarities encourages viewers to read Sarah Jane's character in relation to Lora. Sirk's mise-en-scène habitually depicts both women through tropes of feminine display: both characters are associated with mirrors and both are frequently posed in formfitting costumes that flatter and eroticize their breasts and legs. These parallels, however, merely underscore some basic differences in the performing lives of the two characters. First and most important, Sarah Jane's performances are far more complicated in their political and cultural effects than Lora's are: when Sarah Jane appears onstage, she is "acting" not only in the cultural sphere, but in the public sphere as well, insofar as she "passes" for white whenever she performs. And equally important, the careers of these two performers play out in vastly different cultural registers: the middlebrow Broadway theater and the lowbrow nightclub stage. At first glance, Sarah Jane's nightclub career seems to emulate the structure of Lora's theatrical success. The status of the venues where Sarah Jane performs clearly rises as the film proceeds, from a "lowdown dirty dive" in New York called Harry's Club to a more luxurious cabaret in Hollywood named the Moulin Rouge, in an upscale trajectory that mimics Lora's own progress from model to stage actress to movie star. These apparently similar career paths have radically different outcomes, however. As we have seen, Lora's success brings her increasing independence and cultural authority, so that by the end of the film, she chooses not only the roles she will play, but the conditions under which she will play them—as, for example, when she gets Amerigo Fellucci to "agree to [her] terms" for participating in his film. For Sarah Jane, by contrast, increases in the status connotations of her performance venues seem actually to *decrease* her independence as a performer. At Harry's Club, Sarah Jane sings and dances alone in what amounts to a burlesque star turn; at the ostensibly more upscale Moulin Rouge, by contrast, Sarah Jane is but one anonymous showgirl in a vast chorus line, all of whose members mime the identical scene of autoerotic seduction while seated on an elaborate conveyor belt of mechanized rocking chairs.

For many feminist critics, the disparity between Lora's theatrical fortunes and Sarah Jane's results from the two characters' quite different deployment of female sexuality. In this reading, the emphatically carnal quality of Sarah Jane's stage presence serves to reinforce the film's general proscriptions against the entry of women into the public sphere. Thus, for example, Sandy Flitterman-Lewis suggests that by portraying Sarah Jane through powerful cautionary images of degraded female sexuality—routed to the film audience through the eyes of her shocked and suffering mother—the film severely undercuts Sarah Jane's public autonomy: for Flitterman-Lewis, "[Sarah Jane's] assertion of identity becomes a mere parody of a highly conventionalized female sexuality already existing in the dominant culture. As such it can provide no true liberation, but only the imitation of revolt" (56). Extending this argument, Jackie Byars contends that the sexual emphasis in Sarah Jane's performances gives the film's polemic against female independence in the public sphere specifically racist inflections. In her view, the film builds its narrative of Sarah Jane's career upon a "racist premise": that "Sarah Jane will sell [sexuality], if that's what it takes to get ahead" because she "possess[es] none of the inhibiting attitudes that initially hampered Lora's career progress" (251). In such readings, then, the differences between Lora and Sarah Jane—their varied professional achievements, their contrasting styles of sexual expression onstage—reveal the film's ideological blindness to its own implications within a system of racist and patriarchal values.

When we read the two women's different careers in the cultural sphere in relation to issues of taste and status rather than sexuality, however, quite different meanings emerge. Seen in the light of the postwar status panic, Sarah Jane's story becomes the place where the film comes closest to generating a negative critique of its own vocabulary of female cultural empowerment. The structures of status panic that Lora exploits in her theatrical career are in fact reduplicated in Sarah Jane's narrative—with a difference. In the context of American racial relations, status panic does not provide opportunity for cultural advancement; rather, it assumes the force of a status double bind specific to African American women. In that sense, the whole point of Sarah Jane's story lies in the way it negates status panic as a basis for *collective* female empowerment across the divides of race and class.

It is important to note that the African American women in *Imitation of Life* are not wholly excluded from the status rhetoric that permeates the film. Annie in particular appears acutely conscious of status and taste discriminations. On her deathbed, for example, she assures her minister that the mink scarf that she wants to bequeath to his wife is in fact "genuine." One might thus argue that it is Annie's function to authorize the status rhetoric that Lora uses in the theater for use in the home. Throughout the film, Annie liberally expresses her likes and dislikes with respect to behaviors and commodities, the favorite term of approbation in her critical lexicon being "nice," a word that for her designates a particular combination of aesthetic worth and moral value, and that therefore can be applied uniformly to the landlord with whom she barters her cleaning services in exchange for a reduction in rent, to the "young folks" at her church with whom she wants her daughter to socialize, and to the fifty-dollar bills that she sends every Christmas—in both her name and Lora's—to the milkman who extended Lora credit long ago. Unlike Lora's status rhetoric, however, Annie's taste judgments tend neither to associate her with the ambiguous class identity of the postwar new middle class nor to identify her with the specifically female strategy of cultural empowerment that Lora exemplifies. Rather, it is essential to understand that Annie expresses her tastes within the particular social framework historically associated with black female domestic workers: the quasi-familial, highly personalized, and intensely emotionally cathected relation between employer and employee that, in the words of Judith Rollins, "makes domestic service . . . more profoundly exploitative than other comparable occupations" (156; see also Heung 27–29). In one especially telling scene early in the film, Annie assures "Miss" Lora that she "like[s] takin' care of pretty things" so much that she is willing to do Lora's laundry for nothing. The vicarious pleasure that Annie takes in Lora's "pretty things" suggests that for her, status rhetoric bespeaks an *over*identification with the tastes of those to whom she is socially and economically subordinated as a black domestic worker.

For Annie, this vicarious mode of participation in the postwar status panic bolsters her Christian sense of resignation to her social role on earth; for her part, however, Sarah Jane refuses such accommodation. Unlike her mother, she refuses to subordinate her tastes to anyone's: in her childhood, for example, she expresses outspoken distaste for the black doll that Susie, Lora's daughter, has designated for her use. But this refusal to submit to a taste imposed upon her engenders its own double bind. Although she refuses the tactics of overidentification, she is also unable to exercise independent cultural leverage as an African American woman—an impossible task within the status vocabulary at work in the film. In the incident with the doll, for example, Sarah Jane's rejection of "the black one" chosen for her results in her demanding the same white doll that Susie has cherished "all [her] life," in an episode of racial self-loathing that uncannily repeats the logic of overidentification from which Sarah Jane is trying to escape.[4]

This same double bind structures the cabaret numbers that Sarah Jane performs. In flaunting her sexuality onstage, Sarah Jane rejects the vicarious mode of status striving that her mother has enjoined upon her, even as she takes Annie's overidentification with white tastes to its logical extreme by actually "passing" for white every time she appears onstage. In the cabaret scenes, however, the representation of that double bind takes on a specific critical force. In their staging and performance, Sarah Jane's cabaret numbers scandalize the very end toward which both Annie and Lora strive in their differently defined status vocabularies: good taste itself. In their deliberate tawdriness, their inescapable visual excess, the nightclub scenes emphasize the impossibility of Sarah Jane's position as an African American woman caught within a system that measures class and cultural advancement in terms of the independent expression and recognition of status claims. In that sense, it is in the mode of bad taste that Sarah Jane's performances emphasize the racial fault line that fractures the film's discourse of female cultural empowerment.[5]

The racial contradictions that trouble *Imitation of Life*'s status paradigms are ultimately condensed in two crucial scenes in the film, both involving Sarah Jane. The first occurs before Sarah Jane embarks upon her career as a white showgirl. In it, Lora conducts a business meeting over cocktails at her home with her agent and a representative of the Italian film director Amerigo Fellucci, who wants to cast Lora as Rena in *No More Laughter,* a role that Lora describes as "only the greatest part since Scarlett O'Hara." During the meeting, Sarah Jane embarrasses Lora by carrying a tray of food out to the guests while performing an elaborate parody of abject black servitude, complete with stereotypical "colored" dialect: "No trick to totin', Miz Lora. Ah l'arned it from my mammy, and she l'arned it from old Massa, 'fo she belonged to you." What is of special interest here is the way Sarah Jane's "act" relates to the terms in which Lora characterizes the movie role for which she is a candidate. Significantly, Lora alludes to an image drawn from mass culture to describe an event that we are meant to understand as the culmination of all her status striving. The comment thus displays a classic middlebrow confusion in cultural registers: in Lora's lexicon, "Scarlett O'Hara" designates the high status of the part, even though the allusion is too lowbrow to support that meaning. For our purposes, however, the point of the reference is that it acknowledges how that middlebrow confusion has served *some* women well by providing them with models of female cultural empowerment with which to identify. In this light, it is important to note that Sarah Jane's impersonation of a plantation servant assigns Lora the role of plantation mistress, casting her as a real-life Scarlett, as if to force her to assume the full ideological consequences of the model of empowerment she has chosen. In that sense, Sarah Jane's angry parody involves a double irony. As Marina Heung points out, Sarah Jane here names the real economic relations of servitude that the film's characters have been at such pains to disguise (31). But more important, her "act" also names what has gone unspoken in Lora's status vocabulary of female cultural empowerment: the racial privilege that makes such rhetoric possible.

This exposure of the racism implicit in the film's status paradigms gets papered over, on the narrative level at least, in the final scene involving Sarah Jane: the spectacular funeral sequence, where, in short order, Sarah Jane acknowledges her racial identity, disavows performance, and returns "home" to occupy a position in the Meredith household much like her mother's, even to the point of calling Lora "Miss." Alongside this conservative narrative closure, however, the last scene also contains the film's own highly tentative construction of a cultural space and a status rhetoric that might accommodate women across the divide of race. As many critics have pointed out, the funeral scene constitutes the film's one gesture toward representing the African American community that might have given Annie and Sarah Jane emotional support and public cultural sustenance. It is important to note, however, that the cultural space represented in the funeral scene is not *categorically* different from the theatrical milieu that Lora inhabits. Rather than constructing the funeral as an example of "authentic" black folk culture set in opposition to the "imitation" white world of Broadway theater, Sirk's mise-en-scène instead emphasizes the performance tropes that span *both* cultural styles: costume, spectacle, choral participation, solo star turns, and intense audience engagement. What is most important—and most distinctively middlebrow—about the cultural sphere imaged in the funeral, in other words, is that it allows both the "authentic" folk culture of the African American community and the "imitative" commercial culture of the white Broadway theater to exist on-screen simultaneously.

Read from a highbrow perspective, of course, such coexistence symbolizes the tendency to absorb inherently hostile cultural strata that made middlebrow culture the particular *bête noire* of American intellectuals seeking to preserve an authentic national folk culture (Agee 404–10). Read, however, from a perspective more historically attuned to the way middlebrow taste cathected the class and gender anxieties associated with the postwar status panic, the linkages between white theater and black folk culture visualized on-screen in the funeral sequence instead provisionally reconfigure the paradigms of status differentiation and female cultural empowerment that defined the American 1950s—in a tentative but nonetheless significant gesture toward the representation of a genuinely heterogeneous cultural sphere. Thus, the final moments of *Imitation of Life* demonstrate how the film's social concerns are part of the premier cultural vocabulary of its day, how completely the film's critical imagination—its complex dialectical knowledge of the simultaneous promise and double bind of female cultural empowerment in the 1950s—is itself intelligible only *as* a middlebrow phenomenon. It is the contradictory promise of cultural coexistence glimpsed in the funeral sequence that perhaps most strongly links the middlebrow culture of the postwar era to the present political challenges of our own postmodernity.

Notes

I presented an early version of this essay at the annual meeting of the Society for Cinema Studies in 1992. I am grateful to Orrin Wang, Lauren Berlant, Miriam Hansen, and W. J. T. Mitchell for their generous commentary and encouragement.

1. The seminal postwar statements on middlebrow taste include those of Lynes, Macdonald ("Theory"; "Masscult"), Fiedler, and "The State of American Writing." For more recent attempts to defend middlebrow literary culture and to trace its development, see Ross, Rubin, and Radway ("Scandal"; "Mail-Order"). Ross's work is particularly valuable for its analysis of how the intellectual critique of middlebrow culture relates to Cold War political alignments.

2. This term was coined by Mills in *White Collar* (239–40); other helpful studies of stratification include those of Lipset, Hofstadter, Riesman, and Packard.

3. For a competing account from the 1950s of this transformation in class identity, see Bell (37–68).

4. For audiences in the 1950s, moreover, this incident would have a more specific historical referent, as it alludes to the well-publicized studies in which Kenneth Clark investigated children's awareness of and identification with racial categories by asking them to choose between black and white dolls. Clark's studies figured in the NAACP *amicus* brief in *Brown v. Board of Education*.

5. A fuller analysis might consider how the figure of the "tragic mulatto" has functioned historically to define taste as well as racial borders. On this point, see Berlant (110–15); see also Carby (89, 148).

Works Cited

Agee, James. "Pseudo-Folk" (1944). In *Agee on Film: Reviews and Comments.* Boston: Beacon, 1958. 404–10.

Bell, Daniel. *The End of Ideology: On the Exhaustion of Political Ideas in the Fifties.* Glencoe, Ill.: Free Press, 1960.

Berlant, Lauren. "National Brands/National Bodies: *Imitation of Life.*" In *Comparative American Identities: Race, Sex, and Nationality in the Modern Text.* Ed. Hortense Spillers. New York: Routledge, 1991. 110–40.

Bourdieu, Pierre. *Distinction: A Critique of the Social Judgement of Taste.* Trans. Alan Nice. Cambridge: Harvard University Press, 1984.

Butler, Judith. "Lana's 'Imitation': Melodramatic Repetition and the Gender Performative." *Genders* 9 (Fall 1990): 1–17.

Byars, Jackie. *All That Hollywood Allows: Rereading Gender in 1950s Melodrama*. Chapel Hill: University of North Carolina Press, 1991.

Carby, Hazel. *Reconstructing Womanhood: The Emergence of the Afro-American Female Novelist*. New York: Oxford University Press, 1987.

Clark, Kenneth. *Prejudice and Your Child*. Boston: Beacon, 1955.

Conroy, Marianne. "Acting Out: Method Acting, the National Culture, and the Middlebrow Disposition in Cold War America." *Criticism* 35 (Spring 1993): 239–63.

Dyer, Richard. "Four Films of Lana Turner." *Movie* 25 (1977): 30–52.

Fiedler, Leslie. "The Middle against Both Ends." In *Mass Culture*. Ed. Bernard Rosenberg and David Manning White. Glencoe, Ill.: Free Press, 1957. 537–47.

Fischer, Lucy. "Three-Way Mirror: *Imitation of Life*." In Imitation of Life: *Douglas Sirk, Director*. Ed. Lucy Fischer. New Brunswick, N.J.: Rutgers University Press, 1991. 3–28.

Flitterman-Lewis, Sandy. "*Imitation*(s) *of Life*: The Black Woman's Double Determination as Troubling Other." *Literature and Psychology* 35, no. 4 (1988): 44–57.

Friedan, Betty. *The Feminine Mystique*. New York: W. W. Norton, 1963.

Halliday, Jon. *Sirk on Sirk*. New York: Viking, 1972.

Heung, Marina. "What's the Matter with Sarah Jane? Mothers and Daughters in *Imitation of Life*." *Cinema Journal* 26 (Spring 1987): 21–43.

Hofstadter, Richard. "The Pseudo-Conservative Revolt" (1955). In *The Radical Right*, rev. ed. Ed. Daniel Bell. Garden City, N.Y.: Doubleday, 1963. 63–80.

Kronenberger, Louis. "Highbrows and the Theater Today: Some Notes and Queries." *Partisan Review* 26 (Fall 1959): 560–72.

Lipset, Seymour Martin. "The Sources of the 'Radical Right' " (1955). In *The Radical Right*, rev. ed. Ed. Daniel Bell. Garden City, N.Y.: Doubleday, 1963. 259–312.

Lynes, Russell. *The Tastemakers: The Shaping of American Popular Taste* (1955). New York: Dover, 1980.

Macdonald, Dwight. "Masscult & Midcult" (1960). In *Against the American Grain: Essays on the Effects of Mass Culture*. New York: Vintage, 1962. 3–75.

———. "A Theory of Mass Culture." In *Mass Culture*. Ed. Bernard Rosenberg and David Manning White. Glencoe, Ill.: Free Press, 1957. 59–73.

Mills, C. Wright. "The Sociology of Stratification" (1951). In *Power, Politics, and People: The Collected Essays of C. Wright Mills*. Ed. Irving Louis Horowitz. New York: Oxford University Press, 1963. 305–23.

———. *White Collar: The American Middle Classes*. New York: Oxford University Press, 1951.

Packard, Vance. *The Status Seekers: An Explanation of Class Behavior in America and the Hidden Barriers That Affect You, Your Community, Your Future*. New York: David McKay, 1959.

Radway, Janice. "Mail-Order Culture and Its Critics: The Book-of-the-Month Club, Commodification and Consumption, and the Problem of Cultural Authority." In *Cultural Studies*. Ed. Lawrence Grossberg, Cary Nelson, and Paula A. Treichler. New York: Routledge, 1992. 512–30.

_____. "The Scandal of the Middlebrow: The Book-of-the-Month Club, Class Fracture, and Cultural Authority." *South Atlantic Quarterly* 89 (Fall 1990): 703–37.

Riesman, David, with Nathan Glazer and Reuel Denney. *The Lonely Crowd: A Study of the Changing American Character*. New Haven, Conn.: Yale University Press, 1950.

Rollins, Judith. *Between Women: Domestics and Their Employers*. Philadelphia: Temple University Press, 1985.

Ross, Andrew. "Containing Culture in the Cold War." In *No Respect: Intellectuals and Popular Culture*. New York: Routledge, 1989. 42–64.

Rubin, Joan Shelley. *The Making of Middlebrow Culture*. Chapel Hill: University of North Carolina Press, 1992.

Selig, Michael. "Contradiction and Reading: Social Class and Sex Class in *Imitation of Life*." *Wide Angle* 10, no. 4 (1988): 13–23.

"The State of American Writing, 1948: Seven Questions." *Partisan Review* 15 (August 1948): 855–85.

Chapter 7

Compromised Liberation: The Politics of Class in Chinese Cinema of the Early 1950s

Esther C. M. Yau

Confronting Class as Empty Signifier

In the 1990s, it is not possible to discuss "class" without considering its discursive, historical trajectory in existing socialist countries. The historical performance of "class"—how as a political category it has redefined the meaning of social existence of people living under "socialist" systems—means more, indeed, than its theoretical elaboration alone. Subsequent to what amounts to a collective disavowal of "class struggle" in the 1980s, the drive to modernize has become a major social force in those countries eager to partake in global capitalism, including China. The causes of the disavowal are complex, but one has to do with the persistence of inequality despite a long-standing rhetoric on "proletarian leadership." Arguably, the failure to sustain processes that would have led to truly democratic social relations quickened the public's shift from the pursuit of social equality to that of individual wealth. Access to social privileges, once possible only by way of politics, is now sought through market economy, and little attention is paid to the negative consequences of intense modernization and commercialization.[1] Notwithstanding this eclipse of a "principle of intelligibility of social transformation,"[2] class remains a continuing, integral dimension of cinema as a cultural intertext. It enters into a complex, historical modulation with the ideology of socialist "modernization."

In this essay, I address the contribution of "class" and its related concepts in the elaboration of a new mode of cinematic representation in China at the time when its distinctive aesthetic/political form was being regulated by the ideological demands of a socialist state cinema. It is generally accepted that there are three distinct periods during which class has played different roles in the political life of Chinese audiences. In the first, pre-Cultural Revolution period, from 1949 to around 1965, "class" was identified as a matrix indicating the source of inequality and social conflict. On the question of articulation of class consciousness, the creation of a new proletarian cinema in "worker-peasant-soldier films" departed from prerevolutionary cinema. In the second, the Cultural Revolution period, from 1966 to around 1978, "class struggle" on screen became an extension of the actual power struggles among political leaders that were taking place on a massive scale off-screen, with violent repercussions among cadres and students of all regions.[3] These first two periods are often conflated in popular Western accounts of Communist China, but they need to be separated for reasons that will become evident in this essay. In the third, post-Cultural Revolution period, "class" has a diminished visibility in the arts. By the mid-1980s, human quality, national/racial character, local color, and personal style began to diversify the screen. The logic is revisionist: because the orthodox definition of class is seen to have dominated China's political culture, a thorough critique of this culture would entail challenging "class struggle" as its single most important principle. Associated with a rigidified hierarchy established by the Communist Party itself, class was drained of its radical meaning and sentimental value. In this context, rethinking the liberating qualities associated with class as a critical and creative principle for cinema must acknowledge the full implications of its historical performance in the social realm and in the life of the audience.

The negative role of class in contemporary Chinese cinema is itself, however, somewhat deceptive, for in those versions different from the classical Marxist-Maoist ones, class remains pertinent in popular perceptions. The epic films made in 1990 and 1991 that extol China's political leaders illustrate an alternative conceptualization of class.[4] They underline spectacular revolutionary battles, details that enhance characterization, and ways of incorporating an art cinema style into official hagiography. To the extent that the public understands its leaders as no longer truly interested in being equal with ordinary citizens, these films tell an interesting truth by *not* focusing on the leaders' commitment to a classless society. Class now means two different things: an empty signifier and a real hierarchy. The deliberate omission of the familiar class struggle on film unconsciously reveals the existence of class barriers as an unspoken fact. To many writers and directors, Party politics have been disengaged from socialist ideals and only opportunists would brandish "class struggle" in the 1980s in the same ways as in previous decades. Ernesto Laclau has written that "theory will become contaminated, deformed and eventually destroyed by a reality that transcends it. But it is precisely in this destruction that all thought . . . meets its 'destiny.' "[5] The historical performance of class in China and the persistence of inequality between the leaders and the nameless masses (between *lingdao* and *laobaixing*) have undone the orthodox version of class. In its place is a skepticism based on an acute awareness of antagonisms arising from bureaucracy and inequality, a skepticism sometimes called postsocialism. Antibureaucracy, or the protest against those privileged cadres abusing their official power, was one of the important causes brandished in the Tiananmen Square demonstrations.[6] Yet this class consciousness in the form of acute criticism of hierarchy was mostly lost amid Western media accounts (and often among the Chinese people themselves), whose depiction of people's protests is mostly elided into a projection that Communism has simply failed in China.

In less politicized ways, Chinese film and society have always retained another long-standing view of class (*jieji*, rungs on a ladder) as a system of social differentiation. This view accompanies a class-status system in which an individual's socioeconomic position is perceived as owing to his or her family origin, education, occupation, and social status.[7] Transposed onto a new classification system since the early 1950s, the class-status system has always been operative. Equally active are the intra- and interclass maneuvers within a complex social network that inform the everyday politics of class. In other words, although most films implicitly or explicitly reject the notion of immanence (*jiejixing*)—a prescriptive definition of class identity or class character as being uniform and predictable among members of the same class—these films have not disposed of class as a symbolic referent significant in the representation of social relations.

The Critical and Creative Potential of Class

Ideological and cross-cultural barriers exist in the West regarding the character of political critique in contemporary Chinese cinema. Class has always been the negation of democracy and universal humanity in anti-Communist rhetoric. This view seeks confirmation from comments made by Chinese filmmakers who reportedly have rejected "class struggle" for the same reasons as those proposed in Cold War rhetorics. Thus, even though many well-known "Fifth Generation" films have a more complex engagement with China's history and culture, their critical efforts are often described by Western journalists merely as one-dimensional works of auteurs that are unambiguously anti-Communist. Simplification such as this reflects a superficial understanding of the political culture to which the critical efforts of contemporary Chinese films are directed. Discussion of socialist cinema of the 1950s, by identifying some of the prominent motifs of that political culture, places "Fifth Generation" and other films of the 1980s within a context informed by the genealogy of class in Chinese cinema and addresses the ideological problems in certain cross-cultural interpretive frameworks applied to contemporary Chinese film.

The notion that China's socialist cinema prior to the 1980s is a product of political pressures reveals inadequate definition of cinema as a cultural institution.[8] Explicitly political aspects, including the personal involvement of CCP leaders in motivating the creation of specific works and censoring them subsequently, and the commissioning of films to support government policies make socialist cinema very different from market-based cinema. Yet, overt Party interventions aside, other questions remain, such as, What is the relationship between cinema and society when both are in the midst of radical transformation? What kinds of mediations exist between politics and film in a socialist context? Is sensitivity to peasants' comprehension and taste merely "politically correct," whereas sensitivity to an urban shopper's comprehension and taste is natural? As one examines Chinese films of the 1950s, it becomes clear that the arts and social discourse are repositories of values that do not have a one-dimensional relationship to politics. The common argument that Confucian morality thrived along with socialism in China is one indication of a more complex relationship.[9]

The argument that Chinese films of the Maoist period were ruined by their focus on class is myopic to its own assumptions, such as the existence of spontaneous filmmaking, and the nonideological nature of universal humanism. This argument is sometimes accompanied by the more confusing suggestion that class can be useful as an analytic instrument, even if potentially disastrous as a guiding ideology.[10] Viewings of didactic socialist films that speak for oppressed groups apparently strengthen the argument that the use of class as a creative focus has made Chinese cinema too optimistic in outlook and thus less sophisticated, but a critic's awareness of class can produce sophisticated criticism of bourgeois art. If this argument turns into a principled aversion to films that privilege class struggle coupled with enjoyment in performing "against-the-grain" readings on ideologically problematic texts, then a self-defeating split is unavoidable. That is, if class can be refined as a theoretical category but reserved for criticism only, then the bias cannot be more obvious. Such a separation of critique-oriented practices from creative ones is always a difficult ideological undertaking, one that still troubles, for example, feminism in the United States.

To the extent that socialist films give class a privileged role in a national cinema, they allow us to explore the successes and failures of its discursive performance. Class that is understood simply as a repressive mechanism in the arts is, according to Foucault's discussion on the juridical dimension of social discourse,[11] a misunderstanding of the socialist discourse on class, or what is said and what is regulated by way of class. Instead of approaching class as a silencing mechanism, therefore, I would argue that it articulates social antagonisms and establishes new networks among the population. On film, it refashions the image of society. It is this creative role of class, one that sets in motion a variety of elements that make up new forms of textuality and textual politics, that has been inadequately explored.

Hegemony and Nonessentialist Conceptions of Class

Responding to the era of "Lenin in ruins" and the low visibility of class, Western Marxists have examined Marxism's founding concepts. Notably, Etienne Balibar points out that a misreading of the arguments in *Capital* has produced a prevalent but mistaken representation of class struggles as symmetrical conflicts personified by material and ideological agents whose identities are predestined and affiliation based rather than conjuncture based.[12] Balibar establishes a theoretical basis to account for the structural and historical overlap, rather than complete segregation, of classes. The existence of contradictions within classes, moreover, is crucial to the Marxist conception of social relations.

In a neo-Marxist vein, Stuart Hall rejects the mistaken notion that a unified class and similarly unified class consciousness exist on the basis of shared material interest and position in the social structure. Under Thatcherism, the territories of the dominant and subordinate classes have been effectively penetrated and fragmented.[13] Hall understands, therefore, that classical Marxist concepts of class interest, class position, and material factors cannot adequately account for the actual disposition and movement of ideas that have produced a substantial ideological fracturing of both the dominant and subordinate classes. Instead, this new cultural dynamic must be addressed by the critical concepts of ideology and discourse conceptualized within Gramsci's notion of hegemony, a concept further developed by Laclau and Mouffe.[14]

Balibar's and Hall's reworking of concepts of class struggle and class consciousness come out of two disparate but connected tasks: the rearticulation of the relevance of class in spite of state socialism's disintegration, and the explanation of the absence of class symmetry in postmodern ideological formations. Both Balibar and Hall recognize the role of the state in the "reproduction of relations of exploitation" and in the constitution of class and ideological formation, a role that was undertheorized in classical Marxism. Balibar also suggests that the monopolizing Party in the socialist state has propagated the mistaken self-representation of having achieved a "classless" society. In a revision of Gramsci's notion of hegemony, Laclau and Mouffe argue that the social is irreducible to any unitary principle or an objective entity; it is articulated and constituted only by nodal points of antagonisms. Present and future revolutions in the form of radical democracy, they suggest, involve social agents and relations that come into being through such articulations.[15] Given that Laclau and Mouffe base their revolutionary conceptions on democratic hegemonies, it remains to be seen how the notion of antagonisms and hegemonic articulations may be relevant to a socialist (or "postsocialist") context, described by Laclau and Mouffe as authoritarian hegemony.[16]

The Politics of Class Off-Screen

The nation building taking place after 1949 in Mainland China needs to be recognized for its hegemonic and constitutive, rather than repressive, character. For a country that has experienced in the span of a century three successive crises—Western and Japanese imperialism and a civil war—nation building after the socialist takeover is both infrastructural and symbolic. The constitution of new identities requires consensual management (notably through an anti-imperialist patriotism) and policy adjustments (such as responses to problems in grassroots movements, as in land reform).[17] Especially prior to the antirightist campaign of 1957, the "people's democracy" had a democratic character (by way of weakening the validity attributed to many established institutions and values), and an authoritarian character (by ensuring an imaginary horizon that accompanies the constitution of the Party's correctness).[18] Nation building, to which cinema contributes ideologically, took no less than a hegemonic articulation in the early 1950s, its effective management and containment of antagonisms and differences clearly different from the dynamics of the Cultural Revolution era. To fail to see the "plurality of the social" and the plurality of social antagonisms in Communist countries is to imagine only one type of antagonism—that "between the Party and the freedom-loving people."

The massive official classification of China's population in the early 1950s served as a surveillance system in which everyone participated. Almost immediately it became a new site of antagonism. There were two types of classification: first, an unprecedented documentation of every member of the population, according to occupation, economic income, geographic location, political affiliation (or lack of it), and kinship ties; second, a ranking of state employees, notably cadres, that determined the income, types of government subsidies, and levels of services and privileges they received. Both classifications were completed by the end of 1953.[19] Other than peasants, a diminishing sector of industrial workers, self-employed, and the unemployed, everyone else was directly or indirectly hired by the state and subjected to ranking. Subsequently, a new, composite cadre class began to take shape during the 1950s.

The first type of classification recorded the class and social placement of a person as he or she lived in the presocialist era (to be exact, within three years prior to 1949).[20] As such, it formed a set of household-based, backward-looking criteria, transcended only by membership in the revolution and the Party. That is, in the early 1950s, a CCP membership could transcend "reactionary" kinship ties. These backward-looking criteria, transcendence by honor, and a ranking for the whole population made up the yardstick by which an individual's income, promotion, and sociopolitical placement were decided by the socialist system. In a society in which the giving and solicitation of favors are an integral part of everyday life, everyone's class background and ranking soon become important social knowledge exchanged in private and public channels. Class is constitutive of identity and social network.

Full recognition of the equality effects of such classification cannot be achieved by comparing it with what appear to be less rigid class relations in the past. For example, the argument that education and service in the state bureaucracy offered a social mobility mechanism to lower classes ignores the fact that most of the scholar-officials of the feudal era came from well-off families. As far as the everyday deprivations of inequality were concerned, the poor faced the following: factory work under conditions that were often conducive to sickness and sometimes fatal illnesses; lack of access to adequate medical care; illiteracy and little means to change it; susceptibility to famine, floods, and usury because of their land-bound status; and, for women, even lower-paid labor as well as higher rates of crime and sexual violation than those suffered by men.[21] Although such sufferings may have been overly dramatized and politically exploited by Chinese leftist films of the 1930s and 1940s, we cannot dismiss their historical accuracy.

In the historical context of oppression, the classification process—backward looking, hierarchical, and prone to abuse as it had been—was also the mechanism by which the state ministered to the well-being of the population by redistributing wealth to the previously impoverished and deprived. In the 1950s, this intervention included naming miscreant groups and punishing them (sometimes with penalties as severe as execution), curbing crime and government corruption, enabling better access to government services, and implementing measures and producing discourses that amounted to the creation of a new and healthy social environment resembling a modern state management technology. The liberating effects, therefore, were not illusions resulting from brainwashing sessions, but had a concrete material basis. As the underprivileged were encouraged to indict the old society in "speak bitterness" meetings, class consciousness became for them the key to self-representation and self-liberation. The problem, however, arose from the fact that class consciousness in this context supported a classification system that was clearly hierarchical. As soon as they appeared, the liberating effects of a politicized consciousness became enmeshed with the authoritarian effects of a state technology.

Social differentiation in the postrevolutionary context instigated new antagonisms and alliances. As well as building a politicized class consciousness that encouraged the upkeep of social equality, the classification that transformed people's chances under socialism also nourished a "reactionary," calculation-based class consciousness (*shili*). The latter is linked to a commonsense notion of social investment that apportions favors according to a person's background, occupation, political affiliation, and social placement. As it left the theoretical realm, the classical notion of Marxist class struggle became contaminated, taken over by a pragmatic, culturally nonspecific practice of social differentiation and interpersonal calculation. In China, official classification actually revived (i.e., by giving hegemonic articulation to) this non-Marxist consciousness of hierarchy. A paradox then followed: equality effects were intertwined with hierarchy effects that had their roots in classical Marxism and in China's social practice. For the Chinese living in the 1950s, cross-referencing between a prerevolutionary differentiation scheme and a postrevolutionary differentiation scheme was not just a matter of negotiating memory and new circumstances (which included developing an appropriate attitude to a new class of cadre)—the old and the new schemes and their notions of class had permeated each other in everyday social (and even sexual) politics.

The politics of class as discussed above is better described as the "plurality of the social" (as per Laclau) than as "class struggle" in its orthodox sense, especially because state ownership had altered the relations of production. Instead, old and new antagonisms were intertwined, and they crisscrossed old and new alliances both within and across class boundaries. This situation, which involved both Communists and non-Communists, was codified in the mid-1950s after Mao Zedong pronounced the existence of "contradictions among the people," but it never rose to the prominence of "class struggle."[22] This class politics is often displaced in orthodox accounts and elided in cross-cultural discussions, pro- and anti-Communist ones alike.

Inscription of Class in China's Socialist Cinema

Chinese cinema of the early 1950s participated in the politics of class by way of a consciousness-building mission, an ideological task once undertaken by the leftist films of the 1930s. In films of the pre-1949 era, however, viewer attention was drawn to unresolved social contradictions in the diegesis that implicated conditions outside the cinema,[23] whereas in films of the post-1949 era, political resolutions to contradictions were provided within the diegesis. The resolutions that pointed to CCP intervention outside the cinema were intended to generate an optimistic outlook and positive energies toward rebuilding the nation. Thus, if in pre-1949 films the liberating effects were drawn from removal of ideological barriers to collective participation in struggles still in process, in post-1949 films that adopted a similar logic, the implications had changed: representation of historical contestation of an oppressive social norm in the post-1949 context became inevitably teleological. Since resolutions and clear directions were considered more efficacious in consciousness building at the time, films of the early 1950s were less open than early Chinese leftist films to experimenting with approaches to new and unresolved antagonisms in the postliberation context.

The full implications of the inscription of class in Chinese cinema of the early 1950s go beyond the descriptions above. Films produced within a socialist context are not mere reproductions of the social dynamics outside cinema (such as those arising from liberation movements); rather, the dynamics are necessarily mediated by cinematic and signifying practices in institutional, discursive, and intertextual terms. In other words, institutional and textual reproduction of the dynamics are reformulated and often transposed into new terms by virtue of binding principles that intensify, displace, or resolve (thus functioning as containment of) antagonisms and provide different articulation to the dynamics. The creation of a new rural genre that integrates elements of melodrama and the musical, for example, gives presence to the enhanced political status of peasants, whereas individual films of the genre also reinforce the peasants' otherness and weaken political awareness of their continued deprived existence in relation to urban folk. The institutional, discursive, and intertextual terms that receive plenty of attention with regard to capitalist cinema have often been treated as if they were nonexistent in socialist cinema, especially because the latter's images and meanings are so overtly political. Nevertheless, this investigation is intended to bring to light the character and type of these mediations as they pertain to a socialist cinema and a representative film of the 1950s.

Changes in studio production practices in the early 1950s significantly altered the look and feel of films in the years to come. Replacing commercial entertainment films with worker-peasant-soldier ones, the socialist cinema was to be inspired by an expanded definition of the proletariat and, in its forms, to follow a changed set of ground rules. Without digressing into a long account of institutional changes, I want to note a few major ones. First, film production and exhibition shifted from direct financial investment into direct ideological investment. Instead of profiteering capitalists doing business in the cities, the government was directly involved in the creation of a national cinema with an expanded audience base. Its budget, however, was constrained by political factors such as the country's involvement in the Korean War. Although the tempting monetary gains for executives and stars ceased to exist, there were no threats of bankruptcy either.

Second, instead of appealing to bourgeois tastes, films were made for a state/proletarian alliance. Significantly, stars and star appeal were no longer viable, nor were alluring faces, bodies, and fashions. Following the exodus of film producers, directors, actors, and actresses to Taiwan and Hong Kong, there was a significant change of casts on the Mainland screen. Several notable female stars who stayed because they were either neutral or sympathetic to the Communists were considered inappropriate for proletarian roles. Even though most of them were determined to begin anew, at best they played minor roles during the 1950s.[24] Insofar as human faces constitute a prominent part of image content, the proletarian screen also effected a rupture from the past by either replacing or making over the faces and the bodies.

Third, more concentrated efforts were devoted to forging a national character out of cinema. Despite ambivalences and debates, there were persistent, though flawed, efforts to rid cinema of its foreign, colonial, and capitalist flavor. If inexpensive productions gave the look of austerity to films by doing away with expensive decor, props, and costumes, a nationalizing tendency ("to make films Chinese" or *dianying minzuhua*) further dispensed with prominently Westernized settings and decor, especially those uncalled for by the strict necessities of plot. One needs only compare two films from Kunlun Studio to discern how socialist cinema attempted to stake out its differences from its commercial precedent: *Liren Xing/Three Women,* a prorevolutionary film completed in early 1949, and *Woman fufu zhijian/Between Us Husband and Wife,* completed a year later, both have stories that take place in Shanghai. In the first film, the Chinese traitor lives in a well-furnished Western-style mansion complete with servant, chauffeur, and a lover in mink coat. Such glamorous details disappear completely in the second film, in which the male protagonist's lying down on a sofa for some leisurely reading is indicative of his lack of motivation to mingle with workers during the socialist takeover of Shanghai. Even though socialist cinema of the early 1950s is not conceived as a "cinema of poverty," strategic abandonment of luxury and an intensified work ethic reveal its consciously ascetic and proletarian efforts.

The White-Haired Girl

In all of the feature films made in the early 1950s, "class" serves as the major critical perspective and structuring principle for a narrative and imaging system. The explicit foregrounding of an orthodox Marxist conception of class in a mass edification context was unprecedented, and the films made were experiments by writers, directors, and policy makers in this regard. *Baimao Nu/The White-Haired Girl* (1950), codirected by Wang Bin and Shui Hua, an early and exemplary contribution to a proletarian and national aesthetic, illustrates the inscription of both the liberating and the compromising aspects of the 1950s "class" discourse on film. Wang was dedicated to nationalizing Chinese cinema; he directed *Qiao/Bridge* (1949), the first postliberation film, with the help of railroad workers in Harbin. Shui Hua is known for his meticulous work under the deprived conditions of 1950. His later work, *Linjia Puzi/The Lin Family Shop* (1959), also shot by cinematographer Qian Jiang, who filmed *The White-Haired Girl*, is a classic of the late 1950s.[25]

The White-Haired Girl, a film adapted from a 1944 revolutionary opera and based on a folktale told by peasants in northern Shanxi province, is a heartrending story of suffering and survival.[26] A peasant girl, Xi'er, and her widowed father, Yang Bailao, toil in the fields that belong to a landlord, Huang Shiren, who has kept his tenants enslaved by usury. A seventeen-year-old, Xi'er will be married to a young peasant, Dachun, during the Chinese New Year. Misled by landlord Huang and his aide's equivocation into believing that the Yang family has to either pay off the annual interest of the debt they owe Huang or give Xi'er away as payment, the young lovers work very hard and give their earnings to Xi'er's father. On New Year's eve, Yang takes what he understands to be the agreed amount to landlord Huang's mansion. Much to his surprise, Yang is told that he has previously agreed to repay both the interest and the full amount of the debt, and because he has failed to do so, he must give Huang his daughter as payment. Under force and threat, and despite his resistance, Yang is made to leave

Figure 7.1. Landlord Huang shows sexual interest in Xi'er.

his fingerprint on a contract that sells Xi'er to clear his debt. Guilt-stricken but unable to tell Xi'er what has happened, Yang drinks poison and freezes to death outside the home. The next day, while Xi'er is still weeping over her father's dead body, she is taken away by Huang's men. At first, Xi'er is made to serve Huang's abusive mother. Not much later, she is raped by Huang and becomes pregnant. Meanwhile, Dachun, forced off the land, plots to run away with Xi'er but fails. He leaves the village, crosses the Yellow River and finds the Red Army.

On the night of Huang's wedding, Xi'er finds out that the Huangs have sold her away, and a man is waiting with ropes for her. With the help of a maid, Xi'er flees to the mountains. She takes refuge in a cave, where she gives birth to a baby who dies shortly thereafter. She survives the severe winter by eating wild fruits and small animals, and her long hair turns completely white. The villagers begin to talk about a white-haired fairy-spirit that visits the temple twice a month to receive sacrifices.

Three years later, the Eighth Route Army is fighting the Japanese nearby. Dachun, now a soldier, visits his village and is told that Xi'er died three years before. Meanwhile, Huang fabricates forebodings from the white-haired spirit to discourage peasants from cooperating with the Eighth Route Army. Determined to expose Huang's lies, Dachun and another soldier hide in the temple and startle the white figure as it comes to snatch the food sacrifice. They pursue the figure up the mountains into a cave, where Dachun discovers Xi'er. Soon afterward, a struggle meeting against landlord Huang takes place in the village. In the end, Dachun stays in the village to continue land reform and marries Xi'er, whose hair regains its dark luster. She harvests alongside Dachun, who becomes a member of the local militia.

In a film that stages exploitation and suffering, efforts to survive and the support of community sustain threads of hope. Presented as thesis and antithesis, the peasants' tenacity is challenged by material scarcity and an oppressive force. Initially, two families attempt to combine their resources through marriage, but their plan is crushed by a lustful landlord. The separated lovers wait for the day when they will be unified, but one is raped and the other expelled from the land. The scenes of suffering are also scenes of melodrama in which both father and daughter are victimized: a poor widower whose daughter is cheated away from him commits suicide; a seventeen-year-old woman preparing for marriage is taken away by force, then raped and impregnated by a ruthless landlord. The scenes of survival, however, rise above the melodramatic and reverse the tragic destiny that subaltern characters are driven toward: Dachun crosses the roaring rapids of Yellow River in sheepskin floats and becomes a fighter, and Xi'er survives the wilderness and three severe winters as a hunter and by impersonating a goddess. The backdrop to the scenes of intense suffering is a daunting landscape whose chilly face eventually melts and turns into lush meadows when survival is confirmed and justice is at hand. The sources of the dramatic elements are eclectic: classical plays and modern melodramas that feature suffering and the search for justice, and folktales of the uncanny (such as those about hungry ghosts that roam the land waiting to be appeased).[27] Images and sounds are inspired by operas and musicals both Western and Chinese, as well as the war film. Thus, the representation of class oppression and its undoing draws its expressive strengths from elements that are not designed to build class consciousness.

The aesthetic corroboration of peasant-centered politics in *The White-Haired Girl* takes place on the visual and aural levels, denoting poverty without depriving images and sounds of their affective content. Commercial filmmaking entails fetishization of wealth through sophisticated settings, decor, accoutrements, and elegant bodies along with high production expenses, building in a careful and costly manner a mise-en-scène and ambiance that substantiate the presence of wealth.[28] Hollywood films even go so far as to show poverty as the rich man's fantasy, implying that it is embarrassing to be seen as truly poor.[29] It becomes a challenge for a "Third World" national cinema to construct an alternative ambiance and a positive aesthetic strategy on the basis of simple and deprived lives. This challenge tested writers and directors whose visions of poverty were drawn from urban and Westernized cultural experience and who not only had to forgo these cliches but had to make poverty an inspiring resource for a film's artistic construction. Moreover, there are additional worries—for instance, actors in rags performing in front of bare walls may easily lose the popular audience base that socialist cinema badly wants, but a richly detailed poor peasant dwelling is self-contradictory, and its inaccuracy will incite undesirable responses from peasant viewers. These dual demands, of making a proletarian cinema aesthetically befitting its class consciousness while maintaining its appeal to both urban and rural viewers, point to the different conditions between revolution as discipline and revolution as image that are open to negotiation by individual films. In some cases these negotiations result in composite and fractured aesthetic entities.

The White-Haired Girl negotiates these dual demands in many ways. Two major aesthetic strategies are worth noting here. First, the film retains to a large extent the opera's musical form and its theatrical exposition. In doing so, it not only adopts a form with a wide audience base, it builds on the moral clarity of the revolutionary opera. The audience's prior knowledge of and affection for Xi'er and Dachun's story based on the stage version is no small matter at a time when the film must reach out to film-illiterate rural viewers and communicate clearly to them the urgency of land reform movements. The obvious moral distinctions among the film's characters enable the transposing of class oppression analysis into nontheoretical and emotionally involving situations that presumably are easier to grasp than abstract exposition. It may be said that The White-Haired Girl pioneered a mode of communication geared toward the rural base by merging the filmic with opera as musical theater.

Second, peasant and landlord are differentiated in mise-en-scène terms and by contrasts between musical expression and writing. The dimly lit setting of the peasants' bare shack is warmed by the human presence of characters involved in caring exchanges, activities of feeding, and, most significant, songs sung with regional flavor. Decorations in the landlord's mansion, especially the antique-styled Chinese furniture and writings of Confucian/Buddhist aphorisms, convey their owner's feudal and hypocritical sensibilities. Most notable is the fact that none of the members of the landlord's household sing in the film. This, together with the readiness and ease with which the landlord's aide draws up the slavery contract, establishes writing as the oppressor's apparatus set against the phonic expressiveness of the subaltern.

To illustrate the visual and aural dimensions of the film, I shall describe in detail the scene in which Yang Bailao is forced to sell his daughter in Huang's mansion while Xi'er, Dachun, and Dachun's mother are preparing for the best dinner of the year at home. The scene is important as it condenses in time and space two major consequences of class oppression: the betrayal of trust and the destruction of families. It begins as snowflakes dance around to announce the New Year's eve while Yang Bailao heads toward Huang's mansion. Back at home, a medium shot depicts Xi'er decorating the tiny bedroom window, singing her theme tune:

> The north wind blows, the snowflakes whirl,
> Between the windy sky and snowy grounds two birds fly
> Over a thousand miles, lingering in love,
> Pair themselves while alight on a bough.
> Birds form couples, happiness comes in pairs,
> Half a cottage makes the bedroom for the bride.[30]

Holding a pair of paper-cut mandarin ducks in her hands, Xi'er anticipates the wedding. She pastes the birds on the window right above the paper-cut character meaning "double happiness." A long-shot view from outside the bedroom shows all three in happy silhouette. Back inside, Dachun has just given Xi'er something wrapped in paper. She opens it and finds a roll of thread and two woolen flowers. She shyly turns her face away from him, but as soon as he leaves, the camera shows her radiant face. This intimate

Figure 7.2. An anguished peasant father pleads for mercy.

moment is cross-cut with what is to take place at the landlord's house. A cutaway shot shows Yang arriving at the gate to Huang's mansion, where two large lanterns hang.

Back at home, Xi'er arranges her hair into a bun—the way a married woman would wear her hair—and sings:

> Rich people's weddings are with the finest attire
> Without a penny my father cannot acquire
> Two feet of red wool in my hand
> At the mirror here I adorn my hair.

She looks into the mirror and, seeing a beautiful bride-to-be, smiles coyly and buries her face in her hands. Inside the mansion, Huang wears a fur-lined padded jacket and puts on an impassive face as he tells his aide, Mu Renzhi, to take both interest and the loan sum from Yang. The anguished peasant father in rags pleads in close-up. Huang nods to Mu, who tells Yang that there is only one way to clear his debt: bring Xi'er to Huang as payment. Shocked by what sounds like a command, Yang falls to his knees and pleads for mercy so that Xi'er may get married properly. His weathered face torn with sadness and his body shaken with fear and indignation, Yang pleads over and over again, "Young master, I beg you, have pity, please."

Seeing that Huang is not moved, Yang struggles to get up, crying

Figure 7.3. Meanwhile, Xi'er anticipates a beautiful bride-to-be.

"I must go somewhere to plead my case!" "Where?" chides Mu. "Our young master is the number-two magistrate, this is the ya-men door; where are you going to plead your case?" Yang's horri-fied face fills the screen. Mu begins reading the words as he draws up the contract in brush and ink, "The contractor, Yang Bailao, owes landlord Huang one and a half piculs of grain and twenty-five dollars and five cents . . . " Yang's anguish in close-up is am-plified by Huang's ruthless glee and Mu's indifferent efficiency, and the string instruments on the sound track express anger, help-lessness, and sadness all at once. Mu gets to the end of his writing: " . . . since I am too poor to pay, I agree to sell my daughter to the landlord as payment for the debt. This is my decision and I will not go back on my word . . ." Yang pleads in a frenzy, "Please do good, I have only this one daughter." Huang gives Yang a kick, saying, "Tie this man up and send him to the county jail!" Orches-tral music now wails at full force. The old peasant is no match for vicious strength, and despite his frenzied reluctance, Mu grabs his second finger, dabs it in ink and forces a print on the contract. Yang Bailao utters a shriek, and the dramatic violins wind down as his finger goes limp on the paper—a print is thumped right under his name.

The tune of Xi'er's bedroom song returns softly amid the sounds of chilly winter. Outside the bedroom window, Xi'er in silhouette

Figure 7.4. A father is forced to betray his daughter by
fingerprinting on the slavery contract.

is still holding on to the mirror. She unwinds her bun as she hears
Dachun's mother calling from outside. Mother and son have arrived to make New Year's dumplings. A small lantern with characters *ping an* (peace) lights the door to the shack as they enter.
Outside Huang's mansion, the same happy tune sounds tragic as
Yang bangs the door-rings and throws his whole body against the
gates. "Can't do this, young master." The iron door-rings that
hang down from two fierce-looking lion heads make a harsh
sound in the windy night. Snow is getting thick. Back home, Xi'er
begins to roll dough for the dumplings. Dachun offers to help, but
she spares him. The door opens, and Xi'er's exhausted father enters, helped by another peasant.

   The affective content of the contrasting images and sounds of
these scenes is made more poignant by cross-cutting. The vicious
greed conveyed by the landlord's mansion sequence abruptly halts
the innocent happiness in Xi'er's bedroom sequence. The brutality
of the contract-signing sequence assaults the tenuous bliss of the
dumpling-making sequence. Montage taking place at the level of
sequence builds the drama of two men contending for a young
woman: the paternal protector is betrayed by his landlord and in
turn is forced to betray his daughter's trust, while the lustful playboy sets the stage for rape. Montage within the individual image

and between shots in the landlord's mansion sequence heightens the power difference between the men, as one protests futilely and the other coerces mercilessly. Significantly, the victimization of the peasant father preceding that of his daughter makes it clear that class inequality can deprive the paternal figure of his privileges within patriarchy.

The dramatic elements as they combine in *The White-Haired Girl* are ideologically compelling. Indeed, their paradigmatic role in the socialist signification system is felt to such an extent that *Huang Tudi/Yellow Earth* (1984), a highly acclaimed film that revisions the history and meaning of revolution, works with a very similar set of elements: the representation of peasants and the environment of their survival, the tragedy and resistance of women, the promise and possibility of social change, and the appropriation of folk culture and folk songs in political culture. In this regard, an intertextual reading of the ideological work of *Yellow Earth* against that of *The White-Haired Girl* can provide significant insight into its revisionist project concerning the changes of official and popular understanding of China's revolution in thirty-five years.[31] Without such an intertextual reading, works of the 1980s are too often simply pitted against the polemically painted backdrop of the Cultural Revolution. In itself, *The White-Haired Girl* turns out to be of exemplary status for the rural genre in socialist cinema.

The White-Haired Girl as a film is deeply affected by the discussions on revolutionary art for the masses that took place in the Lu Xun Art Academy in Yan'an.[32] In the adaptation of the folktale into opera, *The White-Haired Girl* took on symbolic significance of a major kind. No more than a year after Mao held his authoritative Yan'an forum on art and literature, serious efforts began to forge a popular and national art form. To what extent the opera of *The White-Haired Girl* had altered the original legend became insignificant, secondary to the story's popularity among the Hopei peasants and its potential to be adapted to a mass-based national art form that had practical value in land reform movements at the time. Reportedly, the story's antifeudal and antisexist themes were regarded as of less central importance than its themes of peasants' suffering in the prerevolutionary society and the fact that they could become their own masters (or *fanshan*). According to revolutionaries and officials examining the legend's political value, the folktale reconceived by way of class condenses the "striking distinction between an old society and a new society." The distinction between "an old society that crushes human beings into apparitions" and "a new society that restores ghosts into humans," accordingly, reveals the "class immanence of events and people."[33] Reversal of personal and collective destinies became a political matter, intertwined with the telling of class oppression and struggle.

In the adaptation of the story so that it would better reveal the essence of class conflicts, several major changes were made to the original tale.[34] The first concerns Xi'er's feelings after she is raped and made pregnant. Xi'er must not be deluded into thinking that by giving the Huang family a male child, she might win a semi-legitimate place in the family. In the folk version, the existence of such an illusion betrays the peasant woman's feudal understanding that her body, once raped by the landlord, can only be redeemed by that man alone and by her contribution to patrilineality. Women's "collusion" in their oppression at the level of sexual politics, as argued by Michele Barrett, is related to questions of relations of production and the class structure.[35] Xi'er's "collusion" can thus be read as an internalization of violence and an attempt to use her own reproductive ability to improve her place in the relations of production. In the opera and film versions of the story, with their purified proletarian consciousness, Xi'er entertains no such illusion about the landlord's kindness. Instead, overcome by fear when she flees to the mountains, she looks back at the mansion glimmering in the dark at a distance and sings:

> I'm water that can't be drained dry,
> I'm fire that can't be quenched!
> My grievances are higher than the heavens,
> My tears have become rivers,
> Oh, I must seek revenge!

She then proclaims, "I'm going to live! And live to be avenged!"[36] This persistence in class hatred, knowing that one is wronged and waiting for justice to dawn, turns out to be an effective narrative strategy that moved soldiers and peasants, men and women alike, and caused spontaneous reactions when the revolutionary opera was performed in villages as agitprop to recruit for the army and to mobilize peasants in land reform in the 1940s. The figure of a raped and suffering woman to illustrate class oppression and to allegorize the country's violation had been well used in urban-based leftist films of the 1930s. This same figure in the opera version appealed successfully to the rural masses as well.

The second major change in the story concerns Xi'er's emotional life and the source of her inspiration. In the folktale, she is not engaged to anyone prior to the rape, and after the rape, she gives birth to a daughter and raises her in the wild. Maternal love is the only emotional inspiration in the survival struggle in the folk version, which also portrays the females being "otherly" together as they both grow animallike hair (Xi'er has a fuzzy white body, and her daughter's name is "Little White Hair"). The prospect of raising someone else's (a rapist's) daughter, moreover, does not stop a man from marrying the woman survivor later. In the adaptation process, paternal love (extending from Yang Bailao to Xi'er) and heterosexual love (mutual between Dachun and Xi'er) replace the intimacy between mother and daughter. If Xi'er is to persist in class hatred, as the new logic goes, the trace of sexual intercourse between the landlord and the peasant must evaporate as soon as possible, and there should be no living daughter coming from the landlord-rapist. In both the opera and the film, thus, the female infant does not survive the critical discussion. Love for a peasant man now prevents Xi'er from having inappropriate illusions about the landlord while it strengthens class solidarity and instills hope in waiting. Dachun's background and his joining the Red Army, moreover, underscore the notion that cadres come from the oppressed brave and therefore are truly interested in bringing about social equality. With Xi'er's daughter gone, it was also argued, cadre Dachun would have no hesitation in marrying the white-haired woman—a notion that contradicts progressive equality and panders to feudal values.[37]

The added relationship between Xi'er and Dachun, in the opera and film versions, becomes the main axis along which proletarian revolution is played out. If the death of the father personalizes the criminal nature of class oppression, slavery and rape of a virgin engaged to another man moralizes it. To drive home a theory of class struggle, the proletarian revolution in rural China becomes a story of frustration and fulfillment of manhood and womanhood, cemented by love and trust between two men (a father, a fiancé) and a woman. As Xi'er longs to see Dachun, she sings,

> Into two is divided a cloth of indigo,
> Into two is separated a family, a couple,
> . . .
> Why must poor people suffer so?
> Why are rich people so cruel?

The familiar tragedy of lovers' separation helps carry a class-based accusation. Yet would the story be less convincing if class sentiments were cemented by the love and trust between a mother and her daughter instead? The adaptations provide no room for such a question, as intraclass alliance and complementarity proceed from heterosexual love and trust that ends in a happy marriage. Conceivably, in the 1940s and early 1950s, the opera's and the film's stakes in recruiting males for political and military activities (where male peasants were generally understood to be more suspicious than females toward the revolution) obligated a negotiation between class and patriarchal values that ended up curtailing female relationships as the axis of proletarian organization. An awareness of the woman's political use and her awkward value for the state must accompany any evaluation of the liberating effects of *The White-Haired Girl.*

Even though class is an accomplice of heterosexuality as the norm, *The White-Haired Girl* is still far from falling into a bourgeois heterosexual fantasy. If one considers the commercial formulas that include a rich man, a poor youth, and an attractive woman (sometimes a virgin) as main characters, many familiar stories come to mind. For example, a poor young man is attracted to a virgin who is seduced by a rich man and becomes his mistress. Later, when the woman is abandoned, the young man stands by her. An employee of the rich man and too shy to express his love to the woman, the young man is tempted to climb the corporate ladder but decides to quit his job instead. His sense of integrity moves the young woman who quits her own job with the company and joins him. In another plot, a young woman schemes to kill her rich

Figure 7.5. A white-haired goddess drives landlord Huang away from the temple.

husband with the help of a young man. The young man, hopelessly attracted to her, murders her husband. After getting her inheritance, the woman betrays and abandons the young man. These plot lines have become Hollywood's *The Apartment* (1960) and *Double Indemnity* (1944), both directed by Billy Wilder. A comparison between *The White-Haired Girl* and these two films shows that although *The White-Haired Girl* is mired in patriarchal logic, it is a logic quite unlike that found in urban commercial cinema.

Frederick Engels, who found the proletarian family lacking in the material basis for male dominance, has argued that female chastity is an ideological expression of the bourgeois family. The Marxist feminist critique of Engels points out the central place of heterosexual familialism in his argument while agreeing to a certain extent that the tenacity of the ideology of masculinity and femininity is not merely cultural but is deeply embedded in the division of labor and relations of production.[38] In attempting to align class oppression and sexual inequality, *The White-Haired Girl* makes the landlord's rape of a poor and indebted tenant's daughter a prototypical, double-edged act. By way of violated female chastity, sexuality is articulated at the same level as class. Sticking these two levels together enables transgressive and illicit male sexual desire to become the figure or trope of class oppression, now literally embodied by a bald-headed playboy. Rape as the prototypical oppressive act is then countered by legitimate monogamous heterosexual marriage, which also signifies a permanent and secure class alliance. It is this double-edged meaning of rape that makes it clear why Xi'er must reach the nadir of deprivation with the death of her infant daughter. As a powerful trope to generate moral outrage at this double oppression, the rape also sets limit to questions of sexuality and power, such as, Dare we imagine Dachun or Xi'er as queer revolutionaries? (Throughout the first two periods mentioned at the beginning of this essay, only heterosexuality exists on the Chinese screen, and woman warriors are at best cross-dressers.) Is there a chance for Dachun to be captured by an urban woman who aspires to revolutionary men and not to return to the village? (But revolutionary cadres' abandonment of their rural wives was a major reason for divorce applications from the army after 1949.) What if Xi'er only has to look to herself and/or to her daughter to find the reason to survive? (Many wives of the Eighth Route Army went on living without their husbands.)[39] In other words, although in reality the history of revolution involved more complications than delivering the oppressed from suffering so that young women and men might form loving and prosperous families, the prototypical narrative text of liberation has compromised the terms of revolution and inadvertently brought class struggle to the promise for family-based economic self-determination that concludes the film.

The third major change in the adaptation of *The White-Haired Girl* from folktale to opera/film concerns the extent of collective struggle in the story. A redemption by the Eighth Route Army without the villagers responding with a struggle against the landlord means that liberation is simply a gift to the oppressed. The folk version subscribes to such a passive perspective, but the notion that villagers need only wait for gifts from the CCP is certainly far from what the latter desires from the masses. The suggestion that socialist realist literature best expresses a "socialist salvation theory" has missed the other side of the appeal of the revolution.[40] Self-redemption efforts that mirror the first saving act are what makes revolution possible in the first place. Thus, even though socialist realist works completed after 1949 began to make popular participation look perfunctory, writers and artists were aware of the fact that China's revolution or political change would not have been accomplished without the volunteer annexation of many similar wills. In material and discursive terms, the CCP could not be without its masses, and revolution was not possible without self-redemption struggles that reverberated throughout the country (despite the fact that they may have arisen from motives such as self-aggrandizement).

Alluding to an existing revolutionary practice but also transforming it into a staged uniformity, the scene in which the whole village struggles against the landlord intends to inspire audience emulation. However, the story casts the struggle meeting as vindication for Xi'er's suffering. Revenge as a popular notion makes the condemnation of landlord Huang a more mechanical (i.e., a device for narrative closure) than revolutionary act. The sequence that most resembles staged opera takes place as a chorus of peasants sings in unison:

Huang Xiren, Huang Xiren, Huang Xiren,
You murderous devil, man-eating animal,
Your crimes will be visited on your head,
For the suffering Xi'er we shall take revenge
. . .
Frozen rivers shall thaw,
Blossoms shall welcome the spring,
Sisters forced to turn into ghosts
Shall today change back into human,
People who suffered in days bygone
Shall be their own masters from now on!

Even with pans and cutaways to the struggle efforts taking place in other parts of the village, collective singing and collective gestures in a stage setting appear overly theatrical in the context of the rest of the story's more realistic efforts. Yet the scene serves as the crucial summation of a "class for itself," a proletariat coming into being by virtue of the people's struggle to stand on their own feet, to throw off the landlord's yoke, and to become their own masters. This scene is more than just another example of class-based plotting. The imagining of empowered peasants also points to revolution's main ideological feature and its historical appeal. Off-screen, active solicitation of voices and actions from the less privileged have been answered by lively, strong, and often violent responses that have amplified and even outdone the initial call. These responses have often been more unbridled, more violent, and more mixed with calculations.[41] Confusions are fascinating and exemplary of the evolving antagonisms, but they have no place in a socialist imaginary that bears the mark of a nonrevolutionary sense of effective governance. Thus, the film ends with an image of Dachun and Xi'er harvesting their grain—a new order is in place. Still, one must not forget that it was the popular success of the empowerment imagination, not the orderliness of a revolutionary nation-state, that appealed to common people to get on the political stage of the Cultural Revolution and to become its once active but now denying accomplices.

By affirming and intensifying peasants' resistance ability, an access to a political imaginary of peasants was being established that otherwise would be blocked by the dominant culture's notion of peasants as peripheral and unrefined. Whereas the depiction of peasants as subaltern gained them a place in the critical discourse of the leftist films of the 1930s, they became important figures in the representation of revolution and the supposed transition to a classless society. The term *nongmin* (those engaged in agricultural production), imagined as a "class for itself," becomes a political signifier through class. In the 1950s films of the rural genre, peasants having a collective will to resist oppression provided a corrective, albeit a problematic one, to their structured absence in commercial cinema as a Westernized and urban-based entertainment form.[42]

In as innocent a film as *The White-Haired Girl*, a subtle hierarchy is established at the end in which Dachun, the revolutionary soldier, is the beneficiary. As the film's title and the story work together to anchor audience attention on Xi'er—the causes of her suffering and her survival—it is easy to be satisfied with the fact that Xi'er returns to her community and lives happily ever after with Dachun. Yet, in comparison to her preliberation saga, her eventual restoration to the place of peasant housewife appears to be minimal reward for her struggles, considering the fact that such a social position would have been hers in the first place had landlord Huang not interfered with her marriage. The narrative focus

Figure 7.6. Dachun heads the peasants' struggle meeting.

on Xi'er, I would argue, camouflages the textual preparation for the political and social ascension of Dachun, who by the end of the film has "escaped" the status of the peasant and, as a member of the local militia, has more political power than both Xi'er and other peasants. After the efforts they both have made, Xi'er is just a woman who has lived in the wilderness for three years, whereas Dachun has been fighting the Japanese in the Eighth Route Army during that time—a record that counts in the real hierarchization that separates cadres from ordinary people. Of course, Dachun is also subordinated to a new chain of command as he becomes a part of the postrevolutionary state institution. Access to political power in the text is nevertheless given to the male, *borrowing*, as it were, from the suffering and the wonderful struggle efforts of the female that make the final struggle meeting worth the undertaking. Argued this way, Yang Bailao's death is not simply a case of class oppression, but becomes a textual opening for Dachun to take his place as the new paternal figure in the postliberation social realm. My reading thus anticipates the institutionalization of a new hierarchy based on patriarchal interest that ultimately helped defeat the promises of liberation.

What is unanticipated by *The White-Haired Girl*—and, indeed, by most films of the early 1950s—is the state's appropriation of individual labor in subsequent years when agriculture as collective enterprise was made to support heavy industrial development. In the film, the spirit of "land to each tiller" marks the end point of the class struggle. Indeed, images of Dachun and Xi'er harvesting together suggest that as the result of revolution, the peasants are able to enjoy the fruits of their labor. Still, in relation to the productivist program that emerged in the 1950s, the film more or less foreshadows the ambitions of the nation-state and its stake in eradicating traditional power structures. In subsequent years, the state and its agents became "newly powerful claimants" on the harvest.[43]

Enlightened Projections

The new role assigned to the subaltern as displayed by the "worker-peasant-soldier" film entailed unexpected problematic implications. Zheng Junli's *Between Us Husband and Wife* (1951) shows that such implications had been thought of at the time but only obliquely articulated. There are two protagonists in the film: a cadre who is a college graduate from Shanghai committed to working in the countryside, and a resilient peasant woman who was abused as a child and wife and who liberates herself in the revolution. The cadre marries the peasant woman and they both participate in the takeover of Shanghai. In the film, the cadre is extremely frustrated by his wife's unrefined taste and her audacious manner as she corrects his urban habits, which she considers wasteful. Put off by her overzealous participation in the takeover work, he retreats into his reading. After endless arguments and fights, they begin to live in separate dormitories. Despite its unconvincing saving of the difficult marriage at the end, *Between Us Husband and Wife*, a film subjected to severe criticism at the time, reminds its viewers that the notion of peasants as resilient revolutionaries is an ideology whose enlightened false consciousness may be easily exposed. Any "excessive" assertion of peasant power threatens social dislocation, especially regarding the revolutionary male ego and the assumption of urban, non-self-critical superiority.

Proffering paradigmatic instances of peasant resistance and liberation, *The White-Haired Girl* comes off as a sincere and carefully crafted work dedicated to the masses. Yet, bound by this dedication to proletarian consciousness and aesthetic in support of an emerging state technology, it becomes mythical and is unable to depart from the ideological underpinnings of an enlightened patriarchal urban revolutionary imaginary. *The White-Haired Girl*'s participation in the class politics of the early 1950s has national implications for both urban and peasant viewers. The classification process of the early 1950s has affixed peasants to rural habitat and has forbidden all but a small number of cadres and soldiers to become urban residents because peasants must contribute toward the nation as peasants. As agriculture is made the material base for the country's urban sector to make cultural and technological advances, peasants (as *nongmin*) are rewarded symbolically as a welcomed political signifier on-screen.[44] There is no unequal and awkward exchange between revolutionary cadre and peasant woman in *The White-Haired Girl*, and peasant becomes a fulfilled entity on screen. This making over of peasants is what *Yellow Earth* director Chen Kaige came to realize while a temporary peasant during the Cultural Revolution. Ultimately, it is not the discursive privileging of peasants as fulfilled proletarian entity but the poignant awareness of their Otherness as a continued deprived class and their often nonrevolutionary attempts to transgress this boundary that haunts ongoing urban imagination of and speaking for the subaltern.

An unequivocal affirmation of the liberating prospects of class struggle in Chinese films of the 1950s may have obfuscated their containment of potentially conflicting political and social interests. The textual structure of governance, between urban enlightenment and expropriation of the rural surplus, as well as between gender equality and patriarchal interests, in an exemplary film illustrates the tenuous equilibrium established among potential forces of antagonism in the postliberation context. This undertaking was the point of departure for the new Chinese cinema's reevaluation in the 1980s of entering modernity and its attendant complications.

Notes

1. Those interested in arguments on the implications of existing socialist states for global capitalism may want to read Arif Dirlik's "Post-Socialism/Flexible Production: Marxism in Contemporary Radicalism," *Polygraph* 6/7: 133–69. I differ with Dirlik's statement that "now that socialism is dead, Marx-

ism can once again come home to capitalist societies" for the reason that it may encourage one simply to shift attention away from the conditions in existing socialist societies.

2. This phrase is from Etienne Balibar, "From Class Struggle to Classless Struggle?" in *Race, Nation, Class: Ambiguous Identities,* ed. Etienne Balibar and Immanuel Wallerstein (London: Verso, 1991), 156.

3. Beginning in 1986, Chinese scholars began publishing accounts of China's Cultural Revolution. A well-known example is Yan Jiaqi and Gao Gao's *Wenhua dageming shinian shi, 1966–76* [Cultural revolution: ten-year history, 1966–76] (Tianjin: Tianjin People's Press, 1986).

4. Examples include Yang Guangyuan's *Da Juezhan Yi: Liaoshen zhanyi/Liaoxi-Shenyang Campaign* (1990) and Ding Yinnan's *Zhou Enlai* (1991).

5. Ernesto Laclau, *New Reflections on the Revolution of Our Time* (London: Verso, 1990), 205.

6. Stephen Resnick and Richard Wolff, "Remarx: China Today and Class Analysis," *Rethinking Marxism* 3 (Spring 1990): 157–64. Resnick and Wolff fall back on an ahistorical category, "ancient class processes," when they try to describe what is not clearly capitalist or communist.

7. Philip Kuhn, "Chinese View of Social Classification," in *Class and Social Stratification in Post-Revolution China,* ed. James Watson (Cambridge: Cambridge University Press, 1984), 16–28. See also Mayfair Yang, "The Modernity of Power in the Chinese Socialist Order," *Cultural Anthropology* 3, no. 4 (1988): 408–27.

8. Both Jay Leyda's *Dianying: Electric Shadows, An Account of Films and the Film Audience in China* (Cambridge: MIT Press, 1972) and Paul Clark's *Chinese Cinema: Culture and Politics Since 1949* (Cambridge: Cambridge University Press) try to address the cultural aspects of socialist cinema, but at times they are also overwhelmed by its political aspects.

9. Studies of socialism's impact on Chinese villages support this view. See Richard Madsen, *Morality and Power in a Chinese village* (Berkeley: University of California Press, 1984).

10. A good example of this argument can be found in Rey Chow, "Against the Lure of Diaspora: Minority Discourse, Chinese Women and Intellectual Hegemony," in *Gender and Sexuality in Twentieth-Century Chinese Literature and Society,* ed. Tonglin Lu (Albany: University of New York Press, 1993). Chow's skepticism produces a highly debatable argument, here quoted in full: "Perhaps the greatest and most useful lesson modern Chinese culture has to offer the world is the pitfall of building a nation—the People's Republic of China—on a theory of social change—class consciousness—the disappearance of class itself—can actually materialize in human society. . . . But when the force of class consciousness is elevated to official ideology rather than kept strictly as an analytic instrument (as it was in the text of Marx), it also becomes mechanical and indistinguishable from other ideological strongholds of government power" (p. 31).

11. Michel Foucault, *History of Sexuality,* vol. 1, *An Introduction* (New York: Vintage, 1980).

12. Balibar, "From Class Struggle."

13. Stuart Hall, "The Toad in the Garden: Thatcherism among the Theorists," in *Marxism and the Interpretation of Culture*, ed. Cary Nelson and Lawrence Grossberg (Urbana: University of Illinois Press, 1988), 58–73.

14. Ernesto Laclau and Chantal Mouffe, *Hegemony and Socialist Strategy: Towards a Radical Democratic Politics* (London: Verso, 1985).

15. Laclau, *New Reflections*, 89–92, 197–245.

16. Laclau and Mouffe, *Hegemony and Socialist Strategy*, 55–88.

17. Lynn White III, "Bourgeois Radicalism," in *Class and Social Stratification in Post-Revolution China*, ed. James Watson (Cambridge: Cambridge University Press, 1984), 124–74. Also see Qian Jaqu, "Dengji senyan de Zhongguo dalu [A rigidly hierarchical Mainland China]," *Xin Bao* [Overseas Chinese economic journal] 27 (October 1991): 4.

18. Laclau, *New Reflections*, 186–87.

19. White, "Bourgeois Radicalism," 142–74.

20. Ibid., 143.

21. See, for example, Gail Hershatter's *The Workers of Tianjin, 1900–1949* (Stanford: Stanford University Press, 1986).

22. Laclau and Mouffe recognize Mao's analysis of contradiction as going beyond the class principle, but arrogantly qualify it as having "near-to-zero philosophical value." See *Hegemony and Socialist Strategy*, 64.

23. See Ma Ning, "Textual and Critical Difference of Being Radical: Reconstructing Chinese Leftist Films of the 1930s," *Wide Angle* 11, no. 2 (1989): 22–31.

24. Wang Renmei, *Wode chengming yu buxing: Wang Renmei huiyilu* [My becoming famous and misfortunes: memoir by Wang Renmei]. (Shanghai: Shanghai wenyi Chubanshe, 1985).

25. Both *Three Women* and *The Lin Family Shop* are available on videocassette from China Video Movies Distribution Co., phone (415) 366-2424, fax (415) 365-2523. To my knowledge, *The White-Haired Girl* exists only in 35mm; it is available for viewing in the China Film Archive in Beijing.

26. The folktale was collected by the poet Shao Zhinan, who took it back to Yan'an. The joint efforts of two writers and seven musicians turned it into a revolutionary opera of five acts and more than forty tunes. In 1949, Wang Bin, Shui Hua, and Yang Runxin worked on the adaptation. The film was completed in March 1950 in the Northeast Studio. It received a special honor in Czechoslovakia's Karlovy Vary Festival. A collection of revolutionary opera created during the Yan'an period has been edited by Ding Yi and Su Yiping, *Geju juan* [Opera section] (Changsha: Hunan renmin chubanshe, 1985).

27. Tales of hungry ghosts are shared by many cultures. For a discussion of the background of the opera and a 1949 version of the operatic text, see the chapter on *The White-Haired Girl*, "Ghost, Goddess, Revolutionary," in *Five Chinese Communist Plays*, ed. Martin Ebon (New York: John Day, 1975), 29–117.

28. See Jane Gaines and Charlotte Herzog, eds., *Fabrications: Costume and the Female Body* (New York: Routledge, 1990).

29. An example is Gregory La Cava's *My Man Godfrey* (1936).

30. The lyrics of many of the songs in the film are quite different from those

appearing in Martin Ebon, ed., *Five Chinese Communist Plays* (New York: John Day, 1975). The English version here combines his translation of the Chinese text and my own.

31. *Yellow Earth* shows peasants' difficult existence, but instead of attributing their suffering to class oppression, it suggests that the powers of nature and tradition are really beyond the influence of CCP revolution. See Esther Yau, *"Yellow Earth:* Western Analysis and a Non-Western Text," *Film Quarterly* 41, no. 2 (1987): 22–33.

32. "Jianjie Baimaonu de chuangzuo gingkuang [A brief introduction to *The White-Haired Girl*'s creation circumstances]," *Dianying wenxue* 1 (1959): 81–82.

33. Yang Runxin, "Cong canjia gaibian 'Baimaonu' dianying juban shuoqi [To begin from my participation in adapting *The White-Haired Girl* film script]," *Dianying wenxue* 1 (1959): 82–84.

34. Ibid.

35. Michel Barrett, *Women's Oppression Today* (London: Verso, 1980), 48–62.

36. In an earlier opera version, Xi'er dances on stage in a red jacket, thinking that she will become Huang's wife. Even though the irony of this scene was considered striking, it was deleted because it damages Xi'er's image. "Jianjie Baomaonu de chuangzuo qingkuang," 82.

37. Yang, "Cong canjia gaibian Baimaonu dianying juban shuoqi," 83.

38. Barrett, *Women's Oppression Today*, 48–62.

39. This fact is acknowledged in Lin Nong's *Daughters of the Party* (1959). In this film, peasant women are lonely but brave, and the Party becomes a symbolic paternal figure to all female revolutionaries.

40. Tonglin Lu, using Meng Yue and Dai Jinhua's arguments, emphasizes the salvation aspect only in her discussion. Tonglin Lu, "Introduction," in *Gender and Sexuality in Twentieth-Century Chinese Literature and Society*, ed. Tonglin Lu (Albany: State University of New York Press, 1993), 2–18.

41. Examples can be found in Judith Stacey's *Patriarchy and Socialist Revolution in China* (Berkeley: University of California Press, 1983).

42. More than 90 percent of the country's population are rural viewers. With Cheng Bugao's *Spring Silkworms* (1933), peasants were politicized on screen.

43. See Vivienne Shue, *Peasant China in Transition: The Dynamics of Development toward Socialism, 1949–1956* (Berkeley: University of California Press, 1980). Also see Jean C. Oi, *State and Peasant in Contemporary China: The Political Economy of Village Government* (Berkeley: University of California Press, 1989).

44. Mao Zedong has been quoted as saying, "The peasants want freedom, but the CCP wants socialism" when he decided to nationalize agricultural cooperation and the people's communes. The failure induced by collectivization caused the deaths of twenty million rural Chinese. See Ding Shu, *Ren Wo: Dayuejin yu da jihuang* [Human-induced woes: the Great Leap Forward and the big famine] (Hong Kong: Nineties Monthly/Going Fine, 1993).

Chapter 8

Out of the Mine and into the Canyon: Working-Class Feminism, Yesterday and Today

Lillian S. Robinson

The sound of a door slamming is heard from below.
—Henrik Ibsen, *A Doll's House,* concluding stage direction

People don't do *such things!*
—Henrik Ibsen, *Hedda Gabler,* concluding line

Modern drama started off literally with a bang. Or rather with two of them: the door that Nora Helmer slammed and its ironic echo in Hedda Gabler's pistol shot through the temple, both of them signaling a challenge to the institutions that oppress women and both of them (loudly) giving the lie to traditional bourgeois strictures about what things simply are not done.

I begin with this allusion not only because I, too, wish to start off with a bang, and not just in tribute to the fact that these ideas and the essay in which they are embodied were initially presented as a conference paper under Norwegian feminist auspices. Rather and principally, I want to remind us all that the question of the dramatic representation of revolutionary ideas about women has been an issue on the Western intellectual and political agenda for more than a hundred years. Translating gender theory into the language of *cinema* is an even more complex matter, combining the verbal project of theater with a new emphasis on the narrative process that occurs through the act of the eye. Nonetheless, if films have not proved as fertile a ground for examining hard questions about gender and power, it is not primarily because of the medium's formal limitations, but because the social function of cinema—American commercial cinema, at least—has been to reinforce rather than to challenge dominant ideology.

Two controversial American films, Herbert Biberman's *Salt of the Earth* (1953) and Ridley Scott's *Thelma & Louise* (1991), do grapple with the problem of how to construct a cinematic representation of the issues and analyses originating in social theory about the oppression of women and the possible means to liberation. Both films, moreover, explore the woman question from a perspective informed by their protagonists' working-class situation. But almost every word I have used to describe their commonalities, from "controversial" through "working-class," means something very different for the two films, each of which reflects certain key elements of its own time, conditions of production, and theoretical grounding.

Salt of the Earth and *Thelma & Louise* can serve, in fact, as complementary examples, because each of them possesses and emphasizes important dimensions that the other lacks. In *Salt of the Earth*, the struggle of women takes place in and through the labor movement, which is to say in a context of class and community solidarity. The special oppression of working-class women, even when the immediate perpetrator is a proletarian patriarch, is clearly portrayed as coming from the capitalist system and its representatives. This means that certain aspects of women's experience—the gender division of labor, the oppressive conditions under which women's domestic work is performed, the lack of power within the household—are foregrounded, whereas certain others—sexuality, domestic violence, and rape, for example—are almost entirely absent. These are, of course, precisely the issues that are most important in *Thelma & Louise,* where the narrative centers on the institutionalization of violence against women and where, as a consequence, the film's other observations about marriage, family, and work in or outside the home become "background" surrounding and reinforcing that center, not organically connected parts of a single oppressive system.

A similar contrast may be drawn between the narrative strategies of the two films. Both films involve the interaction of individual women's narratives with social issues and historical forces. It is a convention of Western narrative fiction in all media to concentrate the social dimension into the life and consciousness of a single individual. A documentary, with its intrinsic assertion that truth lies in "reality," may tell the story of, say, Harlan County on strike, but for a mass audience the conventions of the cinematic medium and of the moviegoing phenomenon entrust conviction to narrative. So the best way to make the Chicano miners' strike "real" is to fictionalize it as the *personal* story of Esperanza and her family. Nonetheless, in their common adherence to this convention, *Salt of the Earth* and *Thelma & Louise* represent narrative approaches that are almost mirror images of one another. In *Salt of the Earth*, the story of Esperanza is deliberately typified, almost archetypal. It is the social, the collective situation that matters, and that is realized through embodiment in the experience of a particular individual whom we come to care about. By contrast, *Thelma & Louise* examines social conditions chiefly as a way of explaining the motives and actions of the particular individuals.

The theories underlying the two films—what my title characterizes as "yesterday's" working-class feminism versus "today's"—thus imply different formal choices as well as different ideological bases. And the issues of the congruities and tensions between individuals and community weave their complex and ironic way through both the formal and the ideological/theoretical sets of considerations.

Although I have described *Salt of the Earth* and *Thelma & Louise* as "controversial," this also has different meanings in each case. *Salt of the Earth* was made by Hollywood left-wingers who established an independent company as a response to McCarthyism in the movie industry. Some of the film's technical problems and just about all of its political integrity are the result of the conditions of harassment under which it was made. The blacklist that shaped the careers of Biberman and his associates, and that made them determine to try to make films independent of the mainstream studios, was also applied to their product. Enormous obstacles were placed in the way of the film's production and processing, and the completed *Salt of the Earth* was denied theatrical distribution. In its first thirty years of existence, it was shown at precisely thirteen theaters in the United States, and I would be very surprised if the ten years that have elapsed since the notation of that astonishing statistic have significantly swelled the figure.[1] "No American film," Dan Georgakas maintains, "has ever faced the harassment endured by *Salt of the Earth*."[2] The box in which the currently available videotape is packaged boasts that *Salt of the Earth* is "the only American film ever blacklisted," making a selling point of this history of persecution and, in the process, draining that persecution of real meaning. For whatever reason, yesterday's transgression has become today's commercial attribute. The result is that *Salt of the Earth* still makes its entrance, after forty years, under the sign of transgression, however denatured, because, in our postmodern moment, transgression itself is good (show) business.

It is not clear whether the actual content of *Salt of the Earth* would have aroused as much contemporary controversy as the efforts to ban it. Many of the preemptive attacks went so far as to invent content (scenes of rioting blacks, for example, or a Mexican American child being pistol-whipped by sheriff's deputies). One member of a citizens' group Biberman had invited to a screening in his (eventually fruitless) attempt to win acceptance for theatrical showings remarked after seeing it that the film was neither "socialistic" nor "communistic" as he'd been warned, merely "feministic," and *that* wasn't against the law. Well, feminism was not illegal in the 1950s and it is not in the 1990s, either, but certain challenges to the existing gender arrangements—arrangements that most commercial films unquestioningly endorse—*are* transgressive and remain highly controversial.

Thelma & Louise was designed, interpreted, and successfully marketed as a mainstream Hollywood movie, yet it provoked extraordinarily widespread and ardent debate (*that* kind of controversy) among its audience about the issues of acquaintance rape and women's recourse to violent self-defense. People were aggressively asking whether this is what feminism means, that women become as violent as men traditionally have been, and whether this is what a feminist film should be promoting—people who never before consciously asked what feminism is or isn't, much less what a feminist work of art should be representing and expressing.

These various points where the two films are tangential yet move in opposite directions suggest that closer examination of each one may have something useful to tell us about feminist theory and its representation in narrative film. It may even be that contrasting the respective statements and silences of the cinematic representations could lead to an enriched feminist theory, one that takes account of class and race, as well as gender, and that also recognizes both the collective and the personal dimensions of women's lives. Film is an excellent medium for confronting the fundamental contradiction in the nature of women's oppression: that it has its origin in social forces but is experienced one at a time, woman by women.

Salt of the Earth: The Old Left Confronts the Old Way

Salt of the Earth is a kind of morality play, with the concepts of Justice and Equality standing in for the canonical pieties and with a textbook Marxism standing in for biblical Christianity. This is not to say that the screenwriter, Michael Wilson (who, just prior to being blacklisted, won an Academy Award for the screenplay of *A Place in the Sun* and who, while still officially interdicted, wrote the screenplays for *The Bridge on the River Kwai* and *Lawrence of Arabia*), created a fiction to embody his Marxist ideology. Instead, reality collaborated with him both figuratively and literally, first by presenting him with an actual historical situation that fit the theory so neatly and then through engaging the active participation in the creation of the screenplay of the people whose story it is. Wilson's brother-in-law Paul Jarrico, another blacklist victim, who became the film's producer, was the first to recognize the cinematic possibilities in the story of the women's role on the New Mexico picket line and its consequences for the zinc miners' strike and for the community. Biberman and his associates, all black-listed, had recently formed an independent company (actually *called* Independent Production Corporation) and were searching for suitable projects. (Another way of telling that part of the story: a man gets out of prison and finds his home and his family are not as he left them and his old job isn't there at all, so he has to move fast to find work. You know that scenario from a hundred movies. Many of them are gangster films, but one of them is *The Grapes of Wrath*.)

Nonetheless, the story of the Mexican American miners and

their community—both as it happened and as it is represented on-screen—does correspond to the traditional Marxist view of "the woman question." Although I have been using the term *feminist* as a kind of shorthand, the issues we currently place under that rubric were long classified—some would say ossified—by left-wing parties as belonging officially to the woman question. (I own a little book issued by International Publishers in New York, a press affiliated with the Communist Party USA, called *The Woman Question: Selections from the Writings of Karl Marx, Frederick Engels, V. I. Lenin, Joseph Stalin.* My own response to what has too often meant the relegation of half the human race to "sectorial status" was to entitle my first chapbook of poems *Robinson on the Woman Question.* In it, I suggest that the real woman question is, "Women?" and the answer, of course, is yes.)[3]

At any rate, the ideology that I call "traditional Marxism" derives in part from the nineteenth-century theories of Marx and Engels, particularly the latter's *Origin of the Family, Private Property and the State,* and in part from the programs and practices of Western Communist Parties in the twentieth century. Both sources stress the connection between gender and class, but they do it differently. The theorists recognized that the essential organization of capitalism entailed property in and domination over women. Indeed, the only joke in the *Communist Manifesto* (admittedly a rather mild one) appears when Marx and Engels refute the bourgeois charge that the Communists believe in holding women in common. We believe in holding *property* in common, they explain, and the bourgeois takes it so much for granted that his own wife is property that he assumes we must believe in common property in women. "He has not even a suspicion," they go on, "that the real point . . . is to do away with the status of women as mere instruments of production."[4] In *Origin of the Family,* Engels elaborates on these remarks by using the anthropological insights of his day to explore the history of the notion of perceiving another person's sexual and reproductive capacity as a form of private property, connecting the dominance pattern within the family to the overall structure of society. Hence it simultaneously is and is not a metaphor when he asserts that, in the family, the husband "is the bourgeois [and] the wife represents the proletariat."[5]

Lise Vogel argues convincingly that

Marx's mature writings offer the rudiments of a theoretical foundation for analyzing the situation of women from the point of view of social reproduction. Marx himself did not, however, develop such an analysis nor did he leave significant notes on the subject. Subsequent attempts by late nineteenth-century socialists, including Engels, to use Marx's theory of social development to examine women's situation fell rather short of the mark. As the years passed, moreover, and the problem of women's oppression became codified in the form of the so-called woman question, the very possibility of taking the perspective suggested in Marx's mature work diminished.[6]

For its "take" on the woman question and its answer, therefore, classical Marxism relied on what Vogel calls the "defective formulation" of Engels.

In practice, twentieth-century movements with a basis in Marxist thought tended to make more mechanical connections between gender and class than Engels's language would suggest, situating their analyses and their actions strictly within the working class and the labor movement. Given that Marxist theory also maintains that the oppression of women originates in and is perpetuated by the sex division of labor and women's consequent isolation from social production, and given that the working class and its movement were perceived as the sole means for struggle against the system, the first step to women's liberation must be for women to become part of the workforce and join the labor movement.

As an only partially ironic extension of this analysis, organizing activity among the wives of workingmen—particularly in strike situations—became characteristic of American left-wing practice from the IWW in the Lawrence, Massachusetts, woolen mill strike of 1912 to the CIO's auto factory sit-down strikes of the 1930s. The strategy was twofold, as it is in *Salt of the Earth*. It made women part of the labor struggle, thereby, according to Engels, creating the conditions to alter the power arrangements within the family. More pragmatically, however, it often provided the means for that struggle to be carried on at all under adverse conditions.

In Lawrence, organizers were working within a theoretical tradition that perceived working-class housewives as a potential obstruction or reactionary element when men (and sometimes workingwomen) went on strike. As the ones responsible for maintaining the home and feeding the family, working-class housewives were often fearful of threats to regular income, whatever the potential long-term gains. So organizing women meant breaking down their isolation in the home (and, in the case of Lawrence, within one of nearly thirty different foreign-language groups), making the wives and mothers of workers feel and act like part of the working class. To tell the story this way is to adopt the organizers' point of view. Recent feminist interpretations of the women's role at Lawrence suggest that the overtly politicized organizing followed and was based on existing support networks within the women's community and culture. The innovative tactic characteristic of the Lawrence strike was the mass picket, and one aspect of its success was its engagement of the entire family.[7]

In Detroit in the late 1930s, during the effort to unionize the auto shops, factory occupations, the famous sit-down strikes, were the principal addition to labor's arsenal. (The first American sit-downs had been carried out by rubber workers in Akron, several years earlier, but their occupation of the plant was less comprehensive and less dramatic than later events in Detroit and did not actively involve women.) At the auto plants, because the male workers were sitting in, someone had to maintain the supply lines as well as the picket lines outside the plants, when neither could be "manned" by men. The recognition of a union's "ladies' auxiliary" as a militant and essential part of strike activity originated in the Detroit actions. The official histories of these events emphasize the women's contribution to the "larger" effort and sometimes mention the consequent changes in their own sense of themselves and their political role. But, although many of them also came from groups with a strong patriarchal tradition, little is said about the challenge that such activity on the part of women posed to male power within the working-class family.[8]

The zinc miners' wives in *Salt of the Earth* take over picket duty for pragmatic reasons similar to those that motivated the ladies' auxiliaries in Detroit. In this case, the Taft Hartley Act of 1947, which restricted union activity in a number of ways, made it easier for employers to obtain a court order—the injunction repeatedly referred to in the film—to criminalize picketing by union members. Because the law specifically regulates union activity, injunc-

tions can restrict behavior of union members only. Hence the necessity, in a historically all-male occupation like mining, for the
women to continue the actions that are vital to the strike's success.
In *Salt of the Earth,* the picket is needed in order to prevent strike-
breakers from coming in. Elsewhere, as in Barbara Kopple's 1977
documentary film *Harlan County, U.S.A.* or Denise Giardina's
1992 novel *The Unquiet Earth,* both about coal-mining communities, the pickets are there to prevent the transport of coal mined
by the scabs. And in all three cases, it is women who, because the
injunction specifies miners, take over the action. I pointed out in a
review of *The Unquiet Earth* that the representation of this moment when the women take collective action to replace men who
are prevented from acting has become almost a convention of
American working-class art. Tracing its origin as a narrative device
back to *Salt of the Earth,* I also added, "I may have seen [the im-
age] before, but it'll take a long time before I get tired of it."[9]

A role reversal, by definition, has two sides. Not only do the
women in *Salt of the Earth* become the active element in the miners' strike, but the men are left with the housework and child care,
the traditional women's work. Many of the men, as we see, resist
the initial proposal for women to take over the picket or even to
have a vote in whether they should. On top of this, the "indignity"
of housework—the very indignity with which the women have
lived all their lives—counts as an emasculating experience. Which
means that change for the men means opening themselves to a new
definition of masculinity. In this sense, the real reversal, at once
simple and complex, is Ramon's realization that the women's demand for running water was indeed a statement about working
conditions, even about occupational health and safety, that it too
was "real" politics, part of what, in the scene where the miners
look at the newspaper photo of the mining company president,
and echoing what he has heard by eavesdropping in the sheriff's
office, he calls "the larger picture."

This side of the gender reversal is also present in the ideology
that the filmmakers brought to the story of the miners' strike, but
it is there in a far more ambiguous fashion. From its foundation in
the 1920s, the Communist Party of the United States was at odds
with organized feminism over such issues as absolute equality
across gender lines versus specifically working-class concerns such

as protective labor legislation for women. In the Stalin era and particularly during World War II, the Party continued to stress the problems of working women, but also adopted a line about family democracy that was intended to strengthen rather than challenge the institution. It never embraced the ardently pronatalist stance of Stalin's Soviet Union, but, in the Popular Front years, followed Soviet models in constructing a "Mother's Bill of Rights," demanding "free birth-control clinics, day-care centers, maternal insurance, and an extensive program of social services to assist working mothers."[10] Nonetheless, although most American Communists personally believed in divorce, a degree of (hetero)sexual liberation, and women's right to contraception and abortion, none of these issues was interpreted as part of the "larger picture," the world of real politics. Yet it was within Communist Party circles in those years that the term *male chauvinism* was born and its practitioners were subject to political criticism. (No one I have interviewed recalls a case of anyone's being expelled from the Party for that offense, however, whereas, in the Party's struggles with issues of race and racism, trials over charges of "white chauvinism" became a frequent weapon in internal power struggles.)

On an anecdotal level, my inquiries into the division of labor in American households in the 1940s and 1950s suggest that the only men of that generation with able-bodied wives who routinely shared the housework were Communists. But in my earliest philosophy course, I learned a syllogism about how the statement that all poodles are dogs is very different from the assertion that all dogs are poodles. So, although almost all the men who did housework on an equal basis in that period were Communist (all poodles are dogs) that doesn't mean that all Communist men did housework (not all dogs are poodles) or that there were any political sanctions against those who maintained the traditional family roles.[11]

This ambiguity is reflected in *Salt of the Earth* through the ironic remarks of Ruth Barnes, the wife of the Anglo union official. He is vocal in support of the women's action, but she points out that never, as his job as an organizer has shifted him from one union local to another, has he taken the initiative to organize the women. And, although he knows what is supposed to be politically correct, he does not always apply it within his own home and family, either. Ruth is portrayed as more outspoken than the Mexican American women, not because she comes from outside their *macho* culture, but because she is a politically conscious activist married to a man who is supposed to be a comrade. In addition to offering a momentary glimpse of American left-wing experience in that period, the scene between the Barneses makes it possible for the filmmakers to critique the patriarchal attitudes and structures of Chicano culture without "othering" the experience of male chauvinism and saying, in effect, "*Those* people sure treat their women badly."

In fact, there is a certain effort—again consistent with the filmmakers' ideology—to stress that the most oppressive aspects of sexist domination within the Chicano family are not intrinsic to the miners' ethnic culture but come from the power structure of society. In Esperanza's most important speech, she encapsulates the leftist analysis of her time. The Anglo boss keeps Ramon down, but he has her to take out his frustrations on. She does not have anyone beneath her, nor does she want anyone to be. Rather, she says, she wants to rise and push everyone else—the family and the community—up with her. Whatever we may think of this notion of working-class men's "passing on the oppression" and of sexism as a force that is disturbing principally because it divides the working class, the speech is masterly, because it does two different and difficult things at the same time: it summarizes a political position that is a piece of theory made concrete, and it serves as a moving piece of individual characterization.

Generally speaking, however, there are limits on the extent to which we see Esperanza and Ramon as individuals, rather than as representatives of a collective body, for *Salt of the Earth* is first and foremost the narrative of a community and, within it, the story of a class and an ethnic group. This is another reason the film concentrates on certain issues, those that have the most evident collective dimension, while it all but ignores others, specifically those that appear most private. There is one brief reference, most of it in Spanish, to women's right to equality in the bedroom. And there is a momentary move on Ramon's part to enforce his domestic tyranny with domestic violence, to which Esperanza responds, "No. That's the old way." Neither of these points is elaborated, and none of the other issues high on the current American feminist agenda—an agenda that began, after all, with the declaration that the personal is political—has any place at all in the film. Esperanza might have said that those issues will come later; the blacklist victims might have questioned whether they belong in a serious political film at all.

Thelma & Louise: Good Ol' Boys and Postmodern Feminism

Well, such issues do have a place in Thelma & Louise, a movie they may or may not have considered a political film. It is a product of the same Hollywood establishment that barred Salt of the Earth's director, its screenwriter, most of its technicians, and its professional actors from the industry and that attempted to keep that film itself from existing. Thelma & Louise came into being at a time when a certain vision of feminism had penetrated the mainstream, but, because it came out with guns literally drawn, it managed to transgress the very norms to which its visual and narrative conventions pay allegiance.

If there is a theory underlying Thelma & Louise, it is not one that director Ridley Scott or first-time screenwriter Callie Khouri (who does at least identify as a feminist) consciously adheres to. The assumptions that I read in the film are those laid out in the early feminist theory of Juliet Mitchell. In her pioneering 1966 New Left Review article, "Women: The Longest Revolution" and in Women's Estate, the book-length expansion of that argument published in 1971, Mitchell applies the categories of Althusserian Marxism to the experience of women. The solution to understanding the female situation, she argues, "must lie in differentiating women's condition, much more radically than in the past, into its separate structures, which together form a complex—not a single—unity. . . . The key structures can be listed as . . . Production, Reproduction, Sex and Socialisation of Children. The concrete combination of these produces the 'complex unity' . . . but each separate structure may have reached a different 'moment' at any given historical time."[12]

Mitchell's position is that the structure most in flux, the "weak link" in the chain of oppressive experience, is the place where the new feminism will arise. And she concludes that "the major structure which at present is in rapid evolution is sexuality." Yet, while sexuality "may contain the greatest potential for liberation, [it] can equally well be organised against any increase of its human possibilities." Observing the capitalist system at the height of the sexual revolution, she remarks that "new forms of reification are emerging which may void sexual freedom of any meaning."[13]

Thelma & Louise, in which the narrative proceeds according to a tragic sense of perceived inevitability, is founded on the conviction that, at the present time, the only experience that could trigger such a series of events, with such perceived inevitability, the only experience that could place these women on the edge, is the experience of sexual violence, with its attendant questions about women as sexual objects and as sexual subjects. The postmodern universe in which the two women operate is the grotesque extension of the changes in capitalism—centering on emphasizing leisure and consumption over labor and production—that Mitchell describes as underlying the changes in contemporary sexual practices. Similarly, the commodified desire they encounter, with its permanent subtext of violence, may be read as one of the new forms of alienation Mitchell warns against.

Both *Salt of the Earth* and *Thelma & Louise* are about the changes that take place inside ordinary people who find themselves in the crucible of history. But "history" for the Mexican American mining community is the class struggle, whereas history for Thelma and Louise is a cacophony of mass cultural events and institutions that tell them meretricious and contradictory stories about their own sexuality and power. They may understand their fate as peculiarly—even uniquely—their own, yet every one of their actions is predicated on assumptions about the kind of world we live in and what it means for women.

Like *Salt of the Earth, Thelma & Louise* is about the limitations of class and gender identity and, beyond that, about the possibilities for change. Whereas *Salt of the Earth* is about both internal change and community change within a Southwestern landscape that remains static or moves slowly, *Thelma & Louise* is about internal change—within a hostile and fragmented culture that is not a community, a culture that has failed these women and all women—accomplished by means of idiosyncratic individual actions that take place on the move within a constantly changing southwestern landscape. The only static image of Thelma and

Louise is the photo they snap at the beginning of their odyssey, grinning, all wrapped up but ready to move, in a semiotic universe where movement invariably means freedom. It is this static image that appeared in the advertisements and posters for the film—a fallacious representation, even though, unlike many movie ads, it does show an actual moment from the film. I would suggest that this vacation snapshot is also the most working-class image of the two women that we get, precisely because it *is* such a static and posed vision of "enjoyment." The real point, after all, is that these women do not simply get away for a vacation. They get as far away as they can from the limits of their class and gender—which is not quite far enough to get them to freedom.

I referred earlier to the number and variety of arguments *Thelma & Louise* provoked in the mass audience. It is not my intention to repeat all these arguments (nor to disparage them—I think the widespread public debate may eventually prove to be the film's most important contribution). But one of the odder discussions I got into about the film helped focus my thinking about the way questions of class shape everything the film has to say about gender and sexual violence. It began when a couple of friends expostulated against the narrative's lack of realism. "But it's a fantasy!" I sputtered. They continued, nonetheless, "*Real* working-class women in that situation wouldn't get involved in this elaborate interstate chase. They'd go to Woolworth's and buy some hair dye and get jobs as waitresses until it all blew over." As a confirmed reader of detective fiction, I protested that homicide investigations never do blow over—there's no statute of limitations. But then I began wondering whether seeing Thelma and Louise as *waitresses* on the run might add something to the interpretation.

Of course, only Louise actually works as a waitress. Thelma is a childless housewife whose husband is in retail management and whose suburban home is chock-full of appliances. But historian Dorothy Cobble calls waitressing "the quintessential female job," and goes on to cite New York performance artist Jerri Allyn, many of whose pieces about food, money, and work express her position that "waitressing is not just a job but a metaphor."[14] Similarly, in Los Angeles, a militant group of women artists who do guerrilla theater to focus attention on the status of women in the art world as reflective of the society as a whole call themselves the Waitresses and use images from that job in their actions. From this perspective, the case could certainly be made for Thelma's marriage as an extension of the waitress role, with husband Daryl as customer, expecting meals, housekeeping, and sex to be served up to his order, and irritably chiding the server for what he is quick to label stupidity or ineptitude in a conceptual system that sees "dumb waitress" as a redundancy. But we know that Louise herself is a *smart* waitress, as is the one who works at the roadhouse where the murder takes place. Even the policeman, who knows her, pays attention to that waitress's judgment of the victim, the crime, and the two women on the run, because hers is a job that requires her to pay attention to people, to learn to read them.

It is also a job that entails a certain sexual subordination—on the level of harassment and innuendo, at any rate—along with the serving of food and drink. Indeed, as Dorothy Cobble points out:

> The waitress plays multiple parts, each reflecting a female role. To fulfill the emotional and fantasy needs of the male customers, she quickly learns the all-too-common scripts: scolding wife, doting mother, sexy mistress, or sweet, admiring daughter. Other customers, typically female, demand obsequious and excessive service—to compensate, perhaps, for the status denied them in other encounters. For once, they are not the servers but the ones being served.[15]

Since the waitress is not even guaranteed the minimum wage and her meager salary is expected to be supplemented by tips, which may be generous or stingy, offered or denied, according to the whim of the customer, dealing with the waitress is one of the few transactions in workingpeople's lives where, materially as well as structurally, *they* are, however briefly, the bosses, which means that the waitress, in her turn, has dozens of bosses a day.

Although arguing that "more than food is being consumed at the restaurant site" and that waitresses, therefore, "are responding to hungers of many kinds," Cobble adds that the job of the waitress is also prototypical of the new service work force.[16] So the most familiar of female working-class jobs becomes a postmodern locus at the crossroads of labor, desire, and power. As the other waitresses in the film provide an attenuated chorus to the tragedy of *Thelma & Louise,* serving as the only remnant of community outside their own dyadic relationship, it is worthwhile to keep in mind that definition of the contemporary waitressing site.

Much has been made of the change that occurs in Thelma as the airhead acquires competence and eventually takes charge of the adventure. Louise, by contrast, is almost always competent—as the roadhouse waitress says, "She's the one with the neat hair" (waitress hair, of course)—although her desperation sometimes restricts her ability to act on or even to think ahead and formulate plans. So the real turnaround is in Thelma's character, and because we have been schooled to perceive women in "either/or" dualisms, this growth is often understood as a role reversal, as Thelma's "turning into," *becoming,* Louise. Sometimes it is even suggested that the two women exchange personalities, so that Louise also "becomes" Thelma.

I think what actually happens is that, as Thelma sheds her bimbo persona, she acquires that of J.D., the young man she spends the night with and whose subsequent theft of the women's money leads to the next phase in their experiences on the lam. J.D. is just what those initials used to signify in American slang, a juvenile delinquent, a young parole violator whose creed—"I have always believed that armed robbery does not have to be a totally unpleasant experience"—is one of the film's funniest lines. It is he who teaches Thelma how to rob a convenience store with grace, and, of course, he who makes it necessary to put his lessons into practice, although here is where my friends of the Woolworth's hair-dye scenario part company with the film's actual narrative. At any rate, Thelma, although visibly nervous, not only follows instructions in her first robbery, but improvises according to the situation she encounters. The fact that we get to watch her performance on the store security camera's videotape, along with her husband and a group of cops, makes us more conscious of it *as* a performance, the carrying out of a lesson that we have also witnessed and the adoption of the style of a model whom we have already met, although the husband and the cops have yet to do so.

Once she has successfully accomplished the robbery, we now see Thelma again through what passes for our own eyes, on the large screen and in full color, instead of on the smaller black-and-white videotape (whose existence she is, of course, unaware of) that is the concrete correlative of the male gaze. In the "real" movie, Thelma takes on a different body language and way of dressing after the robbery, as well as a different attitude toward the obstacles she and Louise face and the male sex in general. Her movements (and almost her body itself) become more streamlined, more controlled and inner-directed. She is not only boyish, she is like the particular boy who showed her how—and who, ironically enough, in giving her what Louise calls the first "proper lay" of her life, would conventionally be supposed to have "made her a woman." I suppose only we English professors in the movie theater thought of Yeats's "Leda and the Swan" at that point and asked, "Did she put on his knowledge with his power . . . ?" But the message gets across, anyway.

She does, in fact, put on J.D.'s power with his knowledge, a power that has very real limitations. J.D. is the rebellious working-class boy, defiant even in police custody, having broken parole and with an unexplained $6,700 in his jeans. He sexually baits both the cops who interrogate him and the husband of the woman he's screwed and robbed. His power, in fact, is a kind of insouciant cockiness (this pun is unavoidable, I'm afraid). And Thelma imitates it just right. But J.D.'s power, as we see from the scene where he's under the thumb of the police, is severely limited. In the long run, what he has is an abundance of *attitude,* not power at all. The only person who has less real power than the smart-mouthed working-class boy is, in fact, almost any working-class girl or woman. Despite J.D.'s defiance, once he's in police custody, he is feminized. His body, which is all the proletarian male has to impose against the conditions of his life, is entirely inadequate in the face of the armed power of the state; Thelma's female body would never have assumed the status of a weapon in the first place. If there is a role reversal here that at all parallels the one in *Salt of the Earth,* it is in this far more restricted and pathetic exchange.

Nonetheless, compared with her options as a woman, particularly the kind of woman she had previously been, Thelma really is empowered by the J.D. persona, which she perfects as she travels through a literal and moral landscape well beyond J.D.'s scope, taking charge in the interaction with the state trooper and assuming the lead in the scene with the oil-truck driver. But it is not enough. The two outlaw women cannot be allowed to make it to the Mexican border. (The same border over which actress Rosaura Revueltas, who plays Esperanza in *Salt of the Earth,* was deported in the middle of filming.) They cannot be allowed to make it over the border, yet their capture would be mythically intolerable. The freeze-frame of the moment when, after kissing one another, they fly into the Grand Canyon is a triumph on the level of myth, but it doesn't take a whole lot of imagination to picture the broken bodies and burning convertible that director Scott refrains from showing us, because we've seen *that* in the movies, too. For the moment of the freeze-frame, I thought of another defiant boy—a boy named Icarus, who flew too close to the sun.

Despite all the images of solidarity in *Salt of the Earth,* there is nothing in that film to match the final moment of bonding between Thelma and Louise, just as there is nothing in *Thelma & Louise* to lay beside the sense of community struggle with an ethnic and class basis that marks *Salt of the Earth.* Indeed, the American Southwest, a region with large Hispanic and Native American populations, is seen in *Thelma & Louise* to contain no Hispanics or Native Americans; it is an arid expanse in which, from time to time, representatives of white male supremacy are confronted. The sole person of color we see in that landscape is the West Indian on a bicycle who incongruously turns up in the New Mexico desert to share second-hand marijuana smoke with the state trooper Thelma and Louise have locked in the trunk of his own car. It is a very funny moment, but his unique presence underlines the absence of any awareness that it *matters* that Thelma and Louise are on the run through a part of the country where much of the population resembles Esperanza. What it matters *for* is how we are to connect the sexual insights of *Thelma & Louise* with the insights about work, community, and race in *Salt of the Earth,* and what each of them and both together can suggest about the future of the family.

Each film gives us clues about what we need, through what is missing as well as through what is there. But neither film gives us the whole thing. Affording this absence its most generous reading, this is because that whole is not something to be given to us, but something we take. What is remarkable is that a fictional representation should turn out to be one of the places we can look for truths about how to proceed to make sense out of women's stories and, out of making sense, to make change.

Notes

Many thanks to Thom Andersen, Electa Arenal, Constance Coiner, Douglas Michael Massing, Heng Gun Ngo, Greg Robinson, Michael Roth, and Alan Wald for their respective shares in helping to make this essay happen. The original version of this essay was presented at the conference "Self, Gender and Society" co-sponsored by the Center for Feminist Studies and the Center for European Studies at the University of Bergen, Norway. When I accepted the gracious invitation to participate in that conference, I submitted the title "Out of the Copper Mines, into the Canyon." Then, as soon as I began work on my paper, I was reminded that the workers in *Salt of the Earth* are zinc miners, not copper miners. It is the sort of thing that someone professing to care about working people ought not to get wrong, so I have sacrificed alliteration and scansion to fact.

1. By contrast, nowadays a commercial film may be booked into nine hundred to two thousand screens in its first weekend in release. Although, in response to a number of social and market changes, the conditions under which films are distributed and shown have changed since 1953, the discrepancy remains striking.

2. Dan Georgakas, "Union Sponsored Radical Films," in *Encyclopedia of the American Left,* ed. Mari Jo Buhle, Paul Buhle, and Dan Georgakas (New York: Garland, 1990), 799.

3. *The Woman Question: Selections from the Writings of Karl Marx, Frederick Engels, V. I. Lenin, Joseph Stalin* (New York: International Publishers, 1951); Lillian S. Robinson, *Robinson on the Woman Question* (Buffalo, N.Y.: Earth's Daughters, 1975).

4. Karl Marx and Frederick Engels, *Manifesto of the Communist Party,* (1847), in Karl Marx and Frederick Engels, *Selected Works,* vol. 1 (Moscow: Progress, 1969), 124.

5. Frederick Engels, *The Origin of the Family, Private Property and the State* (Moscow: Foreign Languages Publishing House, n.d.), 121.

6. Lise Vogel, *Marxism and the Oppression of Women: Toward a Unitary Theory* (New Brunswick, N.J.: Rutgers University Press, 1983), 72.

7. Primary sources on the Lawrence textile strike may be found in "Bread and Roses: The 1912 Lawrence Textile Strike," in *Rebel Voices: An I.W.W. Anthology,* ed. Joyce L. Kornbluh (Ann Arbor: University of Michigan Press, 1968), 158–96. Secondary sources include Bill Cahn, *Milltown* (New York: Cameron & Kahn, 1954); Donald B. Cole, *Immigrant City: Lawrence, Massachusetts, 1845–1921* (Chapel Hill: University of North Carolina Press, 1963); and Samuel Yellin, *American Labor Struggles* (New York: Harcourt, Brace, 1936). For a feminist revision of the narrative of women's activity, see Ardis Cameron, "Bread

and Roses Revisited: Women's Culture and Working-Class Activism in the Lawrence Strike of 1912," in *Women, Work and Protest: A Century of U.S. Women's Labor History,* ed. Ruth Milkman (London: Routledge & Kegan Paul, 1985), 42–61.

8. Firsthand accounts of the Detroit sit-down strikes may be found in Jeremy Brecher, Henry Kraus, and Kermit Johnson, "Sit Down," in *American Labor Radicalism: Testimonies and Interpretations,* ed. Staughton Lynd (New York: John Wiley, 1973), 49–74. A good historical account is found in Sidney Fine, *Sit-Down: The General Motors Strike of 1936–37* (Ann Arbor: University of Michigan Press, 1969). For the role of the ladies' auxiliaries in the auto strikes of the 1930s, see also Loraine Weir's documentary film, *With Babies and Banners* (1978).

9. Barbara Kopple, *Harlan County, U.S.A.* (1977); Denise Giardina, *The Unquiet Earth* (New York: W. W. Norton, 1992) and *Storming Heaven* (New York: W. W. Norton, 1988). The review cited is Lillian S. Robinson, "Coal Miners' Daughter," *The Nation,* December 28, 1992, 816–18.

10. Mari Jo Buhle, "National Women's Commission, CPUSA," in *Encyclopedia of the American Left,* ed. Mari Jo Buhle, Paul Buhle, and Dan Georgakas (New York: Garland, 1990), 511.

11. For primary sources on the Communist Party USA and the woman question, see the Party's journals, *The Working Woman,* published from 1929 to 1935, and *Woman Today,* which appeared from 1936 to 1937. Although there is no Party periodical addressed to women after this date, the works cited below indicate that women's issues continued to be discussed in Communist publications and in books put out by publishers connected with or close to the Party. See Ella Reeve Bloor, *We Are Many* (New York: International Publishers, 1940); Grace Hutchins, *Women Who Work* (New York: International Publishers, 1934); Mary Inman, *In Women's Defense* (Los Angeles: Committee to Organize the Advancement of Women, 1940); Betty Millard, "Women against Myth," *New Masses,* December 30, 1947, 7–10, and January 6, 1948, 7–10; Rebecca Pitts, "Women and Communism," *New Masses,* February 19, 1935. The books by Hutchins and Inman are excerpted and the Pitts article is reprinted in *Writing Red: An Anthology of American Women Writers, 1930–1940,* ed. Charlotte Nekola and Paula Rabinowitz (New York: Feminist Press, 1978).

Recent autobiographical, biographical, historical, and critical commentary includes Rosalyn Fraad Baxandall, *Words on Fire: The Life and Writings of Elizabeth Gurley Flynn* (New Brunswick, N.J.: Rutgers University Press, 1987); Constance Coiner, *Better Red: The Writing and Resistance of Tillie Olsen and Meridel LeSueur* (New York: Oxford University Press, 1994); Peggy Dennis, *Autobiography of an American Communist* (Westport, Conn.: Lawrence Hill, 1977). See also Ellen Kay Trimberger's commentary, "Women in the Old and New Left: The Foundation of a Politics of Personal Life," *Feminist Studies* 5 (1979): 432–50, and Dennis's response, 451–61; Elsa Jane Dixler, "The Woman Question: Women and the American Communist Party 1929–1941," doctoral dissertation, Yale University, 1974; Vivian Gornick, *The Romance of American Communism* (New

York: Basic Books, 1977); Dorothy Healy and Maurice Isserman, *California Red* (Urbana: University of Illinois Press, 1977); Robert Shaffer, "Woman and the Communist Party USA 1930–1940," *Socialist Review,* 5–6 (1979): 73–118; Sharon Hartman Strom, "Challenging 'Women's Place': Feminism, the Left and Industrial Unionism in the 1930s," *Feminist Studies* 9 (1983): 359–86. For some fictional glimpses of family and sexual life in Party circles, see K. B. Gilden, *Between the Hills and the Sea* (Garden City, N.Y.: Doubleday, 1971); Dorothy Doyle, *Journey through Jess* (Santa Fe, N.M.: Ten Star, 1989).

12. Juliet Mitchell, "Women: The Longest Revolution" (1966), in *Women: The Longest Revolution* (New York: Pantheon-Random House, 1984), 26; . see also Mitchell's *Women's Estate* (New York: Pantheon-Random House, 1971).

13. Mitchell, "Women," 48–49.

14. Dorothy Sue Cobble, *Dishing It Out: Waitresses and Their Unions in the Twentieth Century* (Urbana: University of Illinois Press, 1991), 2. Ironically, in the same year that *Thelma & Louise* and Cobble's study appeared, another book with the same title was also published, this one a participant-observer's anthropological study of a New Jersey diner. See Greta Foff Paules, *Dishing It Out: Power and Resistance among Waitresses in a New Jersey Restaurant* (Philadelphia: Temple University Press, 1991).

15. Cobble, *Dishing It Out,* 2.

16. Ibid.

Chapter 9

For a Working-Class Television: The Miners' Campaign Tape Project

David E. James

In one of the first working-class novels in English, Robert Tressell describes a protocinematic event that heralded a genuinely proletarian cinema as vividly as the fandango dancer in *L'Éve Future* portended the commodity industry that in fact took its place. The Christmas party in *The Ragged-Trousered Philanthropists* ([1914] 1955) includes "Bert White's World-famed Pandorama," a candle-lit miniature cardboard stage with rollers that shows "pictures cut out of illustrated weekly papers and pasted together, end-to-end, so as to form a long strip." Bert, an apprentice house painter, uses the toy theater to take his audience on a tour of European cities: to one where "mounted police with drawn swords were dispersing a crowd: several men had been ridden down and were being trampled under the hoofs of horses"; to another where they arrive "just in time to see a procession of unemployed workmen being charged by the military police"; and, back in "Merry Hingland," to scenes of domestic starvation, homelessness, and a procession of "2,000 able-bodied men who are not allowed to work" (324–27). Though the workers' cinema that Bert's Pandorama anticipates never came into being in England, something like it did in the age of television. A century later, working-class people used a similarly rudimentary apparatus and a similarly amateur mode of production to show virtually the same images of popular mobilization against unemployment, impoverishment, and police rioting. This time the medium was video, and the works they produced were collectively titled *The Miners' Campaign Tapes,* their own newsreels about their own strike.

The Miners' Strike of 1984–85—the "longest epic of collective resistance in the annals of British labour" (Anderson 1992, 179)—caused violent divisions within the working class and in British society generally.[1] But it also occasioned a remarkable mobilization of popular suport for labor that, cutting across the lines of class and those of the identities that have displaced class in recent political discourse, was experienced and expressed specifically in class terms. The Miners' Campaign Tape Project was only one of the many cultural initiatives that helped to sustain the strike; working-class people made films, videotapes, still photographs, plays, and songs, presenting them at formal and informal meetings at union branches, trades councils, and community groups, and especially at fund-raisers organized by the hundreds of miners' support groups that sprang up all over the country.[2] But the complicated class stucture of contemporary Britain and the shifting and porous boundaries between the propaganda resources of the state and the miners' own media preempt any simple understanding or celebration of the Miners' Campaign tapes themselves as the spontaneous self-expression of an autonomous working-class culture. Rather, in the specific conjuncture in which they were produced, the binary social divisions of early capitalism had become extensively diffused by the class fractions and cross-class alliances present in both postwar Labourism and postmodern Thatcherism, as well as by similarly complex developments in British culture and the communication industries.[3] Heir as they were to the early Soviet agitprop cinemas and the Film and Photo Leagues of the 1930s, the Miners' Campaign tapes were produced and shaped by quite different political circumstances.

A hermeneutics adequate to these circumstances must have a historical and a theoretical component. The first entails the reconstruction in class terms of both the social developments that erupted as the strike and the developments in British moving-image culture of the same period—the events that intersected to produce the Miners' Campaign tapes. The second requires an understanding of culture as itself the praxis of social life, not merely its representation or reflection. Culture collaborates not only with contemplation, but with human sensuous activity, and interpretation of it must move beyond the aesthetic object or product. Description of a text's formal properties or transcodings from its surface to some deeper meanings must take place within the framework of a materialist analysis of the function of the cultural activity in the other forms of social and political practice with which it is inevitably integrated.

In the case of the miners' tapes, the essential terms of both the historical and the theoretical projects may be illustrated by Deleuze and Guattari's figure of the rhizome (1987), which they use to distinguish between the centralized, hierarchical qualities of *arborescent* or treelike structures and the characteristics of the laterally growing *root:* connection *and* heterogeneity, multiplicity *and* asignifying rupture. These qualities of the rhizome, proposed here as defining what is culturally *radical,* inform (1) the politics of the strike itself, (2) the moving-image culture it generated, and (3) the nature of the relationship between these.

1. The strike was a populist, syndicalist response to a deliberate and premeditated attack on the working class, its institutions, and the role it had secured in state power. Determined to roll back welfare-state, consensus socialism, the Thatcher government manipulated the state's combined repressive and ideological apparatuses so as to make it impossible for the miners not to strike, and then misrepresented the strike as an authoritarian act by the National Union of Mineworkers (NUM), hierarchically, centrally, and dictatorially structured, against the interests of its own members and of the country as a whole—propaganda that, in fact, characterized not the strike but the Thatcherite state itself.

2. In the previous decade and a half, avant-garde and leftist film and video workers in Britain had created a network of democratic, decentralized, cooperatively organized film and video workshops that had varying degrees of support from a number of public bodies but were nevertheless committed to and at least partially integrated in working-class communities. When the strike came, these were immediately mobilized on the miners' behalf.

3. The relationship of the Miners' Campaign tapes to the strike was not simply to contest state propaganda by providing a "truthful," nonideological representation of it, as if from an ontologically separate level; rather, the tapes were an active intervention in

the world, designed to participate in and promote the strike, to be its cultural praxis—in Deleuze and Guattari's terms, an "aparallel evolution" of it (11). Consequently, their formal properties must be approached through functionalist rather than formal or mimetic principles. As *campaign tapes,* that is, as an instance of a specific genre of trade union agitational activity (Spence 1988, 2), their work is not reducible to the concept of representation, the foundational heuristic of bourgeois media theory.

The Miners' Strike

In the British postwar compromise among state, capital, and labor, coal was nationalized along with other major industries, and the National Coal Board (NCB) formed on 1 January 1947. Rather than working for structural social reorganization or the redistribution of wealth, Labourism generally accepted this settlement, but, with the end of the postwar boom, industrial action increasingly challenged it. Harold Wilson's attacks on union power contributed to the Conservative electoral victory in 1970, but then strikes by the miners in 1972 and 1974 for higher wages—the latter in response to attempts to impose a statutory pay norm—brought down the Heath administration with what Perry Anderson (1992) has called "the most spectacular single victory of labour over capital since the beginnings of working-class organization in Britain. . . . the only time in modern European history that an economic strike has precipitated the political collapse of a government" (176).

The new Labour administration headed by James Callahan attempted to renew the social contract, but its "Plan for Coal," proposing new investment and increased production, was forestalled by the series of strikes in winter 1978 that followed the Trades Union Congress's (TUC) rejection of pay norms. Thus, the third government in a row fell to the unions, and Margaret Thatcher became prime minister in 1979. Blaming the consensus and particularly the unions for the decline of Britain, Thatcher committed her administration to a market economy, to dismantling the public sector and privatizing the industrial base rather than investing in it, and to the financial deregulation that allowed the City to grow into an international center for finance capital, dealing especially in the offshore Eurodollar market. For coal, Thatcherism meant the industry's reconstitution in terms of the profitability of each pit rather than in terms of the role of the industry in British society as a whole, increased reliance on oil and nuclear power, and the eventual privatization of energy. Huge cutbacks had already transformed the coal industry since nationalization: the 980 pits employing 700,000 miners in 1947 had by 1970 been reduced to 292 pits employing 297,000 miners (Adeny and Lloyd 1986, 14). But the miners, who formed the strongest and most militant of the unions, still posed an inevitable problem, particularly given the election of Arthur Scargill to the NUM presidency in 1982. A member of the Young Communist League when an active miner, Scargill had since then consistently understood politics as class conflict and looked to class struggle as the road to a fully socialist society with a state-controlled economy; in the opinion of a July 1975 *New Left Review* editorial, he showed "an intransigent pursuit of proletarian class interests that has not been seen for many decades" (Scargill 1975, 11).

The Conservative Party's plans for restructuring Britain's energy policy, and specifically for dealing with the energy unions, had been leaked in 1978 in the Ridley Report, an internal party report prepared earlier in the decade. Because the "most likely battleground" was expected to be the coal industry, coal stocks were to be built up, especially in the power stations; contingency plans for the import of coal were made; the recruitment of nonunion lorry drivers by haulage companies was encouraged; and power stations were to be converted to oil. Opposition from miners was still strong enough in 1981 to cause the NCB to retreat on a pit closure plan, but in 1984 Thatcher appointed as chairman of the NCB Ian McGregor, a known union buster who as chairman of British Steel had halved the number of jobs in that industry after the steelworkers' strike in 1979. In March 1984 the board announced a production cut of four million metric tons, the loss of twenty thousand jobs, and the closure of Cortonwood Colliery in Yorkshire. Breaking industry protocol and commitments to a further five years of life at Cortonwood (on the strength of which men from other pits had recently been transferred there and more than £1 million invested), this was a deliberate provocation and, as in Paris in 1848, the proletariat was forced into insurrection. On 3 March, the

Yorkshire area council voted to strike, and three days later, even though all the advantages were held by the government, the national executive committee of the NUM approved.

Having been reorganized as the instrument of free market capitalism under the direct control of the government, the NCB was now to be used as the agent of the government's offensive in what was clearly a deliberate attempt to destroy the NUM and the union movement generally. It found itself confronted by a militant populism, informed by a vision of coal and its mining as a national resource, and determined to defend that resource and the social life it sustained. In previous strikes the miners had been fighting for higher wages; this time they were fighting to safeguard their jobs, the pits themselves, and the village communities that depended entirely on them. Against them, all prepared in advance, were the entire resources of the state: the judiciary, which was used to sequester NUM funds and withhold almost all social security payments to the families of striking miners, to harass striking miners with restrictive bail conditions that jailed them for persistent picketing, and to restrain secondary action by other unions; the police—a massive nationally centralized paramilitary police force, costing half a million pounds per day, routinely mobilizing eight thousand men at any time, with riot gear, horses, dogs, and road blocks—which was used to prevent the free movement of pickets and to intimidate the strikers and their families; and the press, which was used to demonize Scargill as the sole cause of the strike, to misrepresent the strike's progress and especially the police violence in order to sway public opinion against the miners, and to demoralize the miners themselves with false accounts of returns to work.[4] Against all of these, including the media offensive, the miners had resources of their own.

Alternative Cinema in Britain and the Workshop Movement

Recent scholarship has discovered a substantial history of alternative cinemas in Britain, many of which were explicitly as well as implicitly political.[5] Their postwar renewal, however, followed the U.S. independent cinemas of the 1960s, and specifically the New York Filmmakers' Cooperative, with the major difference being that the London Film Co-op (1967) was organized as an egalitarian, work-sharing collective, designed for production as well as distribution. As in the next decade the "structural materialism" of the inaugural moment gave way before feminist, gay, and eventually black initiatives, so a new regionalism challenged the metropolitanized institutions of British culture. Amber Films, to take a primary example of the new co-ops that were founded, was begun by a group of film and photography students in London in 1968, who moved a year later to Tyneside in anticipation that their desire to work collectively on films about the lives of working-class people would be facilitated by the area's strong industrial base and history of community organization. Aided by grants from the British Film Institute (BFI) and the Regional Arts Associations (RAAs), similar groups developed in Cardiff, Sheffield, Edinburgh, and other cities across the country, groups that were thoroughly versed in the post-1968 debates about the politics of representation and the social organization of filmmaking units. Consequently, they were typically committed to an integrated practice of production, exhibition, and distribution, to a collective or cooperative internal organization, and to developing a working base outside the commercial industry.

Though organized into the Independent Film-makers Association (IFA) in 1974, these groups and the dissemination of their politics in film culture were still debilitatingly marginal. Actual alignment with the working class demanded that these artists enter into both its alienation and the institutions that counter it; they had to become unionized workers in the film industry. But because filmmakers in the independent sector were not waged, they were not eligible to join the filmmakers' union, the Association of Cinematograph, Television and Allied Technicians (ACTT). The logical impulse toward unionization was further spurred by several historical factors, including the fall of the Labour government in 1979, which ended hopes for a state-funded network of wage-paying regional workshops; the deepening recession, which, although it did not affect the film industry directly (in fact the industry was one of the few in Britain that expanded throughout the 1970s and into the first half of the 1980s), nevertheless eroded the outside employment opportunities that had previously sustained independent filmmakers; and Amber Films' precedent-setting success in joining ACTT as a self-contained "shop."

After several years of discussions among BFI, IFA, and ACTT, several people active in ACTT convinced the union to establish a special category that would facilitate independent small-scale production and at the same time bring into the union people who were working independently outside it. The catalyst that allowed the unionization of the independents was another state initiative, Channel Four, the new television channel mandated "to encourage innovation and experimentation" (cited in Petley 1989, 8) and to buy its programming from outside.[6] After negotiations with ACTT, the RAAs, BFI, and IFA, Channel Four agreed to fund selected workshops as franchises in an ongoing way rather than simply to commission specific programs.

In the Workshop Declaration of 1982, ACTT agreed to approve properly funded and staffed noncommercial and grant-aided film and tape work if made by a "workshop"—that is, a nonprofit organization of at least four members with equal participation in control of the undertakings and receiving equal and fixed remuneration. As well as producing programs of a predominantly "cultural" character, workshops were expected to be involved with archiving, education, distribution, and generally furthering film culture in their regions. In cooperation with other funding agencies such as BFI and the RAAs, Channel Four was to contribute to the support of the workshops by paying fixed revenues, totaling 1 percent of its annual budget. At the height of the movement in 1988, there were twenty-five fully franchised workshops in the United Kingdom, of which sixteen were receiving varying levels of funding from Channel Four.

Of ACTT's twenty-seven thousand members, only four to five hundred were from franchised workshops and other grant-aided units, but their aggressive, articulate politics brought new class tensions into the union. The older, highly skilled and well-paid technical and trades membership (including the ITV crews that would cover the strike) were by and large of working-class origin, but had a narrowly defined sense of trade unionism and little wider political awareness; on the other hand, the general secretary and leading officials overwhelmingly supported the miners, as did the highly educated, articulate, and politically sophisticated workshop members, themselves mostly of middle-class origin. During the strike, these differences in class origins and sympathies caused arguments at General Council meetings: on the one hand, complaints about the way the strike was being represented in the mass media or, in the case of mass media crew members, about having themselves been verbally and physically attacked by miners; and on the other, proposals for formal and informal methods of supporting the strike, which eventually included large and regular donations of money to the strike fund.

These differences were compounded by regional issues. The London Film Division of ACTT (which comprised workers in the old feature film industry and freelancers) was subdivided into departments according to trade specialization (camera people, producer/directors, editors, and so on) but created a special Grant-Aid Department, lumping all the workshop people together. Concurrently, the growth of regional freelance production led in 1984 to the creation of a Regional Division in ACTT, which, however, was subdivided only regionally (East Midland shop, North-East shop, and so on), with no distinctions made between film and television, between trades, or between commercial and grant-aided production, so that in the regions workshops were fully integrated into the industry.

By the time the strike began, then, a nationwide network of young film and video workers committed to working-class and feminist politics was in place. These workers had strong regional identification and established local constituencies and were experienced in working for and with working-class people. They were organized into democratic, participatory collectives, virtually autonomous but nevertheless funded by state and local institutions, backed by another network of co-ops already engaged in community outreach and with equipment available for individuals and groups in one-off projects. Having their own distribution apparatus and access to national television, they possessed a guerrilla mobility through all points in a media system that, although ultimately dominated by state and corporate broadcasting, was nevertheless multiple, diffuse, and capable of many different organizational forms. The working-class' self-mobilization allowed these powers to be fully realized.

Voice and Space in the Miners' Campaign Tape Project

At the beginning of the strike, two members of a London workshop (Platform Films), Chris Reeves and Lin Solomon, organized a meeting in London of ACTT members, including Stuart McKinnon from a Gateshead workshop (Trade Films) and representatives from several other workshops across the country, to discuss ways in which they, as film and video workers, could help the miners.[7] They agreed to a project of two parts. First, they would produce ten single-issue, five- to six-minute tapes on topics that included redundancy, pit closures, solidarity with other unions, the police, the contributions of miners' wives and other women, and media coverage of the strike. Second, they would make a longer, thirty- to forty-minute, agitational tape, provisionally titled *The Miners of '84—Together We Can Win*, which would supplement the shorter tapes, arguing the miners' case with a voice-over review of the general national and political background. Project members in the various regional workshops were to tape events in their own areas and send the material for editing to Platform, with distribution by Platform and Trade. All involved contributed their labor free of charge, and a fund-raising appeal for editing expenses netted contributions from individuals and £1,000 from ACTT and £500 from the National Union of Journalists (NUJ). In both organization and function, the Miners' Campaign Tape Project recalls Dziga Vertov's "network of cameramen in the provinces" sending material to the "experimental film station" where the Kinopravda, "a periodical of events summarized into an agitational unit," was edited (Vertov 1984, 22).

In the end, only tapes in the shorter format were actually made. These were assembled in pairs:

Tape A: 1. *Not Just Tea and Sandwiches (Miners' Wives Speak Out)*
          2. *The Coal Board's Butchery (No Pit Is Safe)*
Tape B: 3. *Solidarity (Trade Unions Support the Miners)*
          4. *Straight Speaking (The Strike and the Industry)*
Tape C: 5. *The Lie Machine (Media Coverage of the Strike)*
          6. *Only Doing Their Job (The Police, the Law and the Miners)*

Endorsed by the NUM, between four and five thousand copies of these were distributed in Britain, with others, often appropriately dubbed, sent to sympathetic groups throughout Europe and in Japan, the United States, and Australia. The tapes were free to the miners and the miners' wives' support groups, and otherwise were rented or sold for modest fees on a sliding scale, with profits returned for further production or donated to the miners' Hardship Fund.

The tapes are of two kinds. *Straight Speaking* and *The Lie Machine* are replies to the misrepresentation of the strike by the NCB and the mass media. The other four are essentially collages, similarly structured and organized around specific themes, in which miners and women from the mining communities speak, with cutaways illustrating some of their points. *Not Just Tea and Sandwiches* is concerned with the role of women in the strike, and *The Coal Board's Butchery* with the long-term destruction of the industry. *Solidarity* covers other unions' support for the strike; *Only Doing Their Job* addresses the police offensive. *Not Just Tea and Sandwiches,* for example, begins with a woman describing the origin of her support group and the work it has done; it moves to women in a different region, who describe the extreme poverty in their communities and point out that the "miners are being starved back to work via their children"; another group of women describe the communal meals they are making for their village; the tape returns to the second group, whose members condemn scab miners; a new group of women talk about media manipulation of images of women to undercut previous strikes and affirm their absolute commitment to this one; another new group of women describe joining the men on the picket lines; in a conference speech, Scargill pays tribute to the women's role in the strike; the women in the first group continue the issue of picketing and bring up police violence; another group of women talk about police harassment; and finally, over footage of massed police, simple graphics encourage further support groups.[8]

Though the tapes are framed by short pieces of popular music and rudimentary graphics, and some include historical footage of previous strikes, they appear to be essentially a means of enabling the miners to speak for themselves spontaneously and informally. This more or less complete preoccupation with speech is their most salient, and also their most problematic feature. On the one hand, it invests the tapes with the traditional orality of popular culture and the vivacity of miners' language in particular (speech being the

Figure 9.1. The voice of the working class: the Miners' Campaign tapes. Tape 1, *Not Just Tea and Sandwiches*.

Kaye Sutcliffe
Aylesham
Miners Wives Support Group

Mary Young
Yorkshire

chief art available to the working class in the form of practice), and it supplies the dominant imagery and compositional unit—the brief head shot of working-class people talking. On the other, it opens them to charges of naive and artless realism. Their lack of formal or technical complexity encourages their denigration as "a 'degree zero' documentary form,"[9] while their dependence on talking heads, their implication of unmediated presence, and their similarity to the format of television news all seem to disregard the problematization of representation that had occurred in their immediately prior historical context, the documentary legacy of Straub-Huillet, structural materialism's critique of filmic illusionism, and the "Brechtian" mode of documentaries such as *The Nightcleaners* (Berwick Street Film Collective, 1975). Both objections—that of formal primitiveness and that of uncritical realism and logocentrism—reflect bourgeois political and aesthetic priorities. Ignoring the exigencies of a political crisis in a way that a pragmatic understanding of popular culture cannot afford to do, they ignore historical determination generally, and in their idealism are blind to the proletarian politics of the strike and of contemporary British moving-image culture. The particular combination of these sketched above, which made the Miners' Campaign Tape Project possible, also determined its general shape and structured the fabrication of the works themselves, as well as their textual and social activity. The effect—and the effectivness—of the interdependent political and rhetorical agendas in the tapes' responsiveness to their historical moment may be approached through the general principles at stake in what may be summarized as the tapes' use of video to spatialize and spatially redeploy the temporality of the miners' voices.

A major issue in postmodernism generally, definition of and control over space, is also key in postmodern forms of class struggle. In his elaboration of Henri Lefebvre's observation that "today, more than ever, the class struggle is inscribed in space. . . . Only the class struggle has the capacity to differentiate, to generate differences which are not intrinsic to economic growth," David Harvey (1990) has noted how "working-class movements are . . . generally better at organizing in and dominating *place* than they are at commanding *space*" (236–37). With control of the British state, corporate, police, and media apparatuses all more or less centralized in the metropolis, the only incompletely controlled zones were those of the working class, especially those in the far north and west—precisely the location of the threatened coalfields. In the sociospatial dialectic of Thatcher's attack on the miners, a regional offensive against peripheral industries was intrinsic to a general invasion of autonomous, working-class *places* and their reterritorialization as centralized, core-controlled, free market *space* (the abolition of the Greater London Council and other forms of local government exemplify the same offensive).[10] These spatial issues were primary in the government's instigation and prosecution of the strike, and in the miners' and the tapes' response.

First, the closure of the provincial pits threatened not only the miners' income, but the very existence of entire working-class communities—the single-industry pit villages. It left the miners to choose between defending their own places or becoming deskilled peripatetic workers in the homogeneous space of a post-Fordist economy. Second, through the police and judiciary, the state invaded and occupied all relevant public space; the police refused to allow pickets to connect the dispersed elements of the strike by free movement through the road system or to place themselves close enough to scab workers to be able to speak to them, and once a miner had been arrested, restrictive bail conditions prevented him from picketing on the penalty of jail, that is, total spatial sequestration. These struggles over space—the spatioterritorial form of the class struggle—determined both the mass media misrepresentation of the strike and the Miners' Campaign tapes' own participation in it.

The mass media repressed coverage of the long-term historical developments that caused the strike and sensationalized the miners' reactions to police violence. *Straight Speaking* and *The Lie Machine* respond; based on fragments of mass media propaganda that are incorporated into their own audiovisual mode—rephotography of tabloid articles, for example, or quotations from Thatcher and other members of the government, which are then answered in the speaking voices of strike supporters—they reterritorialize the state's discourse in their own terms. The other four tapes, conversely, manifest the offensive as distinct from the defensive mode of the same imperative. Beginning from where the miners stood and spoke, they attempt to forge the separate voices and *places* of resistance into a polynucleated working-class *space,* a proletarian public sphere. Given this objective, their formal properties and the specifics of their production and consumption, which all appear as deficiencies in aesthetic systems that fetishize immanent textual properties, are revealed as necessary to their practical function and intrinsic to their class position. In doing so, they demonstrate one form of proletarian aesthetics. Their properties may now be listed:

- In the tapes, the miners' voices are reproduced electronically and visually; their otherwise ephemeral and private discourse is objectified, made permanent and public. Turned into electronic information, it became a raw material to which the ACTT technicians—unionized, working-class artists—could add their labor in editing and in the distribution of the finished artifacts. For the NUJ and ACTT members who worked for or financed the project, it was a way of partially redressing their own unions' complicity in the use of state and corporate media to attack the working class.

- Although the miners and their supporters appear to be speaking spontaneously in the tapes, they are in fact replying to questions asked by the video makers (from a list prepared at the initial conference). In editing, the questions were cut and the responses broken into pieces and interwoven with each other according to topic, so that in the completed tapes the working class appears to express itself in a unified, focused, cogent, and absolutely committed voice. This, apparently unanimous, voice of the whole community does contain individual specificity, but unites the separate accounts in the collective social story of the strike. And though the miners speak in a variety of strongly accented local dialects—each the marker of a different place—their unity in the strike cancels the regional differences the government had exploited to divide them. Again as in the Vertovian model, from fragments of many people, the perfect, exemplary working-class subject is created.

- Whereas broadcast television pretends to objectivity and balance, the tapes are overtly and totally partisan in their endorsement of the strike, never questioning or criticizing it in any way.

In this respect the Miners' Campaign Project's failure to produce *The Miners of '84* (the longer tape with the supplementary review of general national background and the voice-over commentary mentioned in the initial prospectus) was entirely appropriate. The tapes' standard is not that of information, but of participation; they are not about the strike, but part of it.

- The tapes do not hierarchically rank the discourses they represent: everyone is equal, no voice is framed by another. Broadcast television news, in contrast, asserts the voice of the newsreader as a center of objectivity that, Chinese-box fashion, contains within itself the partial truths of all other speakers. In Deleuze and Guattari's terms, it is arborescent; the voice of the studio branches into—and so administers—the voices of the field correspondents, the sundry experts, and the "people" they interview, subdividing the program into successively more remote and dependent regions that are always controlled from the center. Even on the rare occasion when a working-class person's voice does appear, it is multiply framed, the lowest level in the hierarchy, the least authoritative because it divides into no others. But the working-class voices in the Miners' Campaign tapes link with each other as equals. Each its own authority, they seem to speak for themselves, not as illustrations of an argument proposed from above. As a result, the text is without internal definition, without climax. It is always complete, yet it may be entered anywhere and taken anywhere. Both textually and socially a rhizome, it can grow in any direction—but only and always on a grassroots level.

- The tapes were made on low-band U-matic video, transferred to VHS: a very cheap means of production, readily accessible and widely familiar in a variety of amateur capacities, and playable on domestic television sets. The achievement of such a collective, disseminated enunciation fulfilled the dream that has haunted the left in modern times, that of a motion picture medium available to the working class as producers and whose distribution they could control.

- Though regional newscasts include varying amounts of locally produced programming, the dominant, national television news networks are directed from and produced in London. But the tapes were only assembled there, as a synthesis of the social and cultural activity whose origin was dispersed throughout the coalfields and in the nationwide regional workshops.

- The tapes are of below broadcast quality; although this deprived them of the audience reached, for example, by the workshop tapes commissioned by Channel Four shot on high-band (such as those mentioned by Alan Fountain in the quotation in note 4), it also prevented their assimilation as one of the plurality of positions in the pseudodemocratic balance of liberal journalism. Reflecting the conditions of their production, the tapes' technical limitations allowed them to be entirely functional in their own spaces and to be assimilable to the discursive arenas of working-class politics, but kept them invisible and silent in those of the ruling classes. Unlike the cultural products of all other postmodern identity politics, they could not be recruited to sustain and renew industrial culture or ratify its corporate agendas.

- Once assembled, the tapes were reproduced from multiple, proliferating, and self-appointing points of reproduction. Anyone with access to two VCRs could join the strike by making new copies and instigating new daisy chains of copies.

- Whereas broadcast news is received at a specific time, organizing information access as it organizes the rhythm of the working day, the tapes could be played and replayed, freely engaged in the liberated time of the nonworking day.

- The tapes create an egalitarian, participatory mode of consumption. Broadcast television news asserts its own authority, a class difference between itself and its audience; its discourse implies and indeed occupies the parameters of what is allowed to be relevant, and it expects the audience to subordinate their discourse to its own. Although scholarship (e.g., Morely 1980) has shown that it is never totally successful in this, nevertheless the program sets the agenda, even if people of different classes receive it in different ways and differently incorporate its discourse into their own. The tapes do not resist this process of participatory consumption; rather, they encourage talking back. Allowing the dispersed working-class voices to speak among themselves, they reject not just the authority of the panoptical mass media, but also the discursive privilege of all industrial media, including themselves. Being very short, they do not preoccupy their own consumption; their turn to speak is soon over, and then they may be spoken to and about, augmented, verified, interrupted. Like other forms of Third Cinema, they are only a "pretext for dialogue, for the seeking and finding of wills" (Solanas and Gettino 1976, 62), a conversation piece to spur more talk by more miners and their supporters.

• Financed by the working class, either forcibly through license fees or indirectly through advertising, broadcast television is a mechanism for silently transferring wealth from the working class to the state or corporate shareholders. Financed voluntarily by the unions and the general public and used to raise funds for the miners and their families, the Miners' Campaign tapes were a means by which people voluntarily and self-consciously decided to contribute to sustaining the strike. Raising "hundreds of thousands of pounds" (Petley 1989, 9), the tapes became a way for nonminers to act in class solidarity, and so to participate in the strike.

Conclusion

The defeat of the strike was a catastrophe for the miners, for the trade union movement, and for workingpeople worldwide. The miners' predictions that the industry would be destroyed have proven true; since 1985, 140,000 coal jobs have been lost, and as I write, today's paper announces the closure of the last working pit in Lancashire, ending a 400-year mining tradition, even as the government is considering the piecemeal privatization of the remaining profitable pits and the licensing of private sector operation of discarded pits (Beavis and Brown 1993). Subsequent defeats for the left, and especially the ascendancy of end-of-class and indeed anti-working-class ideologies, appear to justify the miners' other prediction, that the strike was the last-ditch stand for the working class. In fact, the full implications of its defeat in this instance will not be clear until the long-term effects of the present phase of the international restructuring of capital and the effectivity of the new forms of resistance this will create are known.

Until such resistance emerges, the Miners' Campaign tapes and other miners' videos will speak to us from a moment whose possibilities seem ever more remote. In Britain, for the remainder of the Thatcher years and then under Major, the working class has bounced from defeat to defeat, as it has in the United States under Reagan, Bush, and Clinton. The particular conditions in British moving-image culture that made the Miners' Campaign tapes possible have likewise deteriorated; in 1989, giving notice that it had ceased to fund any more workshops in the manner agreed in the Workshop Declaration, Channel Four began a three-year phaseout of existing funding, followed by the BFI in 1991. Although the production of women's, gay, and ethnically identified film and video continues to expand, in both industrial media and outside it, the working class *as* the working class has virtually neither voice nor space of its own.

Yet the example remains. The Miners' Campaign tapes reproduced in their own moment the conditions of the other postwar alternative cinemas in the West: like, for example, the underground films of the 1960s, their production as texts was crucially determined by the construction of alternative apparatuses of production and distribution; the *prise de la parole* by a subaltern group was made in the face of misrepresentation by hegemonic media; their textual properties were determined by practical, participatory functions in real life beyond those of representation; they negotiated between articulating the miners' own political identity and responding to the apparatus and texts of the industrial media; and despite the overall oppositional project, the alternative practice did not exist as one pole of a simple binary, but as a moment—albeit a crucial and exemplary one—in total field containing multiple positions. In this summariness and in their unique ability to inspire and assemble the political and cultural support of other identities (however temporary this might have been), they were the apotheosis of the populist avant-garde. If it seems that, like Minerva herself, they appeared in the gathering of its evening, we must remember that the night will not last forever.[11]

Notes

The present study is indebted to a number of filmmakers and others involved in the Miners' Campaign Tape Project or collateral initiatives, especially Steve Colton, Bob Davis, Richard Hines, Chris Reeves, Simon Reynell, and Lin Solomon. Additional interviews and correspondence with Martin Spence and Jenny Woodley were invaluable. I would also like to thank H. Bruce Franklin for the inspiration and support of his work. The tapes produced by the project may be obtained from the Northern Film and Television Archive, 36 Bottle Bank, Gateshead, Tyne and Wear, NE8 2AR, U.K., and the Video Data Bank, 112 South Michigan Avenue, Chicago, Illinois 60603, USA.

1. As much as a crisis for the working class, the strike was also a crisis within the working class and its institutions. Divisions among the miners themselves, which had long been exacerbated by the federated (rather than centrally controlled) structure of the National Union of Mineworkers (NUM) and by the government's differential pay scales for more or less profitable pits, were reflected in a series of other divisions: within the miners nationally (miners in the North Midlands were reluctant to support the jobs of miners in Yorkshire or Wales), within the union movement generally (at the 1984 TUC conference, electricians and power station engineers opposed the strike, the Labour Party leadership supported it but also criticized the miners, and the steelworkers, themselves recently radically depleted by state offensives, did not support it), and even internationally (Belgian and Australian miners and dockers supported the NUM, but deliveries of coal from Poland, West Germany, and the United States escalated) (see Benyon 1985, 19).

2. *A Catalogue of Films and Videotapes Produced during the 1984/85 Miners' Strike* (n.d.) describes some forty works produced by individuals or small organizations, independently or with various kinds of sponsorship, but almost all made in collaboration with the striking miners and their support groups. Much more material, including many hours of the miners' own amateur video recordings remains uncollected. Some sixty works have been collected at the Northern Film and Television Archive in Gateshead, England.

3. Negrine (1989, 76–77, 153–54) surveys the research on press and TV bias. For specific examples of newspaper misrepresentation of the miners, see also Schwarz (1985, 124–25). Here I emphasize the tapes' alterity to the hegemonic media, but the latter was not itself internally undifferentiated or without contradiction. Overall, the miners' accusation of bias and indeed active hostility in print and television coverage was justified; 75 percent of national dailies and 84 percent of Sunday newspapers were controlled by a conservative pro-Thatcher oligarchy of three press barons, and the government had close personal relations with many Fleet Street editors (Adeny and Lloyd 1986, 240–45). On television, sporadic attempts at "balance" could not compensate for the ongoing news program identification of picketing miners with violence, the use of selectively loaded language, and the inadequate contextualization provided for reported events (Fountain 1985, 131), let alone for the internalized prejudices of the higher-ech-

elon career administrators in the state-controlled media institutions. But, as one analysis of television news during the strike concludes, "While the public may have all watched the same news they didn't all see it the same way" (Negrine 1989, 17), and that part of public opinion opposed to the miners cannot simply be attributed to press distortion. Nor was the national television immune to co-optation by the miners. NUM president Arthur Scargill took advantage of the charismatic authority that made him a magnet for journalists to broadcast the strikers' arguments and to call for pickets and support from other unions. Until the bitterness of the last wintry months of the strike, the miners themselves recognized differences between BBC news, the most egregious offender, and Channel Four news. On all four channels, the news was supplemented by other kinds of programming. Alan Fountain (1985), commissioning editor for independent film at Channel Four (who commissioned several prominers programs), lists the "loose categories" of these: "a range of current affairs programmes"; "a broad band of apparently 'lighter' coverage"; "regional coverage by ITV companies supplementing the national network"; "various one-off documentaries made from a clearly supportive class perspective, such as Chris Curling's *The Last Pit in the Rhondda* and Ken Loach's *Which Side Are You On?*" (which in fact was never broadcast); and "programmes which, to some extent, have been made with the collaboration of their participants, *Taking Liberties, Coal Not Dole, Notts Women Strike Back,* and *Get It Shown*" (130–31).

4. In 1984 almost nine thousand miners were arrested and two miners were killed on picket lines (Benyon 1985, 4). See Fine and Millar (1985) for detailed investigation of the different forms of state offensive against the miners and the erosion of the independence of the judiciary, democratic accountability, and civil liberties generally.

5. An introduction to alternative cinemas may be found in Macpherson (1980). Hogenkamp (1986) surveys independent left filmmaking in the 1930s, the Workers' Film and Photo League, and other workers' film groups.

6. Created in the 1981 Broadcasting Act, Channel Four is a nonprofit company owned by the Independent Broadcasting Authority, a government-appointed body. It is financed by subscriptions from the fifteen regional ITV companies that receive its programs and that sell advertising time between them. Unlike other television stations in Britain, Channel Four commissions programs rather than producing them itself. Since the 1992 Broadcasting Act, Channel Four has itself sold advertising time, in direct competition with other ITV companies.

7. Eventually the group also included Nottingham Video Project, Community Video Workshop (Cardiff), Amber Films, Films at Work (London), Birmingham Film & Video Workshop, Active Image (Sheffield), and Open Eye Film and Video Workshop (Liverpool). See Harvey (1984) for an interview with members of Platform Films that took place just before the Miners' Campaign Tape Project began.

8. As well as being important in so many other ways, the role of women in the strike was crucial in terms of media contestation, because in the previous strikes the BBC had made shameless propaganda use of images of women op-

posed to the strike; thus, Barnsley Women Against Pit Closures and many similar organizations were formed because of anger at the way in which the media portrayed "women and miners' wives in particular, as the victims of the irresponsible action taken by the NUM" (Stead 1987, 127).

9. The putative "simple form of realism" of this mode is summarized by Alan Lovell (1990) as "the subject—oppression of one kind or another; the structure—talking heads interspersed with vaguely illustrative material; presentation—low key and undramatic" (104).

10. The classic sociological account of miners' communities, *Coal Is Our Life* (Dennis, Henriques, and Slaughter 1956), emphasizes the local nature of mining knowledge and experience, with skills often not transferable from pit to pit, let alone village to village, and also the way the shared misfortunes of mining disasters binds miners to their hometowns and home collieries.

11. Not to be excepted here is the commercial British cinema of the 1980s, which failed to address class issues. Ken Loach has recognized its failure to "put on the screen the appalling cost in human misery that Thatcherite policies had wrought on everybody" (cited in Fuller 1993, 59). This cinema was criticized *avant la lettre* by Alan Fountain as the creation "of a cinema in Britain of a Fassbinder, Bertolucci or Truffaut. We have never had such a cinema in Britain, and we don't want such a cinema; we don't want this tacky glamour of the metropolitan EEC bourgeoisie" (cited in Petley 1989, 7). For a critique of this cinema as a symptom, rather than an analysis, of Thatcherism, see Walsh (1993). A notable exception is the somewhat later *Cwm Hyfryd* (Paul Turner, 1992), a feature-film investigation of the social costs of the pit closures and Thatcherism generally.

Works Cited

Adeney, Martin, and John Lloyd. 1986. *The Miners' Strike, 1984–5: Loss without Limit*. London: Routledge.

Anderson, Perry. 1992. *English Questions*. London: Verso.

Beavis, Simon, and Paul Brown. 1993. "Hanson Seeks to Buy Best Pits." *Guardian* (London), 1 June, 12.

Benyon, Huw. 1985. "Introduction." In Huw Benyon, ed., *Digging Deeper: Issues in the Miners' Strike*. London: Verso, 1–26.

A Catalogue of Films and Videotapes Produced During the 1984/85 Miners' Strike. n.d. Newcastle: Northern Film and Television Archive.

Deleuze, Gilles, and Félix Guattari. 1987. *A Thousand Plateaus: Capitalism and Schizophrenia*, trans. Brian Massumi. Minneapolis: University of Minnesota Press.

Dennis, Norman, Fernando Henriques, and Clifford Slaughter. 1956. *Coal Is Our Life: An Analysis of a Yorkshire Mining Community*. London: Tavistock.

Fine, Bob, and Robert Millar, eds. 1985. *Policing the Miners Strike*. London: Lawrence & Wishart.

Fountain, Alan. 1985. "The Miners and Television." In Huw Benyon, ed., *Digging Deeper: Issues in the Miners' Strike*. London: Verso.

Fuller, Graham. 1993. "True Brit." *Village Voice*, 9 February, 56, 58.

Harvey, David. 1990. *The Condition of Postmodernity.* Oxford: Basil Blackwell.
Harvey, Sylvia. 1984. " 'Those Other Voices': An Interview with Platform Films." *Screen,* 25 no. 6, 31–47.
Hogenkamp, Bert. 1986. *Deadly Parallels: Film and the Left in Britain, 1929–39.* London: Lawrence & Wishart.
Lovell, Alan. 1990. "That Was the Workshop That Was." *Screen,* 31, no. 1, 102–8.
Macpherson, Don. 1980. *Traditions of Independence: British Cinema in the Thirties.* London: British Film Institute.
Morely, David. 1980. *The "Nationwide" Audience: Structure and Decoding.* London: British Film Institute.
Negrine, Ralph. 1989. *Politics and Mass Media in Britain.* London: Routledge.
Petley, Julian. 1989. "Background and Development of Film and Video Workshops." In British Council, *Landmarks.* London: British Council, 6–10.
Scargill, Arthur. 1975. "The New Unionism." *New Left Review,* 92, 1–33.
Schwarz, Bill. 1985. "Redefining the National Interest." In Huw Benyon, ed., *Digging Deeper: Issues in the Miners' Strike.* London: Verso, 123–29.
Solanas, Fernando, and Octavio Gettino. 1976. "Towards a Third Cinema." In Bill Nichols, ed., *Movies and Methods: An Anthology.* Berkeley: University of California Press, 44–64.
Spence, Martin. 1988. *Preaching to the Converted.* London: Association of Cinematograph Television and Allied Technicians and the North East Media Development Council.
Stead, Jean. 1987. *Never the Same Again: Women and the Miners' Strike.* London: Women's Press.
Tressell, Robert. 1955 [1914]. *The Ragged-Trousered Philanthropists.* New York: Monthly Review Press.
Vertov, Dziga. 1984. *Kino-Eye: The Writings of Dziga Vertov.* Berkeley: University of California Press.
Walsh, Michael. 1993. "Allegories of Thatcherism: The Films of Peter Greenaway." In Lester Friedman, ed., *Fires Were Started: British Cinema and Thatcherism.* Minneapolis: University of Minnesota Press.

Chapter 10
Poltergeists, Gender, and Class in the Age of Reagan and Bush
Douglas Kellner

During the past two decades, the horror-occult genre has been one of the most popular and successful Hollywood genres.[1] Horror films have traditionally dealt with universal and primal fears (fears of dying, aging, bodily decay, violence, sexuality, and so on). However, the most interesting post-1960s horror films (*The Exorcist, The Texas Chainsaw Massacre, Carrie, Alien, The Shining,* and others) have presented, often in symbolic-allegorical form, both universal fears and the deepest anxieties and hostilities of contemporary U.S. society. A subtext of these films is the confusion and fright of the population in the face of economic crisis; accelerating social and cultural change; a near epidemic of cancer, industrial diseases, and AIDS; political turmoil; and fear of nuclear annihilation. The wide range and popularity of post-1960s Hollywood horror films suggests that something is profoundly wrong with U.S. society, and a probing of these films may help reveal something about the sources of contemporary fears.

The 1970s and 1980s saw an explosion of horror films, which constitute one of the most popular genres of the era. The 1980s was the time of Reagan and Bush and conservative hegemony, and in this study, I wish to argue that Hollywood films presented allegorically fears concerning social disintegration related to the deteriorating conditions of life for the middle and working classes during this period. The decade of the 1980s was an unprecedented era

217

of class warfare, with massive redistribution of wealth from work-
ing- and middle-class sectors to the rich, and an era of high fear of
unemployment, downward mobility, and crisis for the working
classes.[2] Whereas the 1970s saw a wave of popular films dealing
with the working class,[3] the working class was rarely featured
in 1980s Hollywood films, which focused more on middle- and
upper-class families and individuals. Yet members of the working
class were often presented as threatening others to middle-class life
and, as I attempt to demonstrate in this essay, were often negatively stigmatized in genres such as the horror film.

Horror, the Occult, and Allegory

The broad panorama of popular horror films attests to a resurgence of the occult in contemporary society and a sense that individuals are no longer in control of everyday life. When individuals
perceive that they do not have control over their lives and that they
are dominated by powerful forces outside themselves, they are attracted to occultism. Consequently, during eras of socioeconomic
crisis, when people have difficulty coping with social reality, the
occult becomes an efficacious ideological mode that helps explain
incomprehensible events with the aid of religious or supernatural
mythologies.

In the crisis of German society after World War I, for instance,
there was a proliferation of horror films, and the first great wave
of American horror films appeared in the midst of the Great Depression of the 1930s. After the explosion of the atomic bomb and
with the heating up of the Cold War and the arms race in the
1950s, another wave of horror-occult films appeared, featuring visions of mutant animals and humans or apocalyptic holocausts.
Over the years, American culture has accumulated a treasure-
house of occultist lore to draw upon, and in the 1970s and 1980s
Americans turned to occultism for experiences and ideas that
helped them cope with economic crisis, political turmoil, and cultural malaise. In this resurgence of the occult, repressed fears and
irrational forces sought symbolic expressions that often served as
vehicles for reactionary ideologies in contemporary film (i.e., the
Exorcist trilogy, the *Omen* trilogy, the *Halloween* series, and a va-

riety of monster films, demonic-possession films, and other occult thrillers).

Whereas conservative horror films provide fantasies of reassurance that existing authorities and institutions can eliminate evil, many post-1960s horror films do not reassure audiences that historically specific or universal evils can be suppressed and contained. Instead, they reveal a society in crisis, where destructive forces are rampant and conventional authorities and values are incapable of defeating and eliminating the evils afoot. Consequently, these films often do not legitimate contemporary American institutions and values, but show horrific violence and social disintegration to be ubiquitous and powerful forces in the contemporary social order. This is true to some extent of films that rely on religious institutions to defeat "evil" (e.g., *The Exorcist* and to a greater extent the more nihilistic films of George Romero, Tobe Hooper, Wes Craven, Larry Cohen, and others that show contemporary institutions and ways of life to be the source of horror).[4]

In the following discussion, I disclose how the *Poltergeist* series negotiates middle-class fears and insecurities concerning race, gender, and class in the contemporary era. I interpret these films allegorically as articulating deep-rooted fears that are often explored in genres such as the horror film rather than realist films, where they might be too painful to confront and explore. Allegory serves both as a vehicle for conveying ideology and as a mode of articulation of social hopes, fears, and aspirations. As Jameson has argued, allegories can articulate the specific anxieties and yearnings of social classes or nations striving for national liberation and development. Allegories usually transmit some deeper problematics or ideology under the guise of a conventional story or tale, and thus interpretation of the messages or meanings conveyed requires hermeneutical decoding and analysis of the underlying meanings produced by the narrative.

Horror films, disaster films, and other popular genres often present allegorically, in symbolic expression, such things as individuals' fears of losing their homes or families or more general fears of social disintegration and collapse. The allegories of horror transform private worries into public problems, raising narratives concerning the situation of individuals into more general figures who represent existing social conditions and structures. Allegories can also articulate what ideology often represses, transcoding (i.e., translating into cinematic form) anxieties concerning societal crisis and upheaval. Cinematic allegories may provide material for social critique, but they may also provide ideological legitimations for institutions or values threatened or under attack (as I argue is the case in the *Poltergeist* films). The allegories of cinema thus require ideological deciphering that ferrets out both their socially critical and their conservative moments.

Horror films constitute a reactionary genre to the extent that they blame occult forces for societal disintegration and a life out of control, thus deflecting attention from the real sources of social suffering. Yet they also offer the possibility of radical critique by presenting suffering and oppression as caused by institutions that need to be reconstructed. Horror films of the 1970s, for example, see monsters being produced by families, and thus can be taken as socially critical, articulating the critiques of the family in 1960s political movements (i.e., in *The Texas Chainsaw Massacre, The Hills Have Eyes, Motel Hell*, and so on). But films like *Poltergeist* show good families being attacked by monsters, and thus serve as ideological defenses of the middle-class family, which transcode cinematically the conservative profamily discourses of the 1980s. Yet read diagnostically, even conservative horror films reveal contemporary anxieties concerning the family, downward mobility, and homelessness in an uncertain economy and disintegrating social order. In the following diagnostic reading, I accordingly discuss the *Poltergeist* films as indicators of social anxiety in the working classes concerning fear of falling and societal and familial disintegration.

Poltergeist and Middle-Class Angst

Among the wave of 1980s occult-horror films, *Poltergeist* (1982), directed by Tobe Hooper and coauthored and produced by Steven Spielberg,[5] is especially interesting because it articulates the underlying anxieties of the new middle class in the Age of Reagan. *Poltergeist*, along with Spielberg's *E.T. The Extra-Terrestrial* (1982), explores with sympathy and even affection the environment and lifestyle of the new affluent, suburban middle class and presents symbolic projections of its insecurities and fears. Whereas *E.T.*

presents an optimistic and charming allegory of suburban middle-class life, *Poltergeist* presents its shadow side and nightmares in a story where the Other, the Alien, is not a friendly extraterrestrial who comes from outside the society to help it, but threateningly emerges from *within* the socioeconomic system and social subconscious to terrorize the ordinary middle-class people who are the subject of the film. Thus, whereas *E.T.* is Spielberg's childlike fantasy of hope, *Poltergeist* is a symbolic probing of universal and specifically American fears that takes the form of an allegorical nightmare, the decoding of which should tell us something about the vicissitudes of class, race, and gender in the United States today.

Poltergeist features the adventures with the occult of the Freeling family, who discover that their house is built on top of a graveyard whose spirits seek revenge against the intruding family. In another plot twist, evil spirits attempt to seduce the clairvoyant five-year-old daughter, Carol Anne, into the spirit world. Her parents try to rescue her and are forced to turn to parapsychologists and a diminutive woman medium for help. The narrative thus mobilizes the generic motifs of the ghost and haunted-house story with motifs of the zombie genre.

The family unit in *Poltergeist* contains a father, Steve Freeling (Craig T. Nelson); his wife, Diane (JoBeth Williams); a teenage daughter, Dana (Dominique Dunne); a young son, Robbie (Oliver Robins); and little Carol Anne (Heather O'Rourke), who is the first to make contact with the poltergeists. The Freelings live in one of the first houses built in Phase 1 of a housing project called Cuesta Vista. The father is a successful real estate agent who has sold 42 percent of the housing units in the area—which his boss tells him represents more than $70 million in property. As a reward for his heroic efforts, he has all the commodities desired by the new affluent middle class. Depiction of this class and its fears of losing home, family, and property is a central focus of the *Poltergeist* films.

The Freelings are thus your Middle-Class Everyone, representing the new class sector of affluent middle-class suburbanites. The name "Freeling" evokes the dominant ideology of freedom, and from this perspective a "freeling" is a free being, a member of a class and society free from basic worries and cares, free to celebrate and live the American middle-class dream. "The Star-Spangled Banner," referring to the "land of the free," plays in an opening segment, and the refrain is heard again later in the film, which presents iconic images of American flags throughout. Yet the film deals with the threats to freedom and loss of sovereignty in contemporary middle-class life, and the all-too-real prospects of downward mobility in an American dream gone sour and become a nightmare.

The film opens with the display of the new icons and objects of middle-class status and provides a charming look at the new afflu-ent consumer environment, with its split-level houses, omnipresent multichanneled TV, electronic gadgets, bountiful toys for the kids, dope and sex for the parents, and a treasure-house of commodities for every conceivable purpose. The opening images show the fa-ther asleep on his couch in front of his television. To the tune of the national anthem, we see configurations of television dots forming the scene of marines putting up the flag at Iwo Jima, evoking America's heroic past. But the present is troubled. The camera pans from room to room in the affluent house, showing the family members asleep. The TV's broadcast image goes off and static fills the screen. Carol Anne, the youngest member of the household, gets up, goes downstairs, and stands in front of the TV talking to the strange lights dancing about in the static. The entire family awakes, comes down, and stands looking at her in amazement. Throughout the film, the TV static signals bizarre happenings and menace.

After the opening scenes, *Poltergeist* presents some comic tab-leaux of suburban life. A heavyset man drives down the street on a bicycle, carrying a case of beer precariously balanced on the handlebars. Some playful kids aim their electronically directed toys at him and he falls off the bike. The beer cans spill and ex-plode and he desperately carries the remaining, and still exploding, cans into the house where a group of middle-aged and middle-class men are watching a football game on TV. The pleasures of com-munal TV football in suburbia are soon disrupted: the next-door neighbor's television set is plugged into the same remote control frequency, and the kids next door have switched the channel to Mr. Rogers, to the dismay of the football fans. The husband runs out to negotiate a peaceful settlement with the neighbor, who insists on the rights of his children, and the two fathers blast their remote controls at each other's televisions, switching the channel from the football game to Mr. Rogers to the alternating consternation and joy of the football audience and the kid-show audience—new forms of conflict and consternation in an emergent high-tech environment.

The opening scenes depict images of technology getting out of control that permeate the *Poltergeist* films. Technology out of control serves as a trope for fears of loss of sovereignty and power over one's immediate environment. In particular, in the 1980s there was fear of television taking over leisure activity and young people's minds, and *Poltergeist* articulates this fear in a parable whereby young Carol Anne is sucked into a television set that is the portal to the "other world" of spirits. The young girl talks to the "TV people" in the opening sequence, in which her hands lightly rest upon the static-filled TV screen at the end of the day's broadcasting. As the film proceeds, the television plays a major part in the plot.[6]

The scenes of the Freeling's television and the family's and then the neighbor's interaction with it also ironically depict the dialectic between public and private space in the contemporary suburban environment. Suburban Americans share the public space of television and media and consumer culture, yet for the most part participate in the shared culture in the private spaces of their own homes. The community portrayed is a leisure community bound together by the objects of play and entertainment: toys, television, sports, beer, and other common commodities. This community is a fragile one: without the TV, for instance, the weekend football-watching community dissolves. Most suburbanites do not know their neighbors, unless they share leisure activities in common. The remote control scene shows how shared suburban space overlaps and produces conflicts, as well as how weak, or nonexistent, "neighborliness" is in the suburbs. It also depicts a new communications environment and technology that individuals do not yet understand and do not fully control, a theme articulated as technology out of control in the *Poltergeist* films.

Such leisure communities represent a decline of class solidarities and show different social groups and class segments fusing in media and consumer cultures, yet without the awareness of class difference that characterized earlier working-class communities. The film shows the privatization of life under contemporary capitalism, the assimilation of working classes into suburban culture, and the centrality of a media and consumer culture to everyday life. Yet, as we shall see, the specters of class and especially class downward mobility continue to haunt this seemingly classless leisure culture.

Crucially, we watch the members of the Freeling family withdraw from their suburban community and turn in on themselves when the poltergeist crisis unfolds. Their neighbors are of little help, appearing only when a crisis erupts outside the house. In fact, *Poltergeist* projects a view that the most organic, solid, and viable social unit and institution in suburban life is the middle-class nuclear family. Spielberg and his coworkers present very positive and affectionate scenes of middle-class family life, without the satirical or ironic distance of many contemporary filmmakers (Altman, De Palma, Woody Allen, and other liberal and radical critics of the family).

After introducing the family, in another emblematic scene, the kids are tucked away in bed and Steve and Diane are alone in their bedroom. The wife holds a marijuana cigarette and talks and giggles about past memories, taking us back from the 1980s to the 1960s. The scene suggests that the flower children are grown up, married, and heads of families. Steve, however, is engrossed in a biography titled *Ronald Reagan: The President, the Man*. He eventually drops the book and starts fooling around with his wife. He plays wild animal, whispers in her ear, and Diane sighs, "Oh, I just love it when you talk dirty!" The scene cuts to the children in their bedroom: they are awake in fear during a thunderstorm. In addition to the thunder and lightning, a gothic tree casts weird shadows throughout the room, a clown doll grins menacingly (an iconic image from Tobe Hooper's previous film *The Funhouse,* which periodically reappears in *Poltergeist* as a sign of menace), and the poltergeists begin knocking things around.

The next night, during an even more powerful thunderstorm, branches of a giant tree take Robbie out through the bedroom window, and his parents desperately retrieve him from the forces of raging nature. At this point, Carol Anne disappears, the family enters a state of panic, and the film enters the realm of occultist allegory. *Poltergeist* presents allegorical spectacles of a family holding together in the face of adverse experiences that threaten to pull it apart. The scenes of separation throughout the movie express fear of impending disintegration of the family and fear of separation from the haven of the family. As the poltergeists become more destructive, Carol Anne is spirited away to a netherworld, the teenage daughter spends more and more time with her friends, and the young boy and his dog are sent away to his grandparents. The father, too, is pulled away by the demands of his job, but eventually he chooses the family over his job (i.e., he finally quits his job and moves away with his family). There are frequent affirmations of love and strong portrayals of family bonds. The mother, especially, is the moral and physical center of the family; she shows herself ready to risk her life for her children, while retaining courage in the face of adversity.

Moreover, unlike typical horror films, where individuals frequently blunder into disaster, in *Poltergeist* the individuals act rationally, cooperatively, and courageously. The father goes to Stanford and summons a group of parapsychologists who come to investigate the phenomena, and they in turn call in a diminutive woman spiritualist, Tangina (Zelda Rubinstein), who tells the family how to deal with the poltergeists and how to get their daughter back. With the spiritualist's guidance, the mother enters the spirit world to retrieve her daughter—revealing the depth of her love and concern for her child. Significantly, it is the women who play the key role in rescuing Carol Anne—reinforcing traditional images of women as protectors and nurturers of children.

In addition to representing fears of the family being torn apart, *Poltergeist* deals with anxieties about losing one's home, or watching it fall apart. The American dream has traditionally focused on buying and owning one's own home, and in an era of accelerating unemployment, a weak economy, and diminishing discretionary income, fears of losing one's home, or not being able to maintain it, accelerated during the 1980s. Stephen King, author of such popular books as *Carrie, The Shining, The Stand,* and *It*—which are a fertile source of allegories about contemporary American anxieties—writes of *The Amityville Horror,* a gothic, occult precursor to *Poltergeist:* "The picture's subtext is one of economic unease. . . . Little by little, it is ruining the Lutz family financially. The movie might as well have been subtitled 'The Horror of the

Shrinking Bank Account.' . . . *The Amityville Horror,* beneath its
ghost-story exterior, is really a financial demolition derby."[7]

Poltergeist also shows a house gradually but inexorably falling
apart. Rooms become uninhabitable, machines and technology either do not work or operate out of the family's control, commodities and toys are destroyed. Finally, the house literally collapses
and the family must flee. This allegory of the home under siege is
part of the reason the film is so effective in manipulating audiences: viewers can identify with this very average middle-class
family in a house that constantly gives them trouble and is eventually taken away from them. *This* is a contemporary horror story
for current and would-be homeowners, many of whom lost their
homes during the Age of Reagan and Bush, or did not have the
funds for home improvement.

Indeed, from the 1980s to the present, many individuals have
fallen into lower class brackets, losing jobs and homes as the
economy has undergone dramatic changes such as deindustrialization, the elimination of factory and corporate jobs and positions,
producing what Ehrenreich describes as "fear of falling."[8] During
precisely this period, class divisions have also grown, with many
working-class people falling into the underclass and middle-class
incomes declining. In recent years, the proportion of low-income
earners in the U.S. labor force has continued to rise and their condition has continued to decline, whereas high-income workers'
wages have continued to rise, creating a two-tier wage structure
and growing class divisions, according to a 1994 report issued
jointly by the Labor and Commerce Departments of the Clinton
administration. The report notes that the "real" hourly compensation of American workers stagnated in the last two decades and
actually fell for male workers, a development "unprecedented in
the past 75 years in this country."[9]

The *Poltergeist* films thus articulate middle-class anxieties in a
deteriorating economy and provide material for insights into the
class psychology of a beleaguered middle class. They also appeal to
working- and underclass sectors whose living conditions are even
worse and who themselves fear falling into hopeless poverty, and
even homelessness. Of course, the industrial working class, more
than the middle classes, faced economic disaster during the deindustrialization of America, but this situation, as I suggest later, was

probably too *really horrible* for Hollywood to deal with, thus working-class and middle-class fears were projected into horror films dealing with predominantly middle-class families.

As it turns out, in the film's occult subtext, the source of the poltergeist disturbance is a decision made by the land developing company, for which the father works, to build their project on top of a graveyard after removing the headstones, but without removing the corpses. In zombie scenes reminiscent of the horror classic *Night of the Living Dead*, the dead arise from the earth and terrorize the neighborhood. In a key scene, Steve confronts his boss, Teague, and shouts: "You son of a bitch! You moved the cemetery, but you left the bodies. . . . You only moved the headstones!" The developer Teague thus represents the greedy capitalist who puts private property above all else. Indeed, the very name "Teague" evokes Frank Norris's ruthless capitalist "McTeague" in a novel that describes the drive to power and profit of a prototypical capitalist of an earlier era.

Poltergeist thus plays on fears that land developers will destroy the environment and upset the delicate ecological balance—another contemporary worry that is the site of current struggles to limit growth and urban/suburban development. But it also articulates class fears that a greedy and ruthless capitalist class will stop at nothing to pursue development and profit, destroying the environment, community, and family life in the wake of a relentless capitalist modernity.

Yet the poltergeists also represent fear of race and otherness, and the films can be read as fear of racial invasion and destruction of suburban middle-class utopia. The monsters in *Poltergeist* appear as a radical otherness to white middle-class "normality" and stand in for fear of other classes and races. Fears of racial others are linked to fears of the working class in the film. Some workers appear early in the plot to work on a family swimming pool, itself a symbol of middle-class affluence. The workers are slightly dark-skinned ethnic types, somewhat uncouth and vaguely threatening. Two male workers leer at the teenage daughter, who responds with obscene gestures—to her mother's amusement. Soon after, one worker opens the window to drink the mother's coffee and snack on some food lying on the drainboard. The mother catches him and good-humoredly chastises the vaguely threatening worker, whom she calls "Bluto" (an odd name, perhaps after the menacing working-class character in *Popeye*—a name appropriated by the John Belushi figure in *Animal House* as well).

Horror films thus mobilize fear of the other and draw lines between normality and abnormality, good and evil. In the *Poltergeist* films, goodness resides in middle-class familial normality and otherness resides in working-class and racial others such as ethnics, the poor, and people of color (this problematic is even more sharply articulated in the second *Poltergeist* film, as we will see in the next section). From this perspective, the threatening monsters stand in allegorically for race and class forces threatening middle-class stability. Such cinematic representations transcode the conservative, yet anxious, profamily discourses of the era in their celebration of the family and negative stigmatizing of otherness.

The film has a traditional happy ending as the family leaves the home, pulls together, survives the disaster, and checks into a friendly Holiday Inn. The Holiday Inn site reveals the underlying theme of security versus insecurity in the film. What could be more secure than the Holiday Inn, that icon of middle-class sameness where one knows in advance that one will receive the same room and furnishings anywhere in America? *Poltergeist* points to intense middle-class insecurities in the Age of Reagan, with growing fears of unemployment, losing one's home, and losing control over one's life and possessions. It contains a panorama of fears of growing powerlessness in the face of corporate power and greed, an economy out of control, and rapid cultural change. It reproduces the fears of the disintegration of the family exploited by Reagan and the New Right, as well as fears of television and losing control over one's children. It reveals the Age of Reagan and Bush to be an era of fear and trembling for both the middle and the working classes, who are faced with intensifying threats to their livelihood and well-being.

American Nightmares

Poltergeist thus presents an allegory concerning contemporary American nightmares. It achieves its power by drawing on fears of falling, which it presents in symbolic form that allows people to experience their subconscious anxieties in the safe medium of film in an ideology machine that smoothes over and tranquilizes their fears by showing the family pulling through. Although *Poltergeist* hints that corporate capitalism is rapacious—destroying the earth, exploiting people, and even threatening human survival—the real source of contemporary anxieties is displaced onto the occult. Hence, although *Poltergeist* and other recent horror films contain allegories about contemporary anxieties, the audience is directed by the film toward spectacles of occult horror rather than the horror show of contemporary life in the United States. The irrationalist-occultist metaphysics in films such as *E.T.* and *Poltergeist* therefore weaken the social insights present in the films and strengthen the rampant irrationalism in U.S. society manifest in religious revivalism, cults, New Age spiritualism, and so on.

In fact, several of Spielberg's most popular films are permeated with the fuzzy-minded occultism that T. W. Adorno shrewdly characterizes as "the metaphysics of dopes."[10] Although Spielberg and company's excursions into the supernatural allow individuals to experience anxieties in a symbolic form that they might not be able to face in a more realist narrative form, their occultist films tend to project real fears onto threats by evil spirits, and focus hope on deliverance by beneficent extraterrestrials (*Close Encounters of the Third Kind, E.T.*) or by seemingly superhuman heroes (like Indiana Jones in *Raiders of the Lost Ark*). Spielberg's ideology machines all too often summon his audiences to escapist fantasies, conservative affirmation of middle-class values, and the traditional mythic heroes and forms of traditional popular culture. Unlike more critical Hollywood filmmakers who dissect dominant myths and question dominant values (Altman, Scorsese, Allen, and so on), Spielberg is a storyteller and mythmaker who affirms both the opposing poles of middle-class values and lifestyles and a transcendent occultism.

The turn to the occult in post-*Exorcist* (1973) Hollywood film represents an ideological crisis in American society by presenting a society in crisis whose institutions are under attack by a variety of forces. Some of the most popular horror-occult films (*The Exorcist, The Omen, Carrie, The Amityville Horror, The Shining,* and so on) portray a disintegrating society incapable of dealing with the evils presented in the films. If there is any salvation, or a solution to the problems depicted, in most of these and other Hollywood "blockbuster" films it appears transcendentally in the form of aliens or extraterrestrials, the church or the spirit world, or superheroes from other worlds or other times, like Superman, Batman, Conan, or Indiana Jones. The appeal to the past, or to the transcendental, for heroes, values, and legitimation does not, however, effectively legitimate the institutions of the existing society, and points to a legitimation crisis in contemporary American society.[11]

Poltergeist, it is true, does attempt to portray the family and middle-class lifestyles positively, but there are ideological contradictions in Spielberg's work between attempts to celebrate existing middle-class institutions and values and the search for salvation from extraterrestrials or spiritualism. There are also hints in his films that existing institutions and values lack vitality. In *Close Encounters,* the husband abandons his family to pursue his fantasy of making contact with the aliens in the UFOs; in *E.T.,* the absence of the father (separated from the mother and in Mexico with a new girlfriend) can be seen as a psychological reason for the boy to turn for friendship and love to the extraterrestrial; and in *Poltergeist,* although we have a particularly strong portrait of the family as a viable institution, the rest of the dominant institutions, and especially the corporation, are presented in a critical light. Thus, although an ideology of the family emerges from *Poltergeist,* the film does not provide ideological legitimation of the American political economy. In this light, the turn to the occult and transcendental-spiritual values in recent Hollywood films discloses a failure of the culture industries to provide effective ideological legitimation for contemporary American capitalism.

Nonetheless, whatever one thinks of Spielberg's occultism, or his affirmation of middle-class values, his work is valuable for shedding light on contemporary U.S. society and revealing the fears, hopes, and fantasies of the new affluent suburban middle class. In Steven Spielberg, the new middle class has found its storyteller and ideologue. His fantasies are permeated with ideologies that should be probed, decoded, and criticized by those interested in understanding U.S. society and culture in the contemporary era.

Poltergeist II and the Crisis of Patriarchy

I have argued that *Poltergeist* shows how specific social classes fear other classes and races, and that these fears may be projected in cinematic form. In this section, I wish to show how the problematics of class and race in contemporary film are also connected with gender and sexual politics. In general, these problematics are intimately intertwined, forcing analysis of representations of race, gender, class, and ethnicity to articulate fully the meanings and effects of popular films.[12] The gender problematic comes to the fore in the second *Poltergeist* film.

The original *Poltergeist* is brilliantly produced, combining Tobe Hooper's taste for the macabre and striking images with Spielberg's cinematic talents. The fluid camera is constantly moving throughout the film, producing striking images and juxtapositions; the lighting creates some stunning effects of the supernatural; and the film is gripping throughout. Brian Gibson's *Poltergeist II: The Other Side* (1986), by contrast, is highly mediocre cinematically, and its contrived "plot" travels further into the occult and supernatural. Yet the film's silly and muddled occultism provides an allegory of middle-class fears, including middle-class male fears of losing power, so once again I will engage in an allegorical reading to depict the film's problematics of gender and race.

Carol Clover points out how women are privileged in the first *Poltergeist* film.[13] The daughter and mother are presented as possessing more intuitive and clairvoyant powers than men, and the chief parapsychologist is a woman, as is the medium; thus, women are presented as the more powerful figures. The father is shown to be helpless and is usually depicted looking on from the sidelines, while the women control the discourse and events (only the women, for instance, participate in a long discussion of death and the afterlife). Clover fails to analyze, however, how the film articulates a crisis of patriarchy brought about by the strong women who threaten the power of the father, providing a need for him to reaffirm his power and respond to the crisis of patriarchy in the second *Poltergeist* film. Her intent focus on the important role of gender in the contemporary horror film also occludes the importance of the role of class and race, just as her argument that the horror film often privileges women over men covers over the importance of the resurrection of male power in *Poltergeist II*.[14]

Indeed, whereas the father is rather marginal in the first *Poltergeist*, he is central to the second one. The film opens a year after the events of the first film, with the father out of work and the family living with his wife's mother. The father indicates how much he misses his job and how he wishes they could return to their home. He complains about the failure of the insurance company to reimburse the family for the loss of the house, articulating contemporary anxieties concerning bureaucratic institutions and corporations. He also jokes about his "downward mobility," and he is portrayed as being completely ineffectual and pathetic, unable to better himself. Hence, the family is forced to live in the mother-in-law's house because the father seems to be unable to do anything to get the insurance company to pay the family's claim, and he is unable to get back his old job. The family's situation represents a thoroughgoing crisis of patriarchy and articulates male fears of losing house, job, and self-respect in a declining economy and disintegrating social order.

The scenario also suggests that male power is tied to economic power and that as men lose their economic power in a declining economy, they lose their familial or patriarchal power as well. The crisis of patriarchy also explains how men resort to violence against their spouses as compensation for their diminished status, as the film indeed depicts. Because the situation of downward mobility was a threat to men and families of all classes during this period, the fears articulated in the *Poltergeist* films are real ones, allowing a diagnostic analysis of male psychology in an era of declining economic stability and well-being.

In the narrative of the film, the Freeling family is once again threatened by the loss of Carol Anne, this time through the intervention of a mysterious preacher named Kane, played by Julian Beck, who was at the time of filming dying of cancer and projected a gaunt, haunting, ghastly figure.[15] Kane is presented as an evil force who is trying to abduct Carol Anne into the spirit world, and he is representative of an uneducated and malevolent working-class figure, a cross between the shyster preacher played by Robert Mitchum in *The Night of the Hunter* and the southern thug who threatens the middle class in standard Hollywood horror and crime dramas.

In the occult plot, Kane is said to have led a group of fundamentalist religious fanatics to California during the last century. They dwelled in a cavern underneath the site of the current Freeling house, believing that the world was coming to an end. The members of the religious sect, however, had a collective change of mind and attempted to climb out of the cave when the time for the predicted end of the world had passed, but they were trapped, as Kane had sealed the entrance with a stone. The sect was rumored to have been killed by Native Americans, but, in the occult plot, continue to reside fitfully in the cave beneath the graveyard, over which the Freeling's house was built, unable to go to "the other side." The spirits are attracted to Carol Anne, who they see as good and innocent and able to lead them "into the light," to take them to "the other side." By comparison, the evil Kane seems to want to spirit Carol Anne into the poltergeist world in order to use his power over her to regain control over his "flock." From this perspective, Kane represents the irrational, authoritarian working-class patriarchy that Steve Freeling must overcome to be a good middle-class father.

Read allegorically, the poltergeist disturbances are thus overdetermined, focusing on both spirits of the dead angry over the desecration of the burial site and on the anger of the poor whites trapped in a cave beneath the graveyard. The images of the poor white religious sect members, presented as threatening underclass types, trapped in the cave represent the fears of the middle class, anxious that downward mobility might push them into a similar forlorn state. The flashback images of the poor whites thus subliminally warn the audience that they too could fall into this condition.

Cumulatively, the images of the spirits of poor whites and spirits of the dead haunting the white middle class transcode its anxieties in an era of economic and social insecurity. *Poltergeist II* thus continues the probing of contemporary fears concerning race, class, gender, and sexuality, even more starkly and extravagantly than the first *Poltergeist*. The film was released in 1986, during a Reagan recession in which fear of unemployment, of losing one's home, and of loss of control over one's life was growing. Once again, technology is shown out of control, with an early scene showing a vacuum cleaner refusing to behave and, throughout the film, the father's car breaking down, perhaps articulating fears of loss or failure of one's automobile, a special token of prestige and power for the middle class. Now the family is threatened both by the spirits of the poor whites wanting out of their spirit dimension and the Native American spirits over whose graveyard the house was built. Together, the *Poltergeist* films thus allegorically represent fears that monsters from lower classes and other races will destroy middle-class suburban utopia.

Once again, the poltergeists come to haunt the family, and once again it is the women who are in touch with the spirit world. The film introduces the grandmother (played by Geraldine Fitzgerald), whose house the Freelings are living in, who also possesses occult power and communicates throughout the film from "the other side" with Carol Anne after her death. But this time the father too must deal with the spirits and prove himself "man enough" to lead the family. At one point, the preacher Kane shows up and rants at Steve: "Who do your wife and family turn to with their problems? They turn to *him* [Taylor], now don't they? They don't trust you any more, and what you fear is that you're not *man* enough to hold this family together!" In this scene, Kane plays on the father's fear that he is indeed not "man enough" to be a proper father.

The father is aided by Taylor, a Native American (Will Sampson) who appears as a "magic helper" (a traditional fairy tale motif) and who lectures him on his responsibilities and need to take charge. In one scene, the father goes off to a "sweat lodge" ceremony with the Native American, a scene of male bonding where the father presumably retrieves some of his lost patriarchal power. He is given a feather, which he proudly displays as a totem of his lost and hopefully to be regained patriarchal power.[16]

Yet the father is still lacking power and resolve, and in one frightening scene he turns to the spirits of alcohol, getting drunk on a bottle of tequila, the type with the worm in the bottle. In the occult plot shift, Kane inserts himself into the worm, to use the weak father to spirit away his daughter. The father swallows the worm and becomes demonically "possessed." The possession takes the form of a violent desire to have sex with his wife, whom he attempts to rape when she declines. In a violent struggle with the monster, the worm comes out of the father's mouth, now in the form of a giant snake, who—after a grotesque birthing metamorphosis—assumes the form of Kane! The figure of the worm/snake/monster/Kane symbolizes the dangers of out-of-control working-class sexuality and equates Kane with monstrous and threatening power.[17]

The father, however, eventually redeems himself and once again takes control of his family. The family bonds together to return to Cuesta Verde, the scene of their destroyed home. They go together into the cave under their house where Kane and his followers are trapped. The evil spirits seize Carol Anne and her mother, but with the help of the Native American, Taylor, the father and the son go to "the other side" to retrieve the mother and daughter. The father thus proves that he is worthy of reassuming patriarchal power and restores the family to unity. After escaping the cave, the family is shown once again in their old neighborhood, presumably to resume their happy and affluent suburban life.

Conclusion

The father has thus reconstituted his identity as leader of the family and reestablished a male authority in touch with the irrational, traditional, and heroic to become a proper middle-class patriarch. Likewise, the family is reconstituted as a positive and integral unit, overcoming threats and challenges to its integrity. Unlike the horror films of an earlier era that showed the family producing monstrosities and evil, the family in the *Poltergeist* films survives threats from the monsters who are outside "others" and threats to middle-class normality. Such films thus present ideological defenses and celebrations of the middle-class nuclear family.[18]

In my reading of the *Poltergeist* films, the poltergeists represent threatening class and racial others who menace middle-class normality, and the films articulate contemporary fears of the middle-class family in an uncertain economy and disintegrating social order. The two films show middle-class life as out of control and threatened with dissolution, yet the reestablishment of patriarchal order brings the family back together. The most poignant images in *Poltergeist II* show the family framed together in single shots, bonding together as a unit. Both of these films show families being torn apart and coming back together, a cinematic fantasy in an era in which real families *were* torn apart by a disintegrating economy and social order. Indeed, losing one's house and job and being threatened by crime and downward mobility were and still are all-too-real fears in the contemporary United States, so perhaps film audiences could symbolically confront such fears only in genres such as horror, rather than in realist drama. Indeed, who would want to watch a drama of a family whose members lose their jobs and their home and then are torn apart, an all-too-real series of events during the past decade of economic crisis.

From another perspective, the *Poltergeist* films, like conservative films such as *The Big Chill*, represent the end of the 1960s. In the first *Poltergeist*, the mother and father smoke dope and make love in one scene; the sixties generation has grown up, married, and now lives a cool lifestyle in the suburbs. In *Poltergeist II*, the wife tells the husband, "You were never a hippie," and says that he just assumed hip attitudes to impress another girl. A significant scene revolves around the mother cutting roses in the garden and remembering planting the roses with her mother when she was a girl—a poignant image of the continuity of the generations that some sixties radicals wanted to rupture. In the *Poltergeist* films, the sixties are dead and buried: relentless traditionalism and celebration of the family have returned with a vengeance, and Hollywood is only too happy to return to conservative institutions like the middle-class family, which it has traditionally celebrated.

Yet all is not happy in the home of the brave and the land of the free, and to discover articulations of contemporary class dynamics in the Hollywood cinema, one must deal with genres like the horror and fantasy film to experience fully the vicissitudes of class in the contemporary era and the deep anxieties around class downward mobility, perhaps *the* American nightmare. Horror and fantasy genres provide the material for social allegories that can deal with thematics too painful and real to be confronted in more realist genres. But whereas horror and fantasy can be deployed to criticize existing institutions, they can also deflect attention from the real sources of contemporary suffering onto occult figures. This is the ideological function of the *Poltergeist* films, which are ultimately conservative celebrations of middle-class normality that, read diagnostically, can reveal the threats to the family that it is the purpose of the films to patch over. The project of the *Poltergeist* films is thus ultimately to suture the spectator into desire for middle-class normality after allowing experience of threats to this normality to be played out. They are thus symptomatic of the right turn in U.S. culture after the radical critique and political movements of the 1960s put in question institutions such as the family and patriarchy.

Notes

An earlier study of the first *Poltergeist* film appeared in my work with Michael Ryan *Camera Politica: Politics and Ideology in Contemporary American Film* (Bloomington: Indiana University Press, 1988) and I am indebted here to our study of contemporary Hollywood film. A different version of this study appears in my book *Media Culture* (London: Routledge, 1995).

1. *Variety* claimed that in 1980 horror and science fiction films would generate more than one-third of all box-office rentals and predicted that by 1981, this figure would reach 50 percent. See "Horror Sci-Fi Pix Earn 37% of Rentals—Big Rise during 10-Year Period," *Variety*, January 3, 1981. *Cinefantastique* reported in a decade recap that half of the top ten money making films of all time are horror and science fiction films. See *Cinefantastique* 9, nos. 3–4 (1980): 72. The popularity of the horror film has continued to the present.

2. As Ferguson and Rogers argue: "The combination of social-spending cuts, other budget initiatives, and the massively regressive tax bill produced a huge upward distribution of American income. Over the 1983–1985 period the policies reduced the incomes of households making less than $20,000 by $20 billion, while increasing the incomes of households making more than $80,000 by $35 billion. For those at the very bottom of the income pyramid, making under $10,000 per year, the policies produced an average loss of $1,100 over 1983–85. For those at the top making more than $200,000, the average gain was $60,000. By the end of Reagan's first term, U.S. income distribution was more unequal than at any time since 1947, the year the Census Bureau first began collecting data on the subject. In 1983, the top 40% of the population received a larger share of income than at any time since 1947." Thomas Ferguson and Joel Rogers, *Right Turn* (New York: Hill & Wang, 1986), 130.

3. See Douglas Kellner and Michael Ryan, *Camera Politica: Politics and Ideology in Contemporary American Film* (Bloomington: Indiana University Press, 1988).

4. On "subversive" and "critical" moments in these and other contemporary filmmakers' works, see the studies in Andrew Britton, Richard Lippe, Tony Williams, and Robin Wood, *American Nightmare: Essays on the Horror Film* (Toronto: Festival of Festivals, 1979); and Kellner and Ryan, *Camera Politica*.

5. *Poltergeist* is credited as a Tobe Hooper film and Hooper is credited as director; Spielberg is credited as producer, source of the story, and one of the writers. There have been many discussions concerning alleged tensions between Hooper and Spielberg during the filming, as well as debate over whose film it really is—as if a collective enterprise "belongs" to one person or another. In fact, the film itself is an amalgam of the cinematic styles and concerns of Hooper and

Spielberg. This film exhibits Hooper's flair for the suspenseful, odd, and horrific and Spielberg's affection for the middle class, fuzzy-minded occultism, technical skill, and nose for the market.

6. Fear of television has been an obsession of Spielberg's in many of his films. Early in *Poltergeist*, the children are told not to play so roughly, and Carol Anne is directed to watch TV: she flicks it on and a violent Western is playing! In *E.T.*, when the alien watches television for the first time, he communicates his thoughts and feelings to the young boy at school (they have apparently achieved a "mind-meld," to use *Star Trek* lingo, sharing each other's minds). When E.T. watches a violent scene on TV, the boy is then violent at school; E.T. watches John Wayne kiss Maureen O'Hara, and the boy kisses a little girl at school. The fear that children will imitate what they see on TV is widespread in U.S. society today, and is symbolically portrayed in *Poltergeist* and *E.T.*—the concern has emerged in contemporary discussions of media violence and the impact of shows like *Beavis and Butt-head* on the young. Not accidentally, when the little boy in *E.T.* succeeds in his ploy to stay home from school to be with his new companion, the mother warns, "And no TV!"

7. Stephen King, "Why We Crave Horror Movies," *Playboy*, January 1981, 237. See the fuller articulation of King's theory of horror in his book *Danse Macabre* (New York: Everett, 1981).

8. See Barbara Ehrenreich, *Fear of Falling* (New York: HarperCollins, 1989).

9. Associated Press, June 3, 1994.

10. T. W. Adorno, *Minima Moralia* (London: New Left Books, 1974), 241.

11. See Jürgen Habermas, *Legitimation Crisis* (Boston: Beacon, 1975).

12. See my book *Media Culture* (New York: Routledge, 1995) for fuller demonstrations of this claim.

13. Carol Clover, *Men, Women, and Chain Saws: Gender in the Modern Horror Film* (Princeton, N.J.: Princeton University Press, 1992).

14. Clover also fails to see that *The Exorcist* and many other contemporary horror films are antifeminism and anti-independent and strong women, preferring to see the genre as strongly prowomen; in fact, like most genres, it has its reactionary and progressive wings, as I shall show in this discussion.

15. Beck, of course, was the founder of the avant-garde Living Theater and was himself a lifelong radical.

16. Clover, in *Men, Women, and Chain Saws,* presents the Native American Taylor as representative of a more feminine nature the father must get in touch with (94), but she misses the significance of the crisis of patriarchy that Steve must overcome and the motif of resurrection of male power; she also fails to read the retreat to the sweat lodge as male bonding that resurrects male power. Rather than representing the feminine per se, Taylor represents a more traditionalist supernatural wisdom against "normal" science and reason, so the message is ultimately that Steve must become more masculine and more wise to reassume the phallic power under threat.

17. Clover sees the birthing segment as a positive expression of the transgression/mixing of gender identities and generally valorizes the frequent

birthing images in the contemporary horror film as evidence of the positive and strong role of women in the genre; *Men, Women, and Chain Saws*, 106ff. But these images of monstrous births—which run through horror films such as the *Alien* series, *The Thing*, and many others—can be seen as extremely negative images of biological processes and thus as antiwomen, as projecting negative images of birth as monstrous and women as bearers of monstrosities.

18. I am leaving *Poltergeist III* (1988) out of my discussion because it does not deal with the Freeling family, showing instead Carol Anne visiting relatives in Chicago and the return of Kane to try to abduct her again. The film is so bad that it could be taken as symptomatic of the decline of the horror genre in the contemporary era, though part of the problem with the vague and unresolved plot might be a result of Heather O'Rourke's death, who was then unavailable to shoot scenes necessary for coherence and resolution. O'Rourke's death, following upon that of Dominique Dunne, the young woman who played her teenage sister in *Poltergeist,* fueled occultist folklore concerning the revenge of evil spirits, attention that should have focused on the nature of a violent society and the inadequate state of medical care (Dunne was killed by a jealous boyfriend, and O'Rourke's family sued for medical malpractice, claiming that she was misdiagnosed and was therefore given erroneous medical advice and treatment for an ailment that led to her death at age 13).

Chapter 11

Class in Action

Chuck Kleinhans

Trying to use the concept of class in contemporary cultural analysis presents several problems. Examining these problems clarifies why thinking about gender and race/ethnicity has progressed in recent years while class analysis has stalled. Most analysts start considering class from a Marxist framework, but that tradition does not provide simple answers except to the simplistic.[1] A full elaboration of the concept of class for cultural analysis calls for a reconsideration of class within Marxism and sociology. It would have to include an explanation of production and diffusion as well as texts themselves. It would have to account for class differences in audience reception. It would have to develop across, between, and within diverse media. And it would have to consider the interrelation of class with gender, race, ethnicity, age/generation, region, and so on.

As a starting point, I examine below the representation of class in a currently popular Hollywood genre, the action hero film. Rather than presenting a comprehensive analysis or a definitive model based on one example, I discuss the problems involved in the enterprise. Unpacking the issues seems more productive now than tying up the loose ends. This essay proceeds according to a roughly historical organization. First I explain my immediate interests; I then discuss some work in film studies that is foundational to my concerns with the representation of class. Next, I elaborate my current thinking about issues of class in mainstream film with a discussion of a Steven Seagal film, *Above the Law*. Finally, I address issues that remain for theory and criticism in dealing with class, recognizing that historical developments move faster than the critical apparatus that tries to understand them.

Star in Motion

A newly emerged action hero auteur, Steven Seagal, as actor, writer, director, and producer, has produced six distinctive action films. In his debut, *Above the Law* (1988), he plays a Chicago cop who battles Central American drug pushers protected by the CIA because they help channel money to the Nicaraguan Contras and El Salvador's repressive government. In *Hard to Kill* (1990) he is a cop who, from his deathbed, fights back to health and revenge upon the corrupt cops who, in league with an evil politician, have murdered his wife and tried to kill him. In *Marked for Death* (1990) he is a former Drug Enforcement Administration agent who burns out in Mexico but who then reenlists in the fight when Jamaican drug gangs threaten his Chicago suburban sister and niece. In *Out for Justice* (1991) he is a Brooklyn cop hunting down a drug-crazed killer he has known since boyhood in their Italian neighborhood. In *Under Siege* (1992) he appears as a former Navy Seal, now serving out his time as a cook, who saves the battleship *Missouri* when a former CIA operative's gang tries to steal its nuclear missiles. And in *On Deadly Ground* (1994) he is again a former special forces operative, now an oil rigger who discovers oil corporate greed is threatening the Alaskan wilderness and who, after encountering a murderous trap set up by the oil company, is saved from death by native people and transformed into an avenger who destroys the enviromentally threatening refinery. Throughout this corpus, Seagal distinguishes himself through his highly developed martial arts skill. The actor studied aikido and other martial arts in Japan for fifteen years before moving to Los Angeles as a master teacher and becoming involved in choreographing film fights. Such sequences are obligatory in his films, occur with predictable regularity (if he enters a bar, we know there will be a fight), and reflect his talent for action spectacle. He is not adept at character dialogue except in confrontations preceding a fight, and his films avoid romantic or love interests (unlike Bruce Willis in the *Die Hard* series) and buddy-partner interaction (unlike Mel Gibson with Danny Glover in the *Lethal Weapon* series).[2]

I first encountered Steven Seagal's image in 1988 in neighborhood video stores. Although I was vaguely aware of his theatrical film debut in *Above the Law*, the ads and reviews for that film led me to expect just another Sylvester Stallone clone enhanced with the martial arts skill of Chuck Norris: perhaps a recycled Billy Jack. But when the video appeared in the mom-and-pop rental stores of my Chicago Latino-Polish predominantly working-class neighborhood, suddenly I found the film's poster prominently displayed, multiple boxes of the tape placed for rental, and a continuous pestering of the store operators by people who wanted to rent the film but found all copies rented out. This continued for months. That demand sparked my interest. Why should this film, above so many others, have such a following in my neighborhood? I decided to rent it, but I had to wait along with everyone else.

Eventually I saw the film and discovered one reason for the draw. It had been shot in my part of Chicago, offering a great pleasure of recognition. But clearly the enthusiasm of the renters–who were often but by no means exclusively adolescent and young men–went beyond familiar pleasure. At the same time, although Seagal was so well known and enthusiastically greeted as each subsequent film arrived in the neighborhood (where one video store sign seemed to say it all generically: "Action, Horror, Comedy, Adult"), I knew few would know his films at my workplace. At Northwestern University, a private elite school in professional-managerial class Evanston, Illinois, when I mentioned my interest in his films to fellow teachers and students, the only substantial comment I heard was from one M.F.A. student in the Radio/Television/Film Department, who dismissively said that Seagal's sound tracks always heighten physical combat scenes with the loud crack of breaking bones.[3] It's true—this stylistic trait may derive from cinematic kung fu traditions.

In some video stores Seagal films appear in the martial arts section; in others, they are in the action section. This underlines the generic nature of his corpus. Probably the easiest way to identify the action genre is through the marketing device of video boxes.

Almost invariably an action video cover shows a person with a determined face looking straight out while prominently holding a gun (or other weapon, such as a knife), or a figure in a martial arts pose. This iconography shades off in one direction to the action adventure (e.g., the Indiana Jones series), science fiction, or war film in the direction of spectacle, and in the other in the private eye, cop, gangster, or western genre. The promise is clearly a shoot-'em-up that stresses action over dialogue, spectacle over character drama, and violence as a means of resolving problems. Critical discussion of these issues sometimes involves unreflective endorsement, as in an older model of popular culture studies. At times, recognition of a comic and/or ironic strain in the action film, as in some of Clint Eastwood's roles after the mid-1970s, moderates the analysis. But more often we find a directly negative view of the often obvious masculinist, racial, and political bias of the genre.

Commonplace thinking about the genre posits a primary audience of boys and young men, irrespective of class. In addition, it is common wisdom that the genre appeals more to the working class and the poor than to the educated middle class. Much of the current public discussion of excessive violence in films, television, rap music, and video games contains this unexamined assumption, and arguments for regulation and censorship of violent representations usually assume that such regulation is necessary because working-class and poor boys and young men especially need to be socially controlled. That this attitude interweaves class and race prejudice, especially when the euphemism "urban underclass" is evoked, goes without saying. And obviously the issue replays the construction of "juvenile delinquency" as a social problem and comic books as mental corruption in the 1950s.

In the Reagan era, many critics identified the action genre as especially ideologically reactionary when militant presidential posturing was associated with the filmic heroism of Rambo.[4] But this criticism was often so sweeping that it ignored considerable variation and complexity in the genre. It also attributed a vast sexism, racism, and political reactionism (which was true of some of the films) to all of them. To top it off, the films were often claimed to be aesthetically deformed by spectacle, violence, and postmodern pastiche. In her recent reconsideration, *Spectacular Bodies: Gen-*

der, Genre and the Action Cinema (1993), Yvonne Tasker argues that the genre is not so simple and obvious. Through an examination of gender, race, sexuality, and nationhood, she finds the action films much more ambivalent than critics have allowed; she asserts that they open multiple spectator pleasures.

Those who dismiss action cinema do not recognize how well it produces some of the key pleasures of Hollywood cinema. First, it is based in the presentation of action. It uses movement—of actors, of vehicles, of objects—which, combined with the editing technique of cutting on action, produces a strong kinesthetic pleasure in the audience. Action narratives exploit techniques of crosscutting to build the suspense of search sequences and to escalate the kinetic pace of chase sequences. They have the capacity to provide exotic locales, impressive landscapes, cityscapes, or vast, complex interiors. Further, action is embodied in the physical presence of the actors, who have highly expressive physiques and martial skills. Action also produces (especially in the theatrical viewing setting) the shared group pleasure of anticipation and resolution, both on the large scale of broad narrative development and on the micro level of defeating an opponent by breaking an arm (with a loud sound-track crack).

Because of their kinetic, corporeal, and spectacular foundations, action films, along with other "physical" genres (horror, melodrama, farce, pornography), often receive dismissive consideration from critics and theorists who look down on them from a position of class prejudice. The concept of class remains unaddressed by most film theorists, although some authors have helped to clarify the basic issues. For example, in his pioneering 1974 article, "The Anatomy of a Proletarian Film: Warner's *Marked Woman*," Charles Eckert recognizes the class nature of commercial entertainment cinema:

> My major contention is that the ultimate sources of
> *Marked Woman* [1937] and its tradition are in class
> conflict; but the level at which the film-makers perceive
> this conflict, and the level at which it is lived by the
> fictional characters and perceived by the audience, is
> existential rather than political or economic. . . . The
> expression of the conflict in the films, however, is almost
> never overt. It is instead converted into conflicts of a

surrogate nature—some ethical, some regional, some concerned with life-style, some symbolized by tonal or aesthetic overlays. (Eckert, [1974] 1985, 409)

Through textual processes of condensation and displacement, the deep structure of class conflict is converted into manifest content, but the effect is "to attenuate conflicts at the level of real conditions and to amplify and resolve them at the surrogate levels of the melodrama" (409). The papering over of contradictions is not perfect. The resulting work makes a "disjuncture between the melodramatic and the strongly affective scenes apparent" (409), which provides an entry for further analysis.

Eckert alerts us to the need to understand displacement in popular narrative. Employing the term *melodrama* in its common use in 1930s film criticism to refer to sensational action sequences, he also emphasizes how spectacle can shape narrative, and how it contrasts with domestic, personal scenes. Eckert's work develops understanding of the domestic melodrama and reminds us that the action formula often uses public space as a site for masculine adventure, but it is always crucially paired with domestic space. Often at significant moments the two worlds intersect, as when the villain enters familial space or personal matters are enacted in public places.[5]

Following Eckert, in an earlier essay I discuss two bio films on daredevil Evel Knievel and race-car driver Junior Johnson in terms of the characters as working-class heroes: men who clearly came out of the working class and who are heroes to the working class (Kleinhans [1974] 1985). The characters embody a fairly straightforward version of the U.S. success myth in which adherence to code values and virtues lead to triumph in sport entertainment. I discuss the films in terms of their appeal to working-class audiences, drawing on sociological analyses of blue-collar workers and comparing those with similar figurations in the narrative. Rather than seeing displacement as a central strategy, by dealing with two films that achieved their initial popularity with working-class audiences, I examined how these films portray the U.S. success myth in ways that match the complications of working-class audience expectations and fantasies. My understanding of the films assumes that the representation and narration in the aesthetic object can be fully understood only through a comparison in terms of the sociology of the working class. Audience understanding, then, mediates between the experienced realities of working-class life and the aesthetic representation of the class on screen.

In a series of three articles, Gina Marchetti advances the analysis of class in the action genre. Examining the television series *The A-Team* (1983-86, 1987), she notes a complex play of contradictions that offer various hooks for the mass audience while presenting an action adventure narrative (Marchetti 1987). In a subsequent article on the action adventure genre, she discusses how this genre deals with social inequality while presenting entertainment in action (Marchetti 1989). In her study of *Year of the Dragon* (1985), Marchetti (1991) discusses the contradictions within and among class, race/ethnicity, and gender in the film. Vietnam vet cop Stanley White is assigned to New York's Chinatown, where he tracks down the leader of a new Chinatown gang who has murdered White's wife early on in the film. In the process, White falls in love with a Chinese American broadcast news reporter. During the making and distribution of the film, which is based on a bestselling novel by Robert Daley, it was actively criticized as racist by Asian American activists. Marchetti shows how the contradictions among race, class, and gender are not functions simply of character but also of narration and spectacle. Whereas Eckert's approach emphasizes displacement of class (onto differences of rural/urban, for example), reminding us to look beyond the surface level of the narrative to textual operations, Marchetti emphasizes the film's ability to mask one aspect, such as racism, with another, such as sexism.

> If Stanley has legitimized white, male power over nonwhite woman, he has also allowed for the fulfillment of the working-class fantasy of possessing wealth magically through romance and dominating it through sexuality. A desire for class equality, thus, obscures the text's otherwise too-obvious racism and sexism. Moreover, the film's concluding romantic embrace can be read symbolically as a liberal call for racial understanding and harmony. Stanley's romance with Tracy can also be seen as the way the character comes to grips with and overcomes his own racism by falling in love. In this case, the myth of romantic

love can be seen as not only the cure-all for crises of male identity but also an antidote for the text's rather open racism. According to this reading, the containment of Tracy's possible sexual threat through heterosexual romance can be seen as a function of her gender rather than her race or ethnicity, so the text can use sexism to mask its racism if this interpretation is pursued. (Marchetti 1991, 294)

These approaches to the issue of class and action heroes offer ways of understanding the action film's complicated pleasures. And realizing that the films are complex, however simple they seem in manifest content, is essential. As Marchetti notes, although *Year of the Dragon* was protested by Asian American media activists, the Asian American audience was far less critical and, in fact, often found gratification in the narrative. If we are to develop a sophisticated critique of the dominant forms of mass culture and to construct effective alternatives, we must strive for complexity in our own analysis. In other words, we have to account for the pleasures of the texts we study and the complexities of audience responses to them. Dismissing action films from a position of high-culture elitism or self-assured political correctness amounts to reproducing a biased class attitude rather than investigating a class phenomenon.

In Action

Steven Seagal's action hero characters in his various films share similar traits: they rely on physical strength and skill, they are fearless in the face of danger, and they solve problems with action (but not without wit and cunning). But what particularly interests me in *Above the Law* is the fantasy configuration of masculinity and class positioned between two key social institutions—the family and the police—that are both threatened by drug criminals. Throughout this complicated narrative of masculine achievement, several things remain constant: references to illegal federal intelligence operations that echo public knowledge, the validation of the family and the male role as protector, the flaws and mistakes of large-scale bureaucracies (the police, FBI, CIA, U.S. government), the importance of standing up against corruption, the importance of coworkers, and the necessity of direct physical action as it is represented in hand-to-hand combat and skilled use of firearms.

The story line sets up the key thematic terms. Although spectacle in the fight sequences serves the most important plot functions (and appears every ten to fifteen minutes of screen time) and is the most memorable part of the Seagal films, it is important to note that the plot's turns supply many hooks for masculinity and class as narrative. Although the action film eschews characters' inner psychology, the turns of events make it clear that a "real man" has to struggle. Such effort is narratively accented in *Above the Law*'s introduction, when we see old family photos as we hear Niccolo Toscani's voice describing his Sicilian immigrant background. The first action sequence depicts his apprenticeship in the study of martial arts in Japan. In an episode set in 1973 on the Vietnam-Cambodia border, we see young Toscani as a CIA agent involved in secret operations. He is present at the "chemical interrogation" of prisoners by a CIA physician, which consists of drug injection and torture, apparently in revenge for interference with the doctor's drug running. Toscani intervenes and, after a drawn-gun standoff, he leaves, yelling, "You think you're soldiers! You're fucking barbarians!" He says he's through. The scene dissolves to a Chicago Catholic church in 1988 and the baptism of Toscani's first child. At the subsequent party, we learn that he is now a police detective.

His first investigation involves finding a missing cousin, a teenage girl. At a bar seeking information, he punches out several guys, overpowers one who points a gun at him, and finally rescues the schoolgirl from a room upstairs, where she is in bed with her boyfriend and cocaine. Currying favor when roughed up, the boyfriend tells of an upcoming drug shipment, and in the next scene Toscani is seen illegally wiretapping to get more information. In the next action episode, Chicago police wait for the deal to go down but are interrupted by overzealous federal agents; the scene erupts in a chase, with Toscani hanging on to the roof of the criminals' car. Although apprehended, the criminal Salvano and his henchman are released by the FBI in response to a call from higher up, and the Chicago police are told to hold off investigating Salvano because he is cooperating on some secret matter of importance. Toscani storms out of the meeting with the FBI, disgusted that the biggest drug dealer in town is let go.

Repeating a frequent pattern in cop action films of personal involvement driving an investigation, Toscani continues his pursuit of Salvano on his own and trails the mobster to Toscani's church, which the criminal visits and then leaves. The parish priest spots the detective and reveals a secret basement room where a group of Latin American refugees are hidden, including Father Tomasino, recently arrived from El Salvador. The following Sunday, Toscani is attending Mass with his family when a bomb goes off, killing the senior priest.

One might think that Toscani acts alone because he is the key figure in all the fight sequences, but it is important to note that he is not a loner: the collectivity of the community is embodied in his actions. Here, the church is central to community identity and at the heart of the sovereign identity of the ordinary people. Toscani's widowed mother relates to the priest as a friend and confidant, the "father" takes a parental interest in Nico, and when the church is violated by the bomb, Toscani assumes the patriarchal burden of bringing the perpetrators to justice. In other films Seagal's character also fights for social justice, for the common people against the criminal/corporate/capitalist/government conspiracy. He represents a masculinity that is disgusted by violation and fights against it: on an immediate and local level and on a global, transnational one—in his most recent film, on a global environmental level. In the action cinema, masculinity is a fluid term and is not present only in the hero; it is also embodied negatively in the villain. The dramatic narration shows and finally resolves the conflict between these two kinds of masculinity. Seagal's characters embody a "proper" masculinity, one that is self-assured and that protects and serves the weak. The villains embody a masculinity out of control, a form of male hysteria that is usually quite clearly marked.

While seeking further information about the now missing Father Tomasino, the detective faces off a gang of toughs in an alley. Late that night, a phone call from an old CIA buddy warns Toscani that he and his family are in grave danger. The cop is then put on suspension and faces an assassination attempt by five guys on his way home. After disposing of them, he returns home to move his wife and child out. Toscani then follows the trail to Father Tomasino's hiding place, only to meet up with the CIA hit squad, his old enemy Zargon the torturer M.D., and the drug dealer Salvano "chemically interrogating" the priest to find out if he has told anyone of their plan to kill a U.S. senator who is investigating intelligence agency involvement in drug trafficking.

A gunfight ensues, with Toscani escaping after seeing his police partner shot. Believing her dead, he goes to her apartment and finds the documents Father Tomasino was going to give to the senator. The entire scheme involves the CIA using Zargon's drug money to finance the Contra forces invading Sandinista Nicaragua. Now understanding the plan, Toscani spies on Zargon, who captures and tortures him with chemicals before the planned murder of the politician. Toscani overcomes the drug's effects, kills the criminals, and foils the assassination. The film ends with a shot of the Capitol building and Toscani's voice-over, as if giving testimony before Congress, warning that no element of the government should be "above the law."

Underpinning the entire story in *Above the Law* is a basic displacement of class oppression and class conflict as an issue. At a key point in most cop action stories, the police officer faces a decision to go against direct orders or prescribed rules of law and conduct. The narrative usually posits this as a moment of moral and ethical choice that forces the cop to disregard rules in order to become the agent of justice. Toscani first enacts this "moral choice" in the Vietnam sequence, where his orders are to "observe and assist" the interrogation. He also disregards the rules when he enters the bar looking for his cousin and roughs up some patrons. And again, he acts on his own when admonished to leave Salvano alone. When he is suspended, he must act on his own to protect his family and catch the villains.

But what this common narrative configuration represses is the reality of actual or threatened economic hardship in such a situation. Many ordinary working-class people gain workplace knowledge concerning their employers' illegal or unethical activities. They observe white-collar crimes ranging from false billing to tax evasion, from health and safety code violations to toxic waste dumping. But the workers also know that the cost of whistle-blowing is the loss of their jobs, or, if their reports are kept internal to the organization, a reputation as a troublemaker. Usually, workers who speak up face immediate and tangible economic punishment that affects them and their families. The necessity of keeping their jobs keeps workers, both blue-collar and white-collar, in line. Two signifying absences allow for the central action fantasy in *Above the Law:* Toscani never loses his livelihood (his ability to support his family), and he sees corruption as an aberration that can be corrected, not as a structural condition of the existing order. He is enabled to do what is right, pursue the criminal, find the wrong-doer, stand up for the victims, without regard for his personal economic situation. His personal ethical motivation is granted full expression as a motivating device in the plot. He tells the CIA: "You think you're above the law. You're not above *my* law."

This core fantasy in which one does the right thing without having to calculate economic hardship has a great appeal in films that draw a working-class audience. And this reflects one of the key lessons of the Reagan-Bush era: by making homelessness widespread and visible, the state underlined the reality that most working-class and lower-middle-class people are just a few paychecks from being homeless, thus providing a not-very-subtle lesson about staying in line, not making waves, not acting on principle. In Seagal's films this fantasy finds considerable narrative support in the thematic importance of family and friendship. Toscani's male potency is most dramatically conveyed through his physical strength and martial arts skill, but it also finds expression in his official role as cop and his role in the family as protector. He begins the film-long quest when at the baptism party his grandmother implores him to find his cousin. Later, when his family is threatened, he calls on his Italian male relatives for help. (Earlier, at the party, his police buddies joke that Toscani has more relatives under federal indictment than any other cop in the city, underlining Toscani's position between the Sicilian family-organized Mafia and the police.) The Catholic church reinforces the theme of family, with the baptizing father protecting the refugees. The priest also has an emotional bond with Toscani, as stand-in for the cop's deceased father. When the cleric is killed by a bomb, Toscani carries the martyr's body from the church (Figure 11.1). His wife's pleas for him to stop being proud and to compromise only strengthen his resolve as a cop.

Figure 11.1. Toscani carries the priest's body out of the bombed church.

Although Toscani's partner, Dolores Jackson (Pam Grier, best known for her roles in "blaxploitation" films such as *Coffy*, 1973), reveals her bravery in the shootouts, she is in her last week of police duty before using her newly acquired law degree to work for the district attorney (a common narrative hook in the action genre: the sidekick's imminent retirement increases suspense that the character will be killed in action). Toscani continuously tries to have Jackson play a subordinate role, so she won't be tainted by his illegal ways. As she comes to his aid under fire, the plot emphasizes her loyalty and willingness to face danger, but it also underlines Toscani's patriarchal protector role. This is particularly marked visually when Toscani visits Jackson's place to fetch the political documents. Believing that she is dead, he stops to look at a photo of her with him and his wife and child. Given their relative positions in the photo, it looks like he has two wives (Figure 11.2). Further, the other photos he finds of Jackson show her alone, even as a child. It seems she has no family, except

Figure 11.2. A photo at his partner's apartment shows Toscani flanked by his wife (played by Sharon Stone, left), who holds their baby, and Dolores Jackson (played by Pam Grier).

Toscani's—nor, for that matter, does his wife, who has to be deposited with his Mafia relatives for her own safety.

Although women are subordinate, in terms of race, pure thuggery is an equal opportunity employer. Although Salvano's gang appears to be mostly Latino, Toscani also has to face off a white tough who sees the cop subduing his Latino friend. When another gang of hoodlums comes after him with automatic weapons, Toscani shoots the white guy in the group and tosses the Asian member through a window while subduing the Latinos. Salvano's bully boys even include a red-haired suit-wearing fellow. Whereas the FBI team is black and white, the CIA bad boys are all white, as is Zargon (Henry Silva).[6] The most demeaning racial stereotype in the film appears with a turbaned South Asian who is comically hysterical when the street fighting moves into his grocery store. This "integration" is a trend that Hollywood seems to have turned into a norm in the mid-1970s after extensive criticism about racial casting of villains, and here it both changes and reinforces social prejudices. Although the bad guys and good guys achieve remarkable racial equity (though obviously gender imbalanced), the main struggle is between white men.

Class in Analysis

Given the preceding presentation of *Above the Law,* I can elaborate some of the problems in trying to do a class analysis of film. It is worth mentioning briefly how the discussion of gender and race has developed in film and cultural studies because it suggests how class analysis may fare. In the past twenty years, first with feminist analysis and later with gay/lesbian/queer criticism and more recently with race investigation, media studies have come to terms with gender and race in matters of representation and reception. But class, although often evoked as a term, has yet to be elaborated adequately as a critical concept. Is this just an inconsequential temporal lag that is about to be remedied, or does class as a social phenomenon present challenges to conceptualization? In either case, it must be noted that the strong development of gender and race studies coincided with the growth of identity constituencies within cultural analysis, particularly in higher education. No similar social group pushes for class analysis. Rather, to the extent that it is a concern, it remains an issue for Marxists.

Lenin ([1913] 1971) has pointed out that Marxism has three sources and three component parts. From economics, particularly English political economy, Marx developed his understanding of the production of surplus value as the engine of capitalism. From this perspective, the working class powered the motor. From the history of socialism, particularly French socialists, Marx drew an image of society deeply divided by class and a view of the working class, at that moment a new emerging social group opposed to feudalism while demonstrating a Jacobin resistance to the bourgeoisie, as politically essential to social change. And from the materialist tradition in philosophy, particularly as inflected by German philosophy, with Hegel's emphasis on history and dialectics, Marx found a historical role for the working class as the inevitable agent for changing capitalism into socialism. Thus Marx described the class structure of capitalism in its early stages when accumulation and entrepreneurship supplied key defining characteristics. The result, within the history of Marxism as a political and intellectual movement, has been to place ultimate faith in the industrial working class as the necessary agent of revolutionary change. This faith has been challenged repeatedly in the twentieth century: narrow nationalism overwhelmed proletarian internationalism; actual communist revolutions took place in nations with very small working classes; many workers accepted fascism; industrial production in many fields evolved into automation and robotization requiring far fewer workers; unions drastically declined in the United States in terms of a share of the workforce; progressive social and political movements often found workers on the other side of their issues; and existing communisms imploded.

Marx and Engels never developed a systematic theory of class. The *Manifesto* ([1848] 1973) asserts that in the bourgeois era, "society as a whole is more and more splitting into two great hostile camps, into two great classes directly facing each other—bourgeois and proletariat" (68). Here is the classic statement that seems to predict increasing class polarization. But in his later work, particularly in the *Theories of Surplus Value,* Marx recognized the tendency of the middle classes to blur class boundaries and actually to increase in numbers.

The analytic power of Marxism's three components in accounting for the epochal change from feudalism to capitalism cannot be denied. But a great deal of left-wing thinking (and political organizing) has run aground by confusing the abstract and analytic concept of the working class with actual workers or groups of workers and by using the abstractions for prediction. Without specific study and historical context, Marxist concepts of class are simply dogma. Although I cannot develop a fuller discussion of this topic here, I can refer to some useful starting points for thinking about the U.S. situation. Stephen J. Rose's *Social Stratification in the United States* (1992) provides a clear introduction to the basics of contemporary wealth and income distribution across occupational and gender and race categories. In *Prisoners of the American Dream,* Mike Davis (1986) explains the particular nature of the U.S. working class in political terms. Stanley Aronowitz's *False Promises* (1973) offers an interpretation of U.S. labor, with attention to its cultural dimension. And *Classes,* by Erik Olin Wright

(1985), provides a Marxist analysis rooted in the sociology of the United States.

In media studies, gender and race investigation has tended to move through three overlapping (but by no means mutually exclusive) phases. The first phase consists of finding makers and explicating their works, past and present. This has finite limits for feminist, gay, or racial/ethnic minority inquiries, although it can be extended from directors and screenwriters to stars. However, whatever their class origins, by the time individuals in the commercial industry get to the point of having creative control, they belong to the upper strata, economically and culturally. Only in rare cases are people catapulted from the working class to positions of entertainment industry power. Arguable examples might include Elvis Presley and Roseanne, who flaunts a "white trash with money" image. But power and control in commercial culture reside ultimately in finance and distribution, which are corporate and capitalist. We would have to look in the marginal areas of home movies/videos, student productions, cable-access programming, labor activist documentary, and low-power broadcasting to find working-class media makers.

The second phase of media analysis is impelled by a motivation to examine a group's representations. Although the working class is directly represented in almost all Hollywood films, it is seldom at the heart of dramatic construction. Even films about union struggles, such as *Matewan* (1987), often concentrate on the organizer rather than the rank and file. So we do have workers represented—female and male, white, black, Asian, and Latino—often through a texture of service, sales, secretarial, and other minor characters, but also in displaced forms in which their class situation is usually forgotten: the waitress, the enlisted soldier, the prostitute, the cowboy, the taxi driver, and so on. Or someone who is technically a small owner may be presented as a worker, such as the truck driver-operator hero of *White Line Fever* (1975) (Tress 1975). When working-class people are at the center of the drama, they are often depicted as rising quickly out of their class. In the comedy *Working Girl* (1988), for example, the Melanie Griffith character is brought from the secretarial pool into the upper-class world of executive management; In *Pretty Woman*

(1990), the Cinderella quickly leaves street prostitution for luxury hotels and shops.

Historical study provides an important analytic approach to group representations. Social historian George Lipsitz (1976, 1982, 1990) has considered the presentation of the working class in 1940s film and ethnic working-class sitcoms in 1950s television. In his dissertation on representations of the working class in Hollywood films of the 1970s, Peter Steven (1982) considers a significant group of films plus three works in depth: *Saturday Night Fever* (1977), *Norma Rae* (1979), and *Blue Collar* (1978). Writing in the early 1980s, Steven noted that a shift had occurred and that Hollywood had a new openness to dealing with workers' lives. Although there is always some room for this in the commercial mainstream, in retrospect it seems that the 1970s produced a cycle that arose, flourished, and trailed off rather than marked a decisive change in subject matter. In an essay on media representations of the working class, Stanley Aronowitz (1989) asserts that there has been a definite pattern of decline, quantitatively and qualitatively, from *The Honeymooners* (1950–52, 1952–57, 1966–70, under various Jackie Gleason shows) to the present. This argument matches Aronowitz's (1973, 1981) other analyses of class in the United States, in which he sees a vast change in the workforce that makes traditional left notions of an industrial proletariat obsolete. When he claims there are no more working-class depictions in the popular media, he also tends to extrapolate from short-term changes. Clearly, the sitcom families of *Roseanne* (1988–) *Married . . . with Children* (1987–), *Roc* (1991–94), and *The Simpsons* (1989–) are working-class by husband's occupation and social context. And we often find working-class families in TV movies of the week and made-for-cable "trauma dramas," such as *The Burning Bed* (1984), and working-class women characters at the center of films such as *Silkwood* (1983) and *Mask* (1985), as critic Elayne Rapping (1987, 1992, 1994) points out in several acute analyses of gender and class representations in media. Cable television, with its intense demand for product, has opened up some opportunities, as with *Laurel Avenue* (1994), depicting several generations of an African American midwestern urban working-class family.

Once we move past sitcoms and domestic melodramas into the public sphere, the stories are dominated by (white heterosexual) men, and those men are seldom clearly identified as working-class, except possibly in origin, as in the bio film of the athlete or entertainer. Thus, any further analysis of class in commercial dramatic narrative has to address the question of how class is represented, including, as I mentioned earlier, how it may be displaced. In turn, the critic needs to understand how such displacement is read by the audience. Although many Marxists would argue that the police are not part of the working class, except by origin, in *Above the Law* and Seagal's subsequent *Out for Justice,* the working-class milieu is essential to the hero's progress through the narrative.[7]

The third large area of critical investigation for gender and race analysis has been the audience, or spectatorship. Drawing on the insight that the text is only a pretext and that meaning is constructed through an audience's active involvement, critics have constructed various models of female spectatorship. To the extent that analysts call on their own frames of reference and experience in constructing their analyses, such studies have faced critical correction when it has been pointed out that their models presume heterosexual or white viewers. Robust studies of African American, Latino, and Asian American audiences remain on the agenda. At present, reception studies face two important adjustments. First, investigators must come to terms with diversity within groups—not all people who share one measure of identity are alike in other ways. Second, analysts need to clarify the procedures of ethnographic investigation, which often seem whimsical to skeptics.[8]

Beyond such corrections, which would apply to empirical or speculative studies of working-class audiences/spectatorship, it has to be acknowledged that such studies of cinema do not exist. Bruce Austin's (1989) comprehensive study of social science research on film audiences reveals that class has never been a significant term in such work. And only in some relatively recent work on television, notably David Morley's (1980, 1986) studies and Ellen Seiter's (1989, 1993) research, has class been addressed as an essential category.

How, then, would we look at the action hero, in this case Nico Toscani? Assuming that I am correct in supposing that such figures appeal more to the working class than to the upper levels of the middle class, we would have to elaborate a class-based analysis of identification. But the concept of identification in dramatic narrative remains weakly developed. In the past three decades only two major advances have been made. The first is the concept of cinematic "double identification" elaborated in French film theories by Christian Metz and others. According to this concept, an audience member experiences a primary identification, essentially an activity of the psychoanalytically understood unconscious, that allows the process of film viewing to take place. Primary identification is linked to early childhood development of fantasy and desire. There is also a secondary identification, in which the viewer identifies with the central character and with the camera as a controlling presenter of narrative. This aspect of identification relates more to socially constructed identity. For our purposes here, it is easy to accept this distinction, with the observation that most of the time the action hero genre keeps the narration within the general scene of the protagonist. But clearly action films also trade heavily in fears (such as Zargon's sadism) and desires (the hero's skilled and muscular body) that relate to primary identification.

The second advance in thinking about identification concerns seeing it as gendered, and particularly as masculine and heterosexual in most cases. Arguments about minority spectatorship extend this insight and confirm that identification seems to function in conjunction with actual and perceived social power. But there has been no adequate accounting of how identification takes place across boundaries. Clearly it does take place—to get pleasure from the dominant media, women can follow masculine adventures; racial minorities accept white characters in a white privileged world; homosexuals and bisexuals project themselves into heterosexual characters and narratives; and working-class spectators follow middle-class or capitalist-class heroes. And the reverse is also the case: middle-class spectators can find working-class heroes appealing, especially when this is covered with a certain romanticization of the more "natural," more "masculine" character. The proletarian can function as the narrative Other for middle-class audiences, reproducing the power dialectic of subordination and desire, debasement and idealization so well worked out in media studies of race and gender.[9] In art experience, desire can override identity, and desire often acts subversively.

Genre analysis enhances our understanding of identification, because any specific film and its responses need to checked against others of their kind. Genre study provides access to the larger cultural context, including historical tradition. Although adventure stories with hero warriors are found in many cultures at many different times in history, the cop action film genre seems especially strong in U.S. cinema in the past thirty years. Today the cop narrative dominates much of prime time television the way the western story did earlier.[10] And with docutainment reality TV, such as *Cops* (1989–) and related shows, the police appear again as privileged narrative figures. Why should this be so characteristic of our cultural moment? Part of the answer rests in the position of the cop as someone who must function within a rule-bound bureaucracy and yet who is authorized to be violent in order to be the agent of justice. In terms of appeal to working-class audiences, part of the answer is that the cop is a worker, and may be female (*Blue Steel*, 1990), African American (*Passenger 57*, 1992), or, perhaps in the near future, homosexual. Is the cop then working-class? Sometimes. It is difficult to think of Crockett and Tubbs from *Miami Vice* (1984–89) as working-class, given their frequent impersonation of high rollers. But in the case of Seagal, especially in *Above the Law* and *Out for Justice*, the working-class context is unmistakable. At the narrative micro level of dialogue, voice, mise-en-scène, shot, editing, and dramatic situation, as well as in the depicted environment and the central character's family, the narrative is inscribed with class-conscious markers. Audience understanding draws on lived experience and class context on the one hand and the aesthetic object on the other to produce a kind of "cognitive mapping" of class in cinematic experience. What are the pleasures of these masculine fantasies? A full answer would have to synthesize from and further develop textual analysis and extratextual analysis, spectatorship and audience ethnography, aesthetics and sociology. The study of popular film has advanced through various stages in the past forty years. Genre and authorship studies have established the foundations for the consideration of commercial entertainment film. Gender, race, and ideological analyses have furthered knowledge. From this perspective, class analysis of popular dramatic narrative films is not only desirable but necessary for a full understanding.

Notes

I would like to thank the following people for their helpful comments: Julia Lesage, John Hess, Rick Maxwell, Michelle Citron, Fran Parr, Jim Schwoch, Larry Lichty, the audience for an earlier version of this essay presented at the University of Oregon, anonymous readers for the University of Minnesota Press, and members of my graduate class in contemporary film theory at Northwestern University, spring 1994.

1. For example, the drastic reductionism of Michael Parenti's *Make-Believe Media: The Politics of Entertainment* (1992) understands almost all films and TV programs in terms of a content analysis of the narrative that amounts to propaganda for the capitalist class. No ambiguity or complexity is granted in the works under consideration. In Parenti's view, working-class viewers are helpless victims of the mass media, unable to select, filter, or change meanings.

2. In *Out for Justice* Seagal's character is separated from his wife and reconciles with her at the end. *Hard to Kill* begins with his character in a happy marriage and then develops a romance with the nurse who helps him heal, but otherwise the plots avoid the double structure of a dramatic line of action coupled with a heterosexual romance typical of the classic Hollywood cinema. In most films he is crucially assisted by a woman (variously African American, Native American, or white) or a man of color.

3. I should note, however, that when I started writing this essay, Michelle Citron and Rick Maxwell, two faculty colleagues who strongly relate to class issues in cultural analysis, in part from their own working-class backgrounds, took a special interest in it.

4. Susan Jeffords provides an extensive survey in *Hard Bodies: Hollywood Masculinity in the Reagan Era* (1994).

5. There has been extensive recent critical study of gender as an issue in domestic melodrama, but less attention has been paid to race and class. I discuss a film portraying the effects of working-class unemployment in "Realist Melodrama and the African-American Family: Billy Woodberry's *Bless Their Little Hearts*" (1994).

6. In Silva's career as a heavy, his variation from the physiognomic norms of white European representation allowed him to play diverse as well as unspecified ethnicities.

7. Parenti, for example, in *Make-Believe Media* (1992), says police are not working-class. Inconsistently, in an earlier polemic, he seems to claim that everyone who is not an owner is a worker (Parenti 1989).

8. John Fiske's work is often cited for overgeneralization based on small samples studied for short terms. In *Power Plays Power Works* (1993), Fiske discusses a few homeless men in a shelter watching *Die Hard*. He notes an interesting behavior in which the men get the most pleasure from the film during action scenes of the villains attacking the corporation and its representatives, and then during scenes showing the lone hero fighting against the villains. They don't

watch the ending. Fiske relates this selective reading to his general thesis of underdog subversive reception and re-creation of culture.

9. I discuss some aspects of this in an analysis of *Shampoo* (Kleinhans 1981).

10. The cop genre continues, transforms, and displaces the western genre in an interesting evolution of U.S. masculine fantasy. For recent suggestive analyses of the western, see Slotkin's *Gunfighter Nation* (1992) and Tompkins's *West of Everything* (1992).

Works Cited

Aronowitz, Stanley. *False Promises: The Shaping of American Working Class Consciousness*. New York: McGraw-Hill, 1973.

_____. *The Crisis in Historical Materialism: Class, Politics and Culture in Marxist Theory*. New York: Praeger, 1981.

_____. "Working Class Culture in the Electronic Age." In *Cultural Politics in Contemporary America*. Ed. Ian Angus and Sut Jhally. New York: Routledge, 1989. 135–50, 370.

Austin, Bruce A. *Immediate Seating: A Look at Movie Audiences*. Belmont, Calif.: Wadsworth, 1989.

Davis, Mike. *Prisoners of the American Dream: Politics and Economy in the History of the US Working Class*. London: Verso, 1986.

Eckert, Charles. "The Anatomy of a Proletarian Film: Warner's *Marked Woman*" (1974). In *Movies and Methods*, vol. 2. Ed. Bill Nichols. Berkeley: University of California Press, 1985. 407–29.

Fiske, John. *Power Plays Power Works*. London: Verso, 1993.

Jeffords, Susan. *Hard Bodies: Hollywood Masculinity in the Reagan Era*. New Brunswick, N.J.: Rutgers University Press, 1994.

Kleinhans, Chuck. "Working-Class Film Heroes: Junior Johnson, Evel Knievel and the Film Audience." In *Jump Cut: Hollywood, Politics, and Countercinema*. Ed. Peter Steven. New York: Praeger, 1985. 64–82. Reprinted from "Contemporary Working Class Film Heroes: *Evel Knievel* and *The Last American Hero*." *Jump Cut* no. 2 (July-August 1974): 11–14.

_____. "*Shampoo*: Oedipal Symmetries and Heterosexual Knots." *Jump Cut* no. 26 (1981): 12–18.

_____. "Realist Melodrama and the African-American Family: Billy Woodberry's *Bless Their Little Hearts*." In *Melodrama: Stage, Picture, Screen*. Ed. J. S. Bratton, Jim Cook, and Christine Gledhill. London: British Film Institute, 1994.

Lenin, V. I. "The Three Sources and Three Component Parts of Marxism" (1913). In *Selected Works: One Volume Edition*. New York: International Publishing, 1971. 20–24.

Lipsitz, George. "Rank and File Fantasy in Films of the Forties." *Jump Cut* nos. 12/13 (1976): 24–27.

_____. *Class and Culture in Cold War America: A Rainbow at Midnight*. South Hadley, Mass.: Bergin & Garvey, 1982.

_____. *Time Passages: Collective Memory and American Popular Culture*. Minneapolis: University of Minnesota Press, 1990.

Marchetti, Gina. "Class, Ideology and Commercial Television: An Analysis of *The A-Team.*" *Journal of Film and Video* 39, no. 2 (1987): 19–28.

_____. "Action Adventure as Ideology." In *Cultural Politics in Contemporary America.* Ed. Ian Angus and and Sut Jhally. New York: Routledge, 1989. 182-97, 371–73.

_____. "Ethnicity, the Cinema, and Cultural Studies." In *Unspeakable Images: Ethnicity and the American Cinema.* Ed. Lester D. Friedman. Urbana: University of Illinois Press, 1991. 277–307.

Marx, Karl, and and Friedrich Engels. *The Manifesto of the Communist Party* (1848). In *The Revolutions of 1848.* Ed. David Fernbach. New York: Random House, 1973. 62–98.

Morley, David. *The "Nationwide" Audience: Structure and Decoding.* London: British Film Institute, 1980.

_____. *Family Television: Cultural Power and Domestic Leisure.* London: Comedia, 1986.

Parenti, Michael. "The Stampede from Class." *NST: Nature, Society, and Thought* 2, no. 1 (1989): 137–52.

_____. *Make-Believe Media: The Politics of Entertainment.* New York: St. Martin's, 1992.

Rapping, Elayne. *The Looking Glass World of Nonfiction TV.* Boston: South End, 1987.

_____. *The Movie of the Week: Private Stories/Public Events.* Minneapolis: University of Minnesota Press, 1992.

_____. *Media-tions: Forays into the Culture and Gender Wars.* Boston: South End, 1994.

Rose, Stephen J. *Social Stratification in the United States: The American Profile Poster Revised and Expanded.* New York: New Press, 1992.

Seiter, Ellen. " 'Don't Treat Us Like We're So Stupid and Naive': Towards an Ethnography of Soap Opera Viewers." In *Remote Control: Television, Audiences and Cultural Power.* Ed. Hans Borchers, Ellen Seiter, Gabriele Kreutzer, and Eva-Maria Warth. London: Routledge, 1989. 223–47.

_____. *Sold Separately: Parents and Children in Consumer Culture.* New Brunswick, N.J.: Rutgers University Press, 1993.

Slotkin, Richard. *Gunfighter Nation: The Myth of the Frontier in Twentieth Century America.* New York: HarperCollins, 1992.

Steven, Peter Gaard. "Hollywood's Depiction of the Working-Class from 1970 to 1981: A Marxist Analysis." Doctoral dissertation, Northwestern University, 1982.

Tasker, Yvonne. *Spectacular Bodies: Gender, Genre and the Action Cinema.* New York: Routledge, 1993.

Tompkins, Jane. *West of Everything: The Inner Life of Westerns.* New York: Oxford University Press, 1992.

Tress, Madeliane. "*White Line Fever:* A Collective Drama." *Jump Cut* no. 9 (1975): 3–4.

Wright, Eric Olin. *Classes.* London: Verso, 1985.

Chapter 12

The Hollywood Waitress:
A Hard-Boiled Egg and the Salt of the Earth

Jane Collings

> Serving a man food . . . apparently, was in itself an ancient
> intimacy.
>
> —James M. Cain, *Mildred Pierce*

The late 1980s and early 1990s witnessed the production of several high-profile Hollywood films that use the character of the
waitress: *The Accused* (Jonathan Kaplan, 1988), *White Palace*
(Luis Mandoki, 1990), *Frankie and Johnny* (Garry Marshall,
1991), *Thelma & Louise* (Ridley Scott, 1991), and (in its way),
The Terminator (James Cameron, 1984). This essay represents an
attempt to understand why this figure of a working-class woman
appears here, and whether contradictions and similarities between
the films mentioned can provide insight into the uses of the notion
of class in mass-culture films in general. Why is it important that
the women in these films be working-class, and if working-class,
why they must be waitresses? Some review of the duties of the
waitress, and her relationship with her customers, will begin to
draw the profile of this character.

The waitress serves her male customers much as, within the
"natural order" of patriarchal culture, the woman serves her male
relatives. On the occasions when a waitress serves a female customer, we may say that the waitress serves her in her identification
with either her husband's or her father's class position, or, if the

woman being served is a self-supporting professional woman, in her identification with a predominantly patriarchal socioeconomic structure. In these particular cases, the waitress is performing something close to the role of the domestic servant within the home of wealthy employers.[1] However, as either restaurant employee or surrogate servant, the waitress performs, on a professional level, the age-old duties of woman within the home. In a book on waitresses and unionization titled *Dishing It Out*, Dorothy Cobble analyzes the waitress's position this way: "Waitress work culture drew on aspects of women's culture or the experience common to all women: reproduction and domesticity" (52).[2]

In the period during and after World War I, waitresses were officially considered to be domestic servants (Cobble 36). This allowed employers to have them work much longer shifts than other workers, albeit with long breaks between meals. The comparison with a domestic servant helps to concretize the link between waitress and woman doing work within the home, as does an evaluation of the comparative class status of the waitress and of the woman within the traditional home in her relationship to the patriarchy. As Friedrich Engels has written, "In the private home, the woman is the proletarian and the man is the bourgeois" (quoted in Harvey 23).[3]

Some points regarding the real-life situation of the waitress need to be considered if we are to understand the screen image in perspective. Waitressing is the sixth-largest occupation for women, the other five female-dominated occupations being clerk-typist, secretary, saleswoman, private household worker, and teacher (Cobble 27). Of these six, waiting tables is the fastest-growing occupation, with a projected percentile growth between 1984 and 1995 of 20 to 32 percent (Silvestri and Lukasiewicz 47).[4] These growth figures reflect participation by both men and women, but the profession has been found to be (in a 1972 study) 92 percent female (Cobble 207).

Because waitressing is such a common and highly visible form of work for women, films dealing with this occupation inevitably deal with the whole "problem" of women who work. The domestic nature of the work itself is particularly useful for pointing to the conflict being worked out with regard to the image of women as workers in a public setting versus women as wives, girlfriends, and moms within the private ownership context of the home.

The waitress has powerful connotations of a public sphere mother. Cobble writes that the "act of eating and being fed is overlaid with powerful associations. Diners transferred unconscious memories connected with food onto the waitress. Some had insatiable appetites for recognition, mothering, and emotional nurturance" (45). This particular image is of the waitress who has done the job for thirty years or so, and who seems to be inseparable from her job. One such waitress in a Chicago restaurant, who was called the "Mother of the Sherman Hotel," is labeled by Cobble as an example of the "older waitress as a folk type"(33).

However, that image contains contradictions in that a woman plying her mothering skills for cash is financially independent as well as streetwise and skilled in her dealings with the public.[5] These contradictions become particularly pronounced in the decades of the 1960s and 1970s. Cobble cites statistics showing that whereas in 1950, 29 percent of waitresses worked part-time, by 1960 that figure was 48 percent and by 1970 it was 63 percent. Cobble also shows that in 1940 roughly 30 percent of waitresses were married, as were 44 percent in 1950 and 54 percent in 1960. Only 16 percent were married in 1910 (211). These statistics suggest, first, that by 1960 many married women were working as part-time waitresses and bringing money into their marriages. As highly appreciated as this income might be, it would also inevitably upset the dominance of the breadwinning male as undisputed head of the house and lead to some feelings of hostility.

Second, the fact that the other half of the waitresses were single suggests that they were self-sufficient, picking up a little cash, possibly achieving a minimal level of financial independence that placed them beyond the bounds of familial and patriarchal control. At the same time, they were not working overly long hours, and they had a fair amount of extra time on their hands. For example, a July 1971 advertisement for snack foods in the trade magazine *Food Technology* (43) shows a young woman in a scanty bikini proffering a large tray of assorted potato chips and crackers with her left hand while at the same moment partaking of one of the snacks—lifting it to her mouth with her right hand. The ad copy is headed, in large capitals, "IRRESISTIBLE." A long way from that of the 1950s Stouffer's girl ("five-eyelet shoes, full slips, no hairpins or jewelry and passing the daily girdle check"; Cobble

46), this image of a sexy food-bearing woman simultaneously proffering and partaking of a snack food suggests that she is available to take part in some of the bounty of new freedoms that surround her in the aftermath of the "sexual revolution" and "women's lib."

It is this particular stance for the working woman that presents the greatest threat to a male-dominated familial and economic system. She not only works and pays her own way, but she spends on her own leisure pursuits, and in this way realizes her authenticity within the economic arena. The films discussed here, in contrast, tend to dwell on the ways that the waitress characters represent fringe elements of no social significance. In this way they pass judgment on the proper place for the working woman and attempt to put her in that place through particular narratives.

Heart of Darkness

> As the story unfolds, Nora is shown to be highly admirable, despite her lower-class manner.
>
> —Janet Maslin, "White Palace"

Callie Khouri, the screenwriter of *Thelma & Louise,* has stated that the detective in the film is the audience or "the moral sense of the audience. He is us" (quoted in Rohter C21). This statement raises the question of the position of audience members vis-à-vis waitress (and housewife cum waitress) characters. In *White Palace* and *The Accused,* particularly, the waitresses are presented as heavy drinkers with freewheeling sexuality, dirty and unkempt dwellings, no money to speak of, and no plans for a better life—that is, the antithesis of the American dream. A review of *White Palace* points to the film's emphasis on a pronounced and markedly bawdy sexuality in a description of the waitress character, Nora, as "towering, earth-planted, [and] melon-breasted" (Benson F1). This characterization takes its cue from the novel *White Palace,* upon which the film is based, wherein this character is described as "a woman who didn't know the meaning of the word *lewd*—no more than did a goat or a monkey in heat—whose

Figure 12.1. High meets low. Copyright by Universal City Studios, Inc.
Courtesy of MCA Publishing Rights, a Division of MCA Inc.

sexual nature pervaded her . . . who took to copulation as avidly
and guiltlessly as an animal took to its food" (Savan 75).

Much like screwball romantic comedy of the 1930s, *White Palace* locates its problem in the fact that Max Baron, the male lead,
is of the foolish and self-indulgent upper (middle) class and the
waitress Nora is of the heedless and dissipated lower. If only he
could sink just a bit, and she could rise quite a bit, then the twain
could meet in the solidly middle class, and this they do by the end
of the film. One production still from the film shows Max in a tux
encountering Nora in her uniform behind the cash register (Figure
12.1). The wide class divisions suggested in their dress in this scene
are reminiscent of 1930s films wherein dissipated playboys find
their humanity and hardened dames find their femininity (and an
accompanying rise in class position) through marriage.

The newspaper ad for the film depicts Nora in her waitress uniform seducing young Max in black tie. The tag line is "the story of
a younger man and a bolder woman." This line, in combination
with the waitress uniform, confirms the impression that it is Nora's nature as a working-class woman that gives her license for
sexual aggression. In this film one reason Nora must be working-

class is so that she can be sexually aggressive and unconstrained in her use of language without being threatening.

White Palace and *The Accused* share similarities in that in each film the waitress encounters a middle-class person and changes that middle-class person's life. In each case, this middle-class person, after undergoing a journey of discovery with the waitress, comes to an important realization about him- or herself. In *White Palace,* the film builds to the pronouncement by Max Baron, in the final scene, "People discover things about themselves and only hope it isn't too late."

In both films, the middle-class character must overcome the challenge of the seeming impossibility of understanding the waitress character. In the case of *White Palace,* Max must figure out how to reconcile his friends and his musical, literary, culinary, interior decorating, and conversational tastes with the fact that he has an overpowering sexual desire for a woman who often disgusts him. (The book on which the film is based refers frequently to Max's ambivalent response to Nora's meaty smell.)

In *The Accused,* the impossible challenge is to the middle-class woman lawyer who has the seemingly impossible task of prosecuting the perpetrators of a gang rape committed against (of all people) a waitress who was dancing suggestively before a crowd of men before the rape began. (This public dancing may be seen as an acting out of the performance of waitressing itself.) However, the originally disdainful lawyer comes to understand the desire of this waitress to prove her *innocence,* and in so doing she undergoes a powerful sea change; she becomes markedly coded as "feminine," even to the point of showing an interest in astrology. In a scene toward the end of the film, the waitress character offers to do the astrological chart of the lawyer, mentioning that her own chart is full of "mystery, intuition, and feelings." Enviously, the straitlaced lawyer asks, "Do I have any of that [in my chart]?"[6]

White Palace and *The Accused* also contain similarities in means of exposition, in that the middle-class character voyages frequently to the lair of the working-class waitress, in each case there is a scene in the middle-class person's home that shows clearly how out of place the waitress is there, and the action of each film revolves around a sleazy out-of-the-way dump—in one case a hamburger stand, and in the other, the bar where the rape takes place. These venues are constructed as places where the middle-class character feels uncomfortable and audiences are not expected to feel comfortable either.

Violence

> *The Velvet Trap* (Ken Kennedy, 1966) is the story of a waitress who is assaulted and raped by her employer . . . elopes to Las Vegas with a [man who] deserts her after one night, leaving her destitute, and she pawns her wedding ring to buy a bus ticket. . . . A pimp . . . steals her ticket . . . and forces her into prostitution. Her first customer . . . dies of a heart attack. [She] runs out of the brothel and is struck and killed by a passing truck.
>
> —description in Kenneth W. Munden,
> *The American Film Institute Catalog of Motion Pictures
> Produced in the United States 1961–1970*

Several of the recent waitress films raise questions about why the waitress is such a disturbing figure that she must be brutalized. *White Palace* is relatively kind and gentle, as it allows Nora to escape to New York, a kind of New World where she and her lover may live out of the public eye. Nevertheless, Nora undergoes multiple slights and unwarranted blows to her pride in the course of the film. In contrast, both *The Terminator* and *Thelma & Louise* center on the relentless pursuit, to the death, of waitresses. *The Terminator* concerns a waitress who is the target of a robot from the future, who has been sent to kill her before she can give birth to a child who will grow up to save humanity in a future war against the machines. It is typical of horror films to use "average" characters to provide the fantasy with a sickening sensation of plausibility. It is as a symbol of the quotidian that the waitress is used here.[7] Other waitresses, such as Frankie of *Frankie and Johnny*, are depicted as having endured a history of domestic violence, and Cora of *The Postman Always Rings Twice* (Bob Rafelson, 1981) is frequently roughed up by her paramour.

Thelma & Louise, like *The Accused*, centers on an incident of rape. The two women of the title must flee the law because Louise has killed a man who attempted to rape Thelma. They cannot turn to the law because Thelma was seen dancing intimately with the man beforehand. Thus, as in *The Accused,* the crime of rape is very hard to prove, given the sexually charged behavior of the woman in question. In this sense, the women of both films consider themselves to be dealing with a legal system that does not take their experience into account and in which they cannot get a fair trial. They do not feel themselves to be citizens with full rights under the law; indeed, this is how women generally had been characterized in the enlightened age of Rousseau's social contract and since: "Women were viewed as creatures of passion rather than rationality, lacking the capacities required to participate as citizens and indeed capable of bringing considerable disorder into the public sphere" (Crompton 148).

The two films have different responses to this predicament. *The Accused* poses a female attorney as someone inside the system who can make a difference as a result of a personal transformation, and in that sense is the more conservative film. In *The Accused,* based on the clinching testimony of a male middle-class eyewitness, the waitress wins a courtroom battle and achieves legal vindication (which incidentally shows the primacy of the judicial system and its infallible ability to adapt each challenge to its institutional power—in this case the rapists are not convicted of raping the girl per se, but of clapping and cheering the rape on—therefore the punishable crime is not so much rape as the pronounced enjoyment of viewing a rape).[8]

Thelma & Louise is less hopeful. Here, the scenes of the greatest harmony and peace are out west among the open spaces, a favorite spot for fugitives of all stripes and eras. The two women who are so misunderstood and so relentlessly pursued by a staggering array of law enforcement find wonder at night on the desert, among the stars. Then finally, they must bow out entirely. They can be seen either to have killed themselves or, on a more textual level, to have left the film—if the crowd of cars, lights, and equipment standing behind them as they take the leap over the edge of the Grand Canyon can be seen as the crew and apparatus of the classical industry tale.

The hostile encounter between Thelma and Louise and a lascivi-

ous truck driver on the road flies in the face of a historical solidarity between waitress and truck driver during the formation of a
waitresses' union. *Dishing It Out* points to the solidarity between
waitresses and the Teamsters during the struggle of the Hotel Employees and Restaurant Employees International Union (HERE) to
unionize businesses. Teamsters staged sip-ins, lingering all day
over cups of coffee and tying up tables so that dinners and lunches
would go unsold. They also refused to deliver food and other items
to restaurants and hotels where the struggle to unionize was on
(Cobble 98–99). However, these acts of solidarity took place in the
late 1930s and early 1940s, and were well before the time when a
couple of women (one a waitress and one a wife/domestic worker)
would take off across country in skimpy T-shirts and an open convertible. In so doing, these women behave in an extremely threatening manner, hence the aggressive response from the truck driver.
Perhaps a film scenario contemporary with the real-life cooperation between waitresses and truckers during the 1930s would find
Thelma and Louise hiding out in the cab of an 18-wheeler as a
means of making their escape, enjoying the protection of a cadre of
friendly truckers at a weighing station, finally marrying the
manager/boss, à la *Only Angels Have Wings* (Howard Hawks,
1939). The fact that in this 1991 film the women attempt (at least)
to solve their own problems, taking off on their own, suggests the
ways that they pose a threat and the ways that they represent a
striving for independence on the part of late-twentieth-century
women. The fact that this independence is not largely obtained, in
real class terms, is moot.

Waiting as Redemption

The waitress Louise bears a relationship to the waitress Frankie of
Frankie and Johnny in that both have been hardened by domestic
violence. Whereas it is suggested that Louise has killed Thelma's
attacker because of an attack Louise herself endured in the past, it
is suggested that Frankie is burying herself alive in response to a
violent and abusive relationship in her past. Frankie's dark secret is
that she was so severely beaten by an old boyfriend that she cannot
have children. The story seems to find that she thus chooses a kind
of living death as full-time waitress among a group of waitresses

who are all depicted as leading dismal and meager (read: single and childless) lives. Frankie, clearly their superior by dint of magnificent cheekbones, toils among them as she secludes herself from the world. Flying in the face of statistics that show that half of all waitresses are married (and the other half, according to Susan Faludi, would be the happier ones with the greatest longevity anyway), this film takes great pains to show that the group of women who work at the restaurant live alone in seedy rooms; one of them even dies a lonely unattended death.

Much of the romance of *Frankie and Johnny* has to do with Johnny, the restaurant cook, investing the blank page of Frankie with a gamut of hopes, emotions, and dreams. As a caption for a photo in a review of the film puts it, "He's high on life, she's a teetotaler" (Turan F12). In this sense, along with Louise, Frankie represents the image of the sexually repressed waitress who lives a lonely, relatively unattached existence. Although the issue of repression must be left to speculation, in actual fact, waitresses do have a greater tendency to be the heads of their households (whether single or married) than do women in the other five major female-dominated professions—a position for the working woman that presents the greatest problem for the society at large.[9]

Images of the three women in *Frankie and Johnny* together tend to dwell on the disparity between them and other female screen women. The waitress Nedda, in particular, is shown to be comically "unattractive" and in fact looks like a stereotypical mental patient—with her disarrayed hair and clothes and chain smoking. The over-the-hill flashiness of the waitress Cora speaks to another stereotype of undesirable women.[10] Frankie herself, without makeup or hairstyle, is presented as a blank page—she reminds me of a penitent, or a Falconetti in a New York deli. Her face is one that can be invested with a range of fantasy personalities by audiences—much as customers might do with a pretty and unassuming waitress delivering a tray of ham sandwiches to their table (Figure 12.2).

Besides this blankness, as Frankie, Michelle Pfeiffer is directed to behave in an unkempt fashion similar to that evidenced by Nora in *White Palace*. In a gesture that is an outrageous affront to waitresses everywhere, she is continually wiping her nose with her hand. Like Nora, she never combs her hair, and she continually

Figure 12.2. Waitresses Frankie, Cora, and Nedda at team bowling. Courtesy of Paramount Pictures. *Frankie and Johnny* copyright 1991 by Paramount Pictures. All rights reserved.

chews gum with her mouth open. Within the film's general emphasis on creating a whole world of "lower-class" characters, much is made of the chaotic and broken-down surfaces of New York City and the haphazard nature of life without money in that city.

In an interview about *Frankie and Johnny,* director Garry Marshall described the way at one point he used a chalk outline of a dead man on the street as a place for kids to pitch pennies into. He called this a special sort of tough New York City humor, and noted that the film is full of the spirit of this brand of realism. In keeping with this concept, many of the scenes for the film were shot outdoors on the streets of New York. Further, Marshall stated about Pfeiffer: "I knew she'd be ready to take the risks. . . . No beauty, no makeup, no glamour stuff. . . . A lot of times I looked in the camera and said 'too pretty' " (Weinraub 1). The role of Johnny was developed in a similar manner: "[Al Pacino] hung around with ordinary Joes at a diner on West 23rd Street . . . picking up the techniques of short order cooking. . . . Mr. Pacino 'worked out' in his trailer, flipping cardboard eggs until he graduated to the real thing" (Carpenter 2:1).

Frankie and Johnny shows some of the solidarity that exists among waitresses. In one episode, after one of them is pinched (by "the professor from the college again"), the waitresses work together to punish the offender—one pouring ice water into his glass while another bumps into her as she pours, sending the stream of water into the man's lap. "You pour, I'll bump," says Frankie, her brevity suggesting that this happens all the time.[11] Cobble (57–58) details such understandings among waitresses, suggesting that this is one of the reasons that waitresses exhibited a high rate of participation in HERE. However, much of the sense of family within the film merely helps (in this context) to render Frankie and her sister waitresses, serving their predominantly feeble clientele, as spinster aunts kept on in a large manor to provide domestic duties. As social theorist Rosemary Crompton puts it, "It still remains the case that many, perhaps the majority, of women are still second class citizens." Quoting a 1990 study, she argues that "the transition from the nineteenth to the twentieth-century status of women [has been described] as one from 'private' to 'public' patriarchy" (152).

Glancing Backward

They gave me an address where I can go to buy my waitress uniform. Oh God, a waitress.
—Alice, in *Alice Doesn't Live Here Anymore*

In a glance backward to the 1970s, *Alice Doesn't Live Here Anymore* finds a voyage of self-discovery taken by the central character, Alice. At the time (and to this day), it was unusual to find a film with a focus on a female character who was a housewife, mother, and later a waitress. The exception to this would be a noncommercial genre known as "portrait films," made through the 1960s and 1970s, which concern themselves with the anecdotal and mundane as a means of exploring the heretofore unspoken dimensions of women's experience. And in fact, the film appears to be making a nod in this direction, in that it was described by a reviewer at the time as "aiming for a new kind of movie naturalism. . . . [The director] uses real locations and encourages actors to improvise" (Farber 1).[12]

In the film, Ellen Burstyn plays a woman named Alice who is forced to earn a living for herself and her son after her truck-driver husband dies.[13] She uses this crisis to wrest herself from the routines of mother and wife in a lower-middle-class town. She resolves, literally, to find her voice: her ambition is to be a singer and to resurrect the essential Alice, an Alice she lost when she married her husband (when asked, she says she married him because he was a good kisser).

However, she must become a waitress out of dire necessity. She initially lands a job as a cocktail lounge singer, after crying in front of the owner of the bar, and is "courted" by a young man who eventually breaks into her house and threatens her with a knife if she ever disobeys him.[14] The moment he leaves, she packs child and suitcase into her car and leaves town, landing up as a waitress somewhere down the road. While working as a waitress, she meets a man who wants her to come and wait table for him at his house. After some self-examination, she realizes that in fact to do so willingly and in an *examined* way would in fact be in harmony with who she is.

In the film, we see that Alice is never comfortable being a waitress. Just as Mildred Pierce, a waitress of sorts within her private home, finds it difficult to make the transition to working in public and with the public, Alice has similar qualms. Alice finds a friend, however, in the waitress Flo, who embodies many stereotypes about waitresses: she has a southern or western accent (i.e., she is "uncultured"), she has "bad taste" in jewelry and clothes and hairstyles, she has a foul mouth and no illusions about men, and she has a heart of gold. Despite their friendship, Alice has doubts about how far she wants to be drawn by this mentor, and as such demonstrates a gap in audience perception between the essentially domesticated Alice, as she moves from one marriage to the next, and the more self-reliant (and de facto, given the gender gap with regard to the professions), working-class Flo (see Figure 12.3).

Despite the fact that *Alice* was hailed as "revolutionary" (Canby 13; Barthel 17), the film is ironically similar to films from the early part of the century wherein a waitress meets a highly eligible man in the course of her work and marries him, ending the story.[15] This resemblence foregrounds the film's theme of "drop-

Figure 12.3. Alice regards Flo. Copyright 1974 Warner Bros. Inc.

ping out," suggesting that Alice's stint as a waitress is not a part of her real life, but a cathartic way station wherein she discovers herself. This continuity of plot line from the 1910s and 1920s to the 1960s suggests a continuity in expectations about women and their value as workers in the public sphere. Alice's story seems to be unique at first glance because she is the driving character of the narrative and the film devotes a lot of time to examining her thoughts, desires, and hopes.

Alice is depicted as a housewife who has been released from servitude by the happy accident of her bullying husband's death. She goes forth to discover herself, only incidentally and temporarily becoming a waitress as she searches for her true identity. The contradiction between the theme of dropping out of conventional middle-class society and the theme of returning to married life in an examined way rests in the figure of the man she marries in the film, as this character is played by Kris Kristofferson—who as a pop icon represents a gamut of liberal 1960s beliefs and their contradictions with regard to women. Kristofferson represents an ideal catch—an eminently sympatico male who will strive for an equal relationship with a woman. This striving, however, will be under the umbrella of a 1960s/1970s-style simplicity that found many a liberated woman barefoot, pregnant, raising her own food, and weaving her own cloth.

Two other films of roughly the same era use the waitress as a symbol of dropping out. In these, a main male character escapes the upper middle class by living with a waitress, as a hero of another century might have settled down with a Tahitian woman. In *Splendor in the Grass* (Elia Kazan, 1961) we find Warren Beatty's character going off to raise goats with an Italian waitress. In *Five Easy Pieces* (Bob Rafelson, 1970), Jack Nicholson's character's vehicle away from the culture of his intellectual and musical family is a waitress named Rayette. In both these films the waitress is seen as a simple and uneducated person to whom a main character may escape from the fast track, and perhaps, the feminism of his own more-privileged class.

In a *Los Angeles Times* article that discusses changing times, one paragraph reads: "In the 1960's, Bob Bussinger was a stockbroker who abandoned his materialistic lifestyle, became a hippie and ended up in Big Sur as a waiter" (Paddock A21). A movie scenario, in contrast, would find this character dropping out and living with a woman who is a waitress, suggesting that a rigid hierarchy demands that this position within the narrative be held by a female. For example, an obscure film titled *Down and Dirty* (Edward Everett, 1969) contains a scenario in which "Ed, a respectable accountant and family man, drops out. . . . He meets Lisa, a waitress in a coffee house, and they fall in love and marry" (Munden 1976, 284). In fact, according to the American Film Institute catalog, the only American 1960s film in which a man plays a waiter (other than a porno film called *Suburban Confidential;* A. C. Stephen, 1966) is *Viva Las Vegas* (George Sidney, 1964), and the man in question is Elvis Presley, a kind of exceptional creature in his own right.

In *Alice Doesn't Live Here Anymore,* rather than a male character finding himself by dropping out to be with a waitress, Alice herself drops out to become a waitress and subsequently and conveniently realizes her authenticity within the roles provided for her.[16]

Conclusion

The films that deal with working-class waitress characters do so in

order to present tales that deal with female characters in a mode
that is very close to that of wife and mother. Further, the films
dwell on the fact that these female characters work, in a way that
is unusual for Hollywood films—it being a well-known fact that
Hollywood characters tend to be fired or suspended from whatever jobs they have near the beginning of the film.[17] Work is not
generally shown, and if it is shown, it is there as a means of working out personal problems.

The films discussed here deal with problems and challenges
posed to the status quo by working women. *The Accused* makes
the point that even though a woman immodestly places herself before the public, she may not be brutalized; *Thelma & Louise* demonstrates that willful women cannot survive in the world they
know, and their inability to go on sends a disturbing message;
Frankie and Johnny shows that working women who shun dates
and matrimony probably do so because they are infertile (for any
number of reasons) and will in all probability have only three
mourners at their funerals—as did one of the women in the film;
perhaps most frightening, *White Palace* shows that a working
woman can involve a man in her life and end up getting him to
leave a well-paying and prestigious job to move to a new city,
drawn by the power of sexual attraction.

In a final note, summer 1994 saw the release of another waitress
film, *It Could Happen to You* (Andrew Bergman). In contrast to
the films discussed above, this film has a very benign take on the
question of working women. It features an actress who is as finely
drawn as any thoroughbred, namely, the delicate Bridget Fonda, as
the waitress character who marries a cop. This cop and waitress
present the picture of two decent people who give away lottery
winnings, have hearts of gold, play baseball with kids, and look
comfortable and good in middle- and upper-middle-class sur-
roundings. When their luck turns sour, the good people of New
York feel so strongly about their continuation as an iconic couple
that they mail them, in increments, a collective sum of $600,000.
Apparently this is the tip they receive for keeping alive the American dream of the perfect marriage—one comprising a cop and a
waitress. In this film, much as in *Alice Doesn't Live Here Anymore,* the waitress character is happy with her lot, and even when
the cop splits his $4 million in lottery winnings with her she de-

cides to continue to wait tables (despite the fact that she has now bought the restaurant).[18] In this way, waiting tables is an expression of her authenticity, and the fact that she is also the owner of the restaurant (through money given to her by the cop) brings her role very close to that of the wife and mother waiting table in the private home.

Notes

1. This thought relies upon a notion well expressed in the following: "While a significant association exists between wife's class and wife's social imagery, a farther significant association exists between *husband's* class and wife's imagery *and this latter association is much stronger than the former*" (Erickson and Goldthorpe 1988; as quoted in Crompton 95–96). Because the relationship between waitress and diner simulates a family situation, early employers consistently recruited white Northern European waitresses: "Waitressing in the twentieth century was an occupation reserved for white women drawn from the 'old' North European immigrant groups (English, Irish, German, Scandinavian, and Welsh" (Cobble 29).

2. The waitress, as a general rule, may be distinguished from the waiter in that he (like the figure of a manservant or head butler) tends to embody the values and status of his employer in a way that the female food server does not. Although many waiters increasingly work in less lucrative establishments once reserved for the waitress, one nevertheless tends to associate the waiter with expensive restaurants in which the waiter can serve as a focus for the awe a customer might feel for the power and wealth inspired by such a setting. A *New York Times* article about Chuck Norris visiting an expensive French restaurant sums up these ideas very nicely. In it, the author describes the waiters calling the film star "Mr. Norris" (rather than M. Norris) and finds significance in the fact that the waiters don't utter French phrases to Norris, instead simply bidding him a good day. The article sums up its attitude toward the stature of waiters in its title: "Tough Enough to Win the Respect of Waiters" (Berkow B1).

3. It may also be said that the man is the instanciation of the law of the patriarchy within the private home. A good crystallization of this is seen in *It Could Happen to You* (Andrew Bergman, 1994), in which a cop and a waitress are structured as the ideal couple.

4. The other top five growth occupations in the 1990s for both men and women are registered nurse, cleaner, janitor, manager, and cashier (Steinberg and Seo WS13).

5. From the earliest part of the century, waitresses tended to be the primary earners of their households and/or living apart from their families: "More than women in other occupations, waitresses lived outside a traditional family setting and hence turned quite readily to their workplace community for friendship and

support" (Cobble 33, 132). This independence from a man and family brought out the comparison with the prostitute. Writes Cobble: "Indeed, the intimacy of food service, the tip exchange, the decided departure of waitresses from middle-class standards of gentility, and perhaps the association—often unconscious—between eating and sex led to the denunciation of waitresses as 'loose women' and even as prostitutes" (24).

6. The entire dialogue is as follows: *Waitress:* "I did your chart, and you're really going to like this . . . public work . . . law and understanding. . . . you could be president of something." *Lawyer:* "What about you?" *Waitress:* " . . . feelings, faith, intuition, mystery, really useful shit." *Lawyer:* "Do I have any of that?" *Waitress:* " . . . Yeah you do. . . . I was going to sign it, but I figure you're not really into that stuff." *Lawyer:* "Will you sign it please?"

In an extratextual twist, the lawyer is played by Kelly McGillis, who proclaimed as the film came out, on the cover of *People* magazine, that she herself had been a rape victim. The *People* article dwells at length on her prolonged emotional and psychological disability brought about by the crime, effectively counteracting the image of the character she plays in the film as a strong woman ("Memoir" 155–60).

7. The waitress is also an oft-recurring figure in newspaper articles that purport to present the experiences of "common people." One such article published at the time of the 1992 Democratic Convention included some comments made by a waitress at a donut shop near the convention site as a device to demonstrate how little impact such events have for one of the little people. This particle of salt of the earth is introduced as "dragging herself from counter to counter because the baby has been up all night"; she has this to say about the event: "I got to cook, I got to clean. . . . Me watch TV? Never" (quoted in Baum E1).

8. Oddly, the scene of final coupling and reconciliation in *White Palace* takes place to the wild clapping and approval of a crowd at a restaurant, as does the final kiss of waitress Alice and her suitor in *Alice Doesn't Live Here Anymore* (Martin Scorsese, 1975).

9. It seems that much is made of statistics showing that almost one-fourth of recent births are to single women, and the notion of the single woman raising her children on welfare is paraded before the media public with great frequency. One of the issues is that children in these homes are more likely to be poor than are children in two-parent households. However, one senses as well that the prospect of a significant upsurge in female-headed households holds dire and frightening consequences for the basic tenets of patriarchal traditions of inheritance and power.

10. It is no coincidence that Susan Sarandon was drafted to play two of the waitress roles discussed in this essay (Nora in *White Palace* and Louise in *Thelma & Louise*). A trademark unglamorous actress, she has been described thus by one of her directors: "She is the only 47-year-old woman who allows herself to look 47. . . . One of the problems in Hollywood is, if you hire an actress who's supposed to play 45 or 50, they look 30. They've had five facelifts, two

boob jobs, their hair is some insane color, they're too thin, Susan hasn't bought into this" (quoted in Cagle 19).

11. *It Could Happen to You* contains a similar incident of solidarity—waitresses work together to put cigarette ashes in the boss's coffee.

12. Another article at the time commented, "Don't be put off by reports that *Alice* is a woman's picture, which makes the movie sound as if it were going to be terribly solemn and humorless, and perhaps even a little chauvinistic about women's rights" (Canby II:13).

13. The fact that the death of this man, a truck driver (who is stereotypically presented as a boor and a lout), is treated by the film as a happy accident sets up an undertone of anti-working-class sentiment that runs through the film. He is not mourned by either wife or small son.

14. This character is played by Harvey Keitel, who also appears as the detective in *Thelma & Louise*.

15. For example, in one film called *The Heiress at Coffee Dan's* (Edward Dillon, 1916), an innocent waitress is unwittingly at the center of a swindler's master plan. Discovering this, she alerts the police, gets a reward, and returns to her job as a waitress, whereupon she and her suitor (a rich man) marry. In *King of the Saddle* (William J. Craft, 1926), the cowboys "go to a luncheonette, where Mary, the sympathetic waitress, gives them a free meal" (a marriage ensues). In *The Great Night* (Howard M. Mitchell, 1922), a rich man "falls in love with Mollie Martin, a waitress who does not know his identity but agrees to marry him" (Munden 1971, 406, 313).

16. This notion of the redeeming nature of domesticity for a woman can be seen in two films of different periods: *The Snob* (Sam Wood, 1921) seems to coincide with *Maid to Order* (Amy Jones, 1987); both films are about the ennobling nature of service work for uppity women who have perhaps identified a little too closely with their fathers' class position. Regarding *Alice Doesn't Live Here Anymore*, a reviewer wrote at the time of the film's release: "The new film is *less* sophisticated than the romantic comedies of the thirties and forties that starred Rosalind Russell, Jean Arthur and Katherine Hepburn. Although those movies may have ended with an affirmation of marriage, they concerned professional women—journalists, advertising executives, actresses, sometimes even lawyers or psychiatrists—who could survive quite effectively on their own. By contrast, the heroine of 'Alice' admits that she does not know how to live without a man" (Farber 2:1).

17. Some examples of this are *Beverly Hills Cop* (Martin Brest, 1984), in which the Eddie Murphy character is on vacation, and *Dirty Harry* (Don Siegel, 1971), in which Clint Eastwood is suspended. Among the films discussed here, the lawyer in *The Accused* is under threat of losing her job if she pursues her defense of the waitress. In *It Could Happen to You*, the cop played by Nicolas Cage is out of a job near the beginning of the film because of an injury.

18. Said the real-life waitress Phyliss Penzo, on whose life this film is based, "I had considered opening a restaurant, but after 27 years as a waitress, you reach the age where you just can't do those hours anymore" (quoted in Mark 41).

Works Cited

Barthel, Joan. "Ellen Burstyn Plays 'Alice' from the Inside Out." *New York Times*, 3 March 1975.

Baum, Geraldine. "Real Life vs. the Convention." *Los Angeles Times*, 16 July 1992.

Benson, Sheila. "Prime Sarandon on *White Palace* Menu." *Los Angeles Times*, 19 October 1990.

Berkow, Ira. "Tough Enough to Earn the Respect of Waiters." *New York Times*. 12 May 1993.

Cagle, Jess. "Laying Down the Law." *Entertainment Weekly*, 29 July 1994, 16–23.

Canby, Vincent. "Terrific, Tough-Talking 'Alice.' " *New York Times*, 9 April 1975.

Carpenter, Teresa. "Al Pacino: Regular Guy among Ordinary Joes." *New York Times*, 6 October 1991.

Cobble, Dorothy Sue. *Dishing It Out: Waitresses and Their Unions in the Twentieth Century*. Urbana: University of Illinois Press, 1991.

Crompton, Rosemary. *Class and Stratification*. Cambridge: Polity, 1993.

Erikson, R., and J. H. Goldthhorpe. "Women at Class Crossroads: A Critical Note." *Sociology* 22 (1988): 545–53.

Farber, Stephen. "Has Martin Scorsese Gone Hollywood?" *New York Times*, 30 March 1975.

Harvey, Sylvia. "Woman's Place: The Absent Family of Film Noir." In *Women in Film Noir*. Ed. E. Ann Kaplan. London: British Film Institute, 1980.

Mark, Lois Alter. "Reality Check, Winning Personalities." *Entertainment Weekly*, 29 July 1994.

Maslin, Janet. "White Palace: Love and the Class Struggle." *New York Times*, 19 September 1990.

"Memoir of a Brief Time in Hell." *People*, 14 November 1988.

Munden, Kenneth W., ed. *The American Film Institute Catalog of Motion Pictures Produced in the United States 1921–1930*. New York: R. R. Bowker, 1971.

———., ed. *The American Film Institute Catalog of Motion Pictures Produced in the United States 1961–1970*. New York: R. R. Bowker, 1976.

Paddock, Richard C. "Big Sur: Resort Symbol of Changing Times." *Los Angeles Times*, 21 April 1992.

Rohter, Larry. "The Third Woman of 'Thelma and Louise.' " *New York Times*, 5 June 1991.

Savan, Glenn. *White Palace*. New York: Bantam, 1987.

Silvestri, G. T., and J. M. Lukasiewicz. "Occupational Employment Projections: The 1994-95 Outlook." *Monthly Labor Review*, November 1985.

Steinberg, Susan, and Diane Seo. "Home Away from Home." *Los Angeles Times*, 4 August 1994.

Turan, Kenneth. "Boy Meets Grill, Gets Girl." *Los Angeles Times*, 11 October 1991.

Weinraub, Bernard. "Pfeiffer's Blue Plate Special." *New York Times*, 6 October 1991.

Contributors

Paul Arthur teaches film at Montclair State University. He is working on a book about urban representation in film.

Rick Berg is an adjunct. When there is work, he teaches a number of subjects at Occidental College and other colleges and universities in Southern California. He is coeditor of *Vietnam in American Culture*.

Jane Collings is a Ph.D. candidate in the Department of Film and Television at the University of California, Los Angeles. She recently completed her dissertation dealing with the 1930s American newsreel, its cultural context, and the notion of a national audience, titled "Streamlining the National Body: Newspaper Spectatorship in the New Era." Her essay in this volume on waitressing is largely a reflection on lived experience.

Marianne Conroy teaches film and cultural studies at McGill University. She is currently completing a manuscript on middlebrow taste and class identification in the postwar Hollywood cinema titled *Allegories of Affluence*.

Jane Gaines, associate professor of literature and director of the Program in Film and Video at Duke University, is the author of

Contested Culture: The Image, the Voice, and the Law (1991). She is currently working on a book titled *Other/Race/Desire.*

David E. James is professor of critical studies in the School of Cinema-Television at the University of Southern California. His previous books include *Written Within and Without: A Study of Blake's Milton* and *Allegories of Cinema: American Film in the Sixties;* he is also editor of *To Free the Cinema: Jonas Mekas and the New York Underground.*

Douglas Kellner is professor of philosophy at the University of Texas at Austin and author of many books on social theory, politics, history, and culture, including *Camera Politica: The Politics and Ideology of Contemporary Hollywood Film,* (with Michael Ryan), *Critical Theory, Marxism, and Modernity, Jean Baudrillard: From Marxism to Postmodernism and Beyond* (with Steven Best), *Postmodern Theory: Critical Interrogations, Television and the Crisis of Democracy, The Persian Gulf TV War,* and *Media Culture.*

Chuck Kleinhans, coeditor of *Jump Cut: A Review of Contemporary Media,* teaches in the Radio/Television/Film Department at Northwestern University.

Bill Nichols consistently addresses issues of social representation, including class, in his essays and books. *Blurred Boundaries,* his latest work, examines the fuzzy boundaries of fiction/nonfiction, authenticity/truth, and postmodernism and historical consciousness. He is currently at work on a book on cross-cultural representation.

Lillian S. Robinson, the founder of American Marxist-feminist criticism, is the author of *Sex, Class, and Culture* (1978, reissued 1986) and *Monstrous Regiment* (1985), coauthor of *Feminist Scholarship: Kindling in the Groves of Academe* (1985), and editor of *Modern Women Writers* (1995). Her work has appeared in many anthologies, as well as in such periodicals as *New Literary History, Tulsa Studies in Women's Literature, Artforum, College English, Clio,* and *Manoa,* and she is a frequent contributor to *The*

Nation and *Women's Review of Books.* Her work in progress includes two books: *Mixed Company: Race, Rape, and Representation* and (with Ryan Bishop) *Night Market: Thailand in Post-Colonial Sexual Cartographies.* She is currently Professor of English at East Carolina University.

Steven J. Ross is professor of history at the University of Southern California, where he teaches courses in American popular culture and social history. He is author of *Struggles for the Screen: Politics, Class, and the Rise of the Movies* (forthcoming) and *Workers on the Edge: Work, Leisure, and Politics in Industrializing Cincinnati, 1788-1890* (1985). His current project, *Hollywood Left and Right,* examines the interactions of movie stars and politics from the silent era to the present.

Esther C. M. Yau is assistant professor of film at Occidental College. She has published in *Film Quarterly, Discourse, Quarterly Review of Film and Video,* and *Wide Angle,* and is coeditor of *New Chinese Cinemas: Forms, Identities, Politics* (1994).

Index

Compiled by Eileen Quam and Theresa Wolner

289